Journal of
Early
Childhood and
Infant
Psychology

Volume 5
2009

PACE UNIVERSITY PRESS   NEW YORK

ISSN 1554-6144
ISBN 0-944473-97-0

Address Subscription Inquiries to:

Pace University Press
41 Park Row, Room 1510
New York, NY 10038

www.pace.edu/press
(212) 346-1405

Journal of Early Childhood and Infant Psychology

Co-Editors
Anastasia E. Yasik
Pace University—New York City
Barbara A. Mowder
Pace University—New York City

Associate Editors
Florence Rubinson
Brooklyn College of the City University of New York
K. Mark Sossin
Pace University - New York City

Editorial Policy: The **Journal of Early Childhood and Infant Psychology (JECIP)** is a publication of the Association of Early Childhood and Infant Psychologists (AECIP). One aspect of AECIP's mission is to provide a vehicle for networking within early childhood and infant psychology, including fostering research, scholarship, and professional interactions. This journal (JECIP) focuses on publishing original contributions from a broad range of psychological perspectives relevant to infants, young children (up to age 8), parents, and caregivers. Manuscripts incorporating evidence-based research, theory and applications within clinical, community, developmental, neurological, and school psychology perspectives are considered. In addition to data-based research, the journal accepts test and book reviews, position statements, literature reviews, program descriptions and evaluations, clinical studies, and other professional materials of interest to psychologists working with infants, young children, parents, families, and caregivers. Proposals for mini-series may be made to the Co-Editors.

Format: Manuscripts should be original work not currently submitted for publication to other journals. Authors must follow the guidelines of the *Publication Manual of the American Psychological Association (Sixth Edition)*. Manuscripts may not exceed 35 double-spaced pages in length, including the cover page, abstract, references, tables and figures.

Submission: Submit an electronic copy of the manuscript for editorial review. Avoid including any identifying author information in the text. Selection of manuscripts is based on blind peer review. Include a cover page with the following information: the title of article, author(s) full name(s), title(s), institution or professional affiliations, and mailing and email address of primary author. The cover page will not be sent to reviewers.

Selection Criteria:
- Importance of topic in early childhood and infant psychology
- Theory and research related to content
- Contribution to professional practice in early childhood and infant psychology
- Clear and concise writing

Submit manuscripts to the Co-Editors at the following address:
Anastasia E. Yasik & Barbara A. Mowder
Co-Editors, JECIP
Psychology Department, Pace University
41 Park Row
New York, New York 10038
(212) 346-1506
Email: jecip@pace.edu

Journal of
Early
Childhood and
Infant
Psychology

Volume 5, 2009

**Mini-Series: Updates and Critical Issues on Medication Use and
Misuse in Young Children**

Guest Editors:
Steven R. Shaw, Ph.D., McGill University
Paul C. McCabe, Ph.D., NCSP, Brooklyn College – City University of New York

General Articles

The Evolution of Medication Use and Misuse for Young Children and Infants:
Changing the Roles of Early Childhood Specialists and Educators to Meet New Challenges and Concerns

Steven R. Shaw
McGill University

Paul C. McCabe
Brooklyn College of the City University of New York

The use of medications with young children and infants has important implications for the study of development and psychopathology. It requires a broad knowledge of developmental disabilities, an understanding of medications, their side effects and treatment outcomes, knowledge of widely described medications for common maladies, and other common medical procedures. The challenge is that medication use with young children and infants is growing rapidly, and often outpaces research examining efficacy and risks with young children. Rapid developmental changes in early childhood and ensuing vulnerability of the neurophysiological systems call for sensitivity and restraint when deciding whether to introduce a pharmacological treatment. The best approach in deciding whether to use medications with young children is to use a collaborative problem-solving process including the prescribing professionals, parents, psychologists, and educators. This approach facilitates communication among all parties and promotes sharing of information regarding medication efficacy and unintended effects. This information, in turn, helps the prescribing professional and collaborative team decide the most efficacious treatment, whether that be medical, behavioral, both, or none.

The science and clinical practice of using medications with young children and infants has important implications for the study of development and psychopathology. The investigation of interventions for developmental disabilities is not complete without consideration of medical management of behavior, cognition, and concurrent health issues (Jackson & Martin, 1998). The study of children with medical issues requires understanding of medications, including

All correspondence should be addressed to Steven R. Shaw, McGill University, 3700 McTavish Street (Room 517), Montreal, Canada H3A 1YA. Electronic mail may be sent to steven.shaw@mcgill.ca.

their side effects and treatment outcomes. The study of typical development requires information on the intended and unintended effects of vaccinations, widely prescribed medications for common maladies, and other common medical procedures (Paul, 2007). The challenge is that medication use with young children and infants is growing rapidly, and often outpaces research examining efficacy and risks of these medications with young children. This means that researchers, clinicians, and advocates must also keep pace with the rapid evolution of medication use to ensure that medications are developmentally suitable for young children and minimize adverse effects.

Prescription Practices for Young Children and Infants

The number of prescriptions for pharmaceuticals of any type for children from birth through 5 years of age has increased five-fold since 2001 (Lasky, 2009). Moreover, over-the-counter drugs such as anti-inflammatory medication, cold and flu remedies, and sleep aids have increased six-fold since 2001 (Crockett, 2005; Taylor-Zapata & Mattison, 2007). Prescriptions for psychotropic medications to address emotional, behavioral, and psychiatric conditions in young children have doubled in the past two decades (Gleason et al., 2007). There is also evidence of a large increase in complementary and alternative therapies, such as homeopathy, vitamin and mineral therapies, Ayurveda (a traditional medicine native to India), and other nutrition-based treatments for medical and behavioral issues (Ente, 2004). Because the use of medication has become pervasive in North America, the study of development and psychopathology without considering medication use and related issues is incomplete (Stevens, 2007).

Despite potential for misuse, increased use of medications to treat chronic and acute illness and injury have resulted in an overall higher quality of life for children (Gazarian, 2009a). However, the increase in prescriptions for medications to address the mental health issues of typically developing children and children with developmental disabilities is far more controversial. The prescriptions of psychotropic medications have increased at a rate higher than medications in general (Hoppu, 2008). For children from birth to age 5, the use of stimulants has risen 300% since 2001 (Mayes, Bagwell, & Erkulwater, 2009). The use of mood stabilizers, anti-depressants, anti-anxiety medications, anti-seizure medications, and anti-psychotic medications has increased significantly for young children and infants (Lasky, 2009). Although many parents and mental health professionals report that the increased use of psychotropic medications has improved the quality of life for many children with difficult to control behaviors, there are also reports of dangerous side effects and worsening behavioral symptoms. Moreover, there is controversy as to whether the use of psychotropic medications are imposing societal expectations on young children, identifying poor parenting or schooling practices, and allowing parents to select a child's personality. The perception of acceptability of psychotropic medications has relevance to modern society, yet a rational investigation requires a review of the science underlying psychotropic medications, including their efficacy and risk (Shaw, Sharp, et al., 2009).

Science and Improved Clinical Practice

There have been significant improvements in the science of medication development. Medication regimens have improved in the areas of chronic illness, acute illness, and mental health. Research trials have become more rigorous, and researchers are now required to acknowledge financial conflicts of interest that could potentially bias the research findings (National Institute of Health [NIH], 2009).

Improvements in the Science of Medication Development

New medications are available for nearly every major chronic, acute, and mental health issue. Prescribers now have a wide range of options for most medical issues. Each year, new medications for children are developed. Many more medications have been developed for adults, but have been tested in trials and are now approved for pediatric cases. For example, at one time methylphenidate (e.g., Ritalin) was the only option to address inattentive and overactive behaviors in children. Now there are over a dozen widely prescribed medications to address patient profiles, susceptibility toward specific side effects, and dosing issues (Mayes et al., 2009). Medications now commonly prescribed for Attention-Deficit Hyperactivity Disorder (ADHD) include several varieties and delivery systems for methylphenidate (e.g., Focalin, Ritalin, Ritalin ER, Metadate, Attenta, Rubifen, Concerta, Equasym, Daytrana). There are also forms of amphetamine salts (e.g., Adderall, Vyvanse), non-stimulant treatments (e.g., Strattera), and even atypical antipsychotic medications that have been used for ADHD (Mayes et al.).

There has been a similar increase in the panoply of medications available to address infections, anxiety, pain, depression, and nearly every other physical and mental health issue (Crockett, 2005). Whether these new medications are markedly more effective than a single medication in managing symptoms or providing a cure is debatable (Mullins, 2009). However, prescribers now have options to address susceptibility to side effects, improve convenience of dosage, and provide options for those who do not respond to the first medication prescribed. Although flexibility in prescription practices is widely considered a positive development for prescribers, the onus falls on prescribers to make effective medical decisions (Stevens, 2007).

Improvements in Clinical Practice

The science of medication improvement does not simply involve production of new medications. There have also been improvements in the applications of older medications to new problems, reduction of side effects, monitoring of effectiveness, parent education, medication regimen adherence, and refinement of diagnoses (Stange, 2009). For example, diagnosis has evolved from simple labels to detailed descriptions of specific symptoms and behaviors (Paul, 2007). Depression is no longer considered a unitary concept. Although major depressive episode may be the primary diagnosis, details involving duration of symptoms, severity of symptoms, co-morbid symptoms, history, medical issues, age, gender, ethnic group status and many other factors are included in making a complex description of problems once labeled simply as "depression."

Knowledge of the complexities of diagnosis assists in matching medication and other therapies to the specific set of presenting problems (Shah et al., 2007; Stevens, 2007). Such multifaceted aspects of diagnoses that affect medication practices apply to asthma, diabetes, acute illnesses, and most other medical issues. Knowledge of diagnostic complexity, development, and biochemistry is required to take full advantage of the variety of medications available. However, advances that are on the cutting edge of medication usage take some time (and significant educational efforts) to affect clinical practice for all prescribers. In many cases, the science of clinical therapeutics is effective, but common prescription practice has not kept pace (Huskamp, 2005).

Sociological Factors in Prescription Practice

Trends in the prescription of medications are as much a sociological phenomenon as scientific or medical (Parnes et al., 2009). Over-the-counter and prescription medications are widely advertised on television. Physicians receive dramatically more hours of pre-service and continuing education hours in the prescription of medications than a decade previously (Taylor, Selbst, & Shah, 2005). There is a societal trend that medications are a common, acceptable, and necessary part of modern life (Jackson & Martin, 1998; Parnes et al.).

Nevertheless, there is also a backlash of popular opinion against the use of medications for young children and infants (Casiday, Cresswell, Wilson, & Panter-Beck, 2006; Harris, 2008). The letters to the editor and opinion pages of major newspapers, television talk shows, and popular internet sites are rife with critical commentary on the appropriateness of prescribing medications to increasingly younger children (Elias, 2006; Harris, 2008). Much of the backlash is due to a primarily emotional response against medications. There is a widespread distrust of large pharmaceutical companies (Casiday et al., 2006). This distrust generalizes from a perception of greed of pharmaceutical companies to a distrust of all of their products. Such distrust has led parents to pursue complementary and alternative treatments for medical and mental health problems (Ente, 2004; Lilienfeld, 2005). As mentioned, increasingly rigorous clinical trials and more restrictive financial reporting requirements for pharmaceutical researchers may begin to restore public faith in the independence and validity of research results.

A second source of backlash is the well-publicized adverse effects of medications (Kaushal et al., 2007). Every medication has some form of unintended effect. The most rare and severe side effects also tend to be the most widely publicized. For example, of the 2,000 children and adolescents with depression participating in trials of selective serotonin reuptake inhibitors (SSRIs), 4% of adolescents with depression experienced suicidal ideation (Khan, Khan, Kolts, & Brown, 2003). The US Food and Drug Administration (FDA) placed the highest level of warning on this class of medications, which is known as a black box warning. Although suicidal ideation is a rare side effect and a not uncommon behavior for children and adolescents with depressive symptoms, SSRIs were widely reported in the media as being extremely dangerous for children and adolescents (e.g., Miller, 2004).

Another example is that vaccinations for measles, mumps, and rubella (MMR) have saved thousands of lives (Casiday et al., 2006). Severe side effects of the vaccinations causing deafness, permanent brain damage, and coma have occurred in less than one in one million administrations. The extremely rare nature of these effects makes it impossible to determine if the MMR vaccine was, in fact, the cause of these conditions (Casiday et al.). In addition, parent and advocacy groups have linked MMR vaccinations to the onset of autism. However, scientific studies investigating this issue failed to support this association (e.g., Fombonne, Zakarian, Bennett, Meng, & McLean-Heywood, 2006). The research on the frequency and nature of side effects of medications for young children is incomplete for many medications (Murray, 2006).

Medication as an Early Intervention

Educators, social workers, and psychologists are often predisposed to a negative bias toward medical interventions (Murray, 2006). This negative inclination is especially apparent concerning medication use for young children and infants. However, the trend toward medication use in younger children is consistent with the belief that the earliest possible interventions are often the most effective interventions. There is no reason to believe that the value of early intervention applies only to educational and behavioral therapies; early intervention may also apply to medication therapies as well.

For example, very early interventions for children with ADHD often prevent school failure and social impairment upon entering school. However, the use of stimulant medications for children 3 to 5 years of age is widely considered an unusual and undesirable practice by many scholars and clinicians (Greenhill et al., 2006). Addressing other behavioral issues such as aggression, mania, and depression at an early age may prevent many social and family relationship difficulties that commonly co-occur with children who have mental health problems. There is evidence that early treatment with medications can prevent the most severe manifestations of mental health and developmental disorders (Greenhill et al.). There is also emerging evidence that some medications, such as SSRIs, can prevent the long-term damage to neuronal networks and brain structures caused by chronic cortisol activation due to the stress of depressive disorders and other psychiatric conditions (Nardi & Barrett, 2005). Still, the preponderance of evidence and recommendations from the FDA requires caution in prescription practices and recommends against prescribing to children less than 3 years of age (e.g., DSM Pharmaceuticals, 2007).

Early intervention is a valuable concept, yet to determine whether medication benefits outweigh risks for young children and infants, there are three major risk factors to be considered (Gazarian, 2009b). First, there must be strong evidence that medications have demonstrated effectiveness for young children and infants. Medications may be effective for adults and school-aged children yet may not be effective or may have a different side effect profile for young children or infants (Gazarian). Second, making accurate diagnoses of medical and mental health disorders in young children and infants is extremely difficult (Taylor et al., 2005). The criteria for diagnosing depression, anxiety, and other developmental issues in childhood, adolescence and adulthood do not completely apply or are difficult to apply to very young children. For example, depression in early childhood has some common yet some differing symptoms than that of older children, adolescents and adults, and the duration criteria are shorter (Luby et al., 2003). Symptoms of guilt and extreme fatigue have been found to be unique markers of preschool depression (Luby, Belden, Pautsch, Si, & Spitznagel, 2009). Without accurate diagnosis, effective treatment is much more difficult (Kaushal et al., 2007). Third, the long-term and cumulative effects of medication are largely unknown (Laskey, 2009). For example, prescriptions for antibiotics given to very young children often disrupt normal and healthy development of the immune system. Moreover, the long-term use of many atypical antipsychotic medications results in permanent neurological problems, although the effects of administering medications to children for 5 to 10 years, or more, are unknown for most medications (Greenhill et al., 2006). Even medications that have been researched for many years, such as psychostimulant medications, have unknown long-term effects. The result is that medical and mental health practitioners must carefully weigh the benefits of early interventions using pharmacology with the risks that arise from medications, including adverse effects.

Administration of over-the-counter medications, prescription medications for illness (including antibiotics), psychotropic medications, vaccinations, and complementary and alternative medications has effects on physiological, cognitive, and/or social development. Whether the treatment effects are positive or negative is due to a complex interaction of the medical issue being treated, medication, compliance with medical regimen, age of the young child or infant, and many other factors (Jackson & Martin, 1998).

Summary

This special issue of the *Journal of Early Childhood and Infant Psychology* explores the tension between early pharmacological intervention and risks of prescribing medication to young children and infants. Posey, Bassin, and Lewis (this issue) review the increasing use of psychostimulant medications with very young children, despite the lack of FDA approval for such practices. Recent empirical evidence indicates improvement in ADHD symptoms in preschool-age children but the long-term physiological and neurological effects are unknown. McCabe (this issue) reports on the increased use of antidepressant medications in early childhood despite a lack of evidence of efficacy and safety with this age. This trend has sparked a growing debate in the scientific and mental health communities regarding the use of medications off label when the long-term effects are unknown (Leckman & King, 2007). In the case of depression, the long-term effects of antidepressants are not known and may have serious consequences on neurotransmitter systems as well as physical growth; however, untreated depression and related stress may cause untoward neurophysiological effects that may be irreversible (McCabe, this issue). Similarly, Shaw, Bruce, Ouimet, Sharma, and Glaser (this issue) review the increased use of atypical antipsychotic medications with early childhood autism spectrum disorders and other developmental disabilities. Although these medications have demonstrated efficacy in reducing deleterious symptoms such as hallucinations, aggression, fear, hyperactivity, and self-injurious behaviors, the long-term cognitive, behavioral, and physiological effects are unknown and side effects can be significant.

In addition to the debate regarding the use of psychopharmacology with young children, there is also evidence of increased use of all forms of medications with very young children. Shaw, Su Lin, and colleagues (this issue) investigate the prevalence and consequence of medication use and abuse with young children due to medical error, administration error, independent parent medication decisions, and medication interactions. The high number of emergency room visits each year due to medication error, misuse, and abuse highlights the significance of this problem and suggests greater collaboration among medical professionals, psychologists, educational professionals, and parents is needed. Likewise, Kozyrskyj, Gill, Klassen, and Forgie (this issue) present their research examining the overprescription of antibiotic medications for young children, especially those in vulnerable classes such as low-income situations. The practice of prescribing antibiotic medications when medically unnecessary leads to antibiotic resistance and chronic conditions like asthma. Further, these consequences can be prevented through clinical practical guidelines and availability of quality evidence, both of which are readily used by physicians working with higher-income families but less utilized among physicians working with lower-income families.

The articles in this mini-series highlight the growing use of medications in society to treat a variety of conditions and symptoms, and the fact that these medications have been used with the early childhood population should come as no surprise. However, as concluded by the authors of these articles, clinical practice needs to be guided by solid empirical evidence documenting the efficacy and safety of the medications. This evidence-based practice is even more crucial when considering the rapid developmental changes of neurological and physical systems in early childhood, and the resultant vulnerability of these systems to outside agents.

Psychologists and educators have traditionally not viewed themselves as active contributors to medical decisions made by treating physicians and families, yet they possess a breadth of knowledge regarding child development, normative and atypical behavior patterns, socio-emotional growth, academic achievement, and psychological functioning that contributes to an understanding of diagnosis and treatment of childhood disorders. Collaboration and communication between medical professionals, psychologists, educators, and parents is essential.

Prescribing professionals need to keep abreast of the latest research on medication efficacy and risk, and use conservative decision-making when considering when to go "off label" when prescribing to young children. These professionals will make better decisions when they have as much information as possible about the child, and this is where psychologists and educators can help parents in communicating information to the prescribing professional. Most medications produce side effects and these symptoms can be monitored and recorded for frequency, intensity, and duration by parents and educators. Psychologists are well trained to work with parents and educators to develop a monitoring system that is sensitive to measuring medication efficacy and any related side effects. Psychologists and educators working in early intervention can develop an expanded role that includes facilitation of medical management and encouraging communication between all parties. The greater the collaboration among medical, psychological and educational professionals and families, the more likely pharmacological interventions will lead to desired results, minimize unintended effects, and shorten the duration of treatment due to enhanced treatment specificity.

References

Casiday, R., Cresswell, T., Wilson, D., & Panter-Beck, C. (2006). A survey of UK parental attitudes to the MMR vaccine and trust medical authority. *Vaccine, 24*, 177-184.

Crockett, A. B. (2005). Use of prescription drugs: Rising or declining? *Nursing Clinics of North America, 40*, 33-49.

DSM Pharmaceuticals. (2007). *Adderall (CII) medication guide*. Greenville, NC. Retrieved October 12, 2009 from http://www.fda.gov/downloads/Drugs/DrugSafety/UCM085819.pdf

Elias, M. (2006, May 2). New antipsychotic drugs carry risks for children. *USA Today*. Retrieved from http://www.usatoday.com/news/health/2006-05-01-atypical-drugs_x.htm

Ente, G. (2004). Prevalence of complementary and alternative medicine use in US children. *Archives of Pediatric and Adolescent Medicine, 158*, 292-296.

Fombonne, E., Zakarian, R., Bennett, A., Meng, L., & McLean-Heywood, D. (2006). Pervasive developmental disorders in Montreal, Quebec, Canada: Prevalence and links with immunizations. *Pediatrics, 118*, e139–50.

Gazarian, M. (2009a). Delivering better medicines to children. *Pediatric Drugs, 11*, 41-44.

Gazarian, M. (2009b). Training pediatric clinical pharmacology and therapeutics specialists of the future. *Pediatric Drugs, 11*, 63-66.

Gleason, M. M., Egger, H. L., Emslie, G. J., Greenhill, L. L., Kowatch, R. A., Lieberman, A. F., et al. (2007). Psychopharmacological treatment for very young children: Contexts and guidelines. *Journal of the American Academy of Child and Adolescent Psychiatry, 46*, 1532-1572.

Greenhill, L., Kollins, S., Abikoff, H., McCracken, J., Riddle, M., Swanson, J., et al. (2006). Efficacy and safety of immediate-release methylphenidate treatment for preschoolers with ADHD. *Journal of the American Academy of Child and Adolescent Psychiatry, 45*, 1284-1293.

Harris, G. (2008, November 17). Use of antipsychotics in children is criticized. *The New York Times*. Retrieved June 20, 2009 from http://www.nytimes.com/2008/11/19/health/policy/19fda.html?_r=1&scp=2&sq=Gardiner%20Harris%20antipsychotics&st=cse

Hoppu, K. (2008). Paediatric clinical pharmacology—At the beginning of a new era. *European Journal of Clinical Pharmacology, 64*, 201-205.

Huskamp, H. A. (2005). Pharmaceutical cost management and access to psychotropic drugs: The U.S. context. *International Journal of Law and Psychiatry, 28*, 484-495.

Jackson, S., & Martin, P. Y. (1998). Surviving the care system: Education and resilience. *Journal of Adolescence, 21, 569-583.*

Kaushal, R., Goldman, D., Keohane, C., Christino, M., Honour, M., Hales, K., et al. (2007). Adverse drug events in pediatric outpatients. *Ambulatory Pediatrics, 7*, 383-389.

Khan, A., Khan, S., Kolts, R., & Brown, W. A. (2003). Suicide rates in clinical trials of SSRIs, other antidepressants, and placebo: Analysis of FDA reports. *American Journal of Psychiatry, 160*, 790-792.

Kozyrskyj, A. L., Gill, P. J., Klasson, T. P., & Forgie, M. D. (2009). Double jeopardy in the low-income child: The case of antibiotic use. *Journal of Early Childhood and Infant Psychology, 5,* 79-99.

Lasky, T. (2009). Estimates of pediatric medication use in the United States: Current abilities and limitations. *Clinical Therapeutics, 31*, 436-445.

Leckman, J. F., & King, R. A. (2007). A developmental perspective on the controversy surrounding the use of SSRIs to treat pediatric depression. *American Journal of Psychiatry, 164*, 1304-1306.

Lilienfeld, S. O. (2005). Scientifically unsupported and supported interventions for childhood psychopathology: A summary. *Pediatrics, 115*, 761-764.

Luby, J. L., Belden, A. C., Pautsch, J., Si, X., & Spitznagel, E. (2009). The clinical significance of preschool depression: Impairment in functioning and clinical markers of the disorder. *Journal of Affective Disorders, 112*, 111-119.

Luby, J. L., Heffelfinger, A. K., Mrakotsky, C., Brown, K. M., Hessler, M. J., Wallis, J. M., et al. (2003). The clinical picture of depression in preschool children. *Journal of the American Academy of Child and Adolescent Psychiatry, 42*, 340-348.

Mayes, R., Bagwell., C., & Erkulwater, J. (2009). *Medicating children: ADHD and pediatric mental health.* Cambridge, MA: Harvard University Press.

McCabe, P. C. (2009). The use of antidepressant medications in early childhood: Prevalence, efficacy, and risk. *Journal of Early Childhood and Infant Psychology, 5,* 13-35.

Miller, C. M. (2004, October 16). FDA orders antidepressant warning. *Miami Herald.* Retrieved June 20, 2009 from http://www.antidepressantsfacts. com/2004-10-16-FDA-orders-antideps-warning.htm

Mullins, D. (2009). Pharmaceutical use and outcomes in children. *Clinical Therapeutics, 31*, 420.

Murray, T. L. (2006). The other side of psychopharmacology: A review of the literature. *Journal of Mental Health Counseling, 28*, 309-337.

Nardi, D. A., & Barrett, S. (2005). Potential effects of antidepressant agents on the growth and development of children and adolescents. *Journal of Psychosocial Nursing, 43*, 22-35.

National Institute of Health. (2009). *Conflict of interest information and resources.* Retrieved June 20, 2009 from http://www.nih.gov/about/ethics_ COI.htm

Parnes, B., Smith, P. C., Gilroy, C., Quintela, J., Emsermann, C. B., Dickinson, L. M., et al. (2009). Lack of impact of direct-to-consumer advertising on the physician-patient encounter in primary care: A SNOCAP report. *Annals of Family Medicine, 7*, 41-46.

Paul, I. M. (2007). Advances in pediatric pharmacology, therapeutics, and toxicology. *Advances in Pediatrics, 54*, 29-53.

Posey, W. M., Bassin, S. A., & Lewis, A. (2009). Preschool ADHD and medication…more study needed!? *Journal of Early Childhood and Infant Psychology, 5*, 57-77.

Shah, S. S., Hall, M., Goodman, D. M., Feuer, P., Sharma, V., Fargason, C., et al. (2007). Off-label drug use in hospitalized children. *Archives of Pediatric and Adolescent Medicine, 161*, 282-290.

Shaw, P., Sharp, W. S., Morrison, M., Eckstrand, K., Greenstein, D. K., Clasen, L. S., et al. (2009). Psychostimulant treatment and the developing cortex in attention deficit hyperactivity disorder. *American Journal of Psychiatry, 166*, 58-63.

Shaw, S. R., Bruce, J., Ouimet, T., Sharma, A., & Glaser, S. (2009). Young children with developmental disabilities and atypical antipsychotic medications: Dual diagnosis, direction, and debate. *Journal of Early Childhood and Infant Psychology, 5*, 37-55.

Shaw, S. R., Su Lin, K., Chiu, T. W., Stern, M., Rezazadeh, S. M., & McCabe, P. C. (2009). Error, misuse, and abuse of prescription and over-the-counter medications for young children. *Journal of Early Childhood and Infant Psychology, 5*, 101-120.

Stange, K. C. (2009). Implementation insights. *Annals of Family Medicine, 7*, 179-181.

Stevens, S. (2007). The good doctor: Eight components of professionals in pediatrics are the "bricks and mortar" of practice. *American Academy of Pediatrics, 28*, 26.

Taylor, B. L., Selbst, S. M., & Shah, A. E. C. (2005). Prescription writing errors in the pediatric emergency department. *Pediatric Emergency Case, 12*, 822-827.

Taylor-Zapata, P. & Mattison, D. (2007). Making progress for how medicines are used in children. *Archives of Pediatric and Adolescent Medicine, 161*, 916-920.

The Use of Antidepressant Medications in Early Childhood:
Prevalence, Efficacy, and Risk

Paul C. McCabe
Brooklyn College of the City University of New York

Prescription rates of psychotropic medications for young children have doubled in the past decade, and antidepressants are the second most prescribed medication in the preschool period. This trend of increased antidepressant use among very young children has occurred despite a dearth of safety and efficacy clinical trials. In fact, there has not been one published clinical trial evaluating the efficacy and safety of antidepressant medication with children under age 5. Yet, some clinicians continue to engage in off-label prescribing practices with young children as they attempt to provide the best possible treatment while minimizing harmful adverse effects. Antidepressant medications may serve a beneficial role in attenuating the harmful consequences of long-term stress on neurodevelopment, but this must be considered against potential adverse effects including activation of mania, agitation, irritability, gastrointestinal symptoms, eating and sleep disturbances, growth retardation and increased suicidal ideation. High-quality research trials are needed to examine the efficacy and safety of antidepressant medication therapy with young children, including the short- and long-term outcomes. Until then, clinicians are advised to avoid antidepressant medications as a first-line treatment, and instead use more proven methods such as play therapy, psychotherapy, and parent training.

The number of young children (birth to age 5) prescribed psychotropic medications to treat emotional, behavioral, and/or psychiatric disturbances has increased significantly over the past 2 decades. Prescription rates for young children receiving psychotropic medications, including psychostimulants, antipsychotic medications, and antidepressants, doubled from the late 1990s to the early 2000s (Delate, Gelenberg, Simmons, & Motheral, 2004; Gleason et al., 2007). As of 2002, the prevalence rate for antidepressant use among children

All correspondence should be addressed to Paul C. McCabe, Ph.D., NCSP, School Psychologist Graduate Program, Brooklyn College of the City University of New York, 2900 Bedford Avenue, Brooklyn, NY 11210. Electronic mail may be sent to: paulmc@brooklyn.cuny.edu.

birth to 5 years old was .10 to .23%. The prevalence rate jumps to 1.4% among children 6 to 12 years old (Delate et al., 2004; Vitiello, Zuvekas, & Norquist, 2006). Since the early 1990s, there has been a 3- to 5-fold increase in prescriptions of antidepressants for children aged 2 to 19 years (Leckman & King, 2007; Zito et al., 2003). Antidepressants are the second most prescribed psychotropic medication for preschool children (psychostimulants are the most prescribed), and prescription rates have doubled over a 4-year period (Zito et al., 2000). Antidepressants have been prescribed to treat a variety of emotional, behavioral, and psychological disorders of childhood, including depression, anxiety, ADHD, selective mutism, autism, and enuresis. Although the prevalence of antidepressant use among young children remains much lower than with older children or adolescents, research indicates that behavioral adverse effects (i.e., irritability, aggression, agitation, hyperactivity) from antidepressant use are more common for younger children (Zuckerman et al., 2007). This finding calls into question the feasibility of antidepressant use in early childhood given adverse effects and lack of empirical support (Luby, 2007).

Despite a dearth of scientific data on treatment efficacy and adverse effects, prescription rates of early childhood psychopharmacology are increasing. This underscores the urgent need for additional research in this area (Luby, 2007). Further, evidence suggests that young children coming from families with the greatest economic need are more likely to be medicated for behavioral and/ or emotional symptoms. For example, Zito and colleagues (2007) reviewed Medicaid insurance records from 2001 and compared the results to similar records from 1995. They found that 2.3% of Medicaid-insured preschoolers received psychotherapeutic medications in 2001, double the rate in 1995, and this increase was largely due to increases across ages 2 to 4 for psychostimulant, antipsychotic, and antidepressant medications. Of the psychotherapeutic medications prescribed, 20.5% were antidepressants (Zito et al., 2007). These results are alarming when considering how little is known about the efficacy of antidepressant medications in early childhood, especially adverse effects, and potentially permanent changes to neurobiological and developmental structures. It is important that mental health professionals working in early childhood carefully consider the available research on treatment strategies for emotional and behavioral symptoms, including a thorough understanding of developmental psychopathology, differential diagnosis, and empirically valid treatment strategies that minimize adverse effects.

Depression in Early Childhood

Major depressive disorder (MDD) in childhood is characterized by intense and persistent sadness, which can alternately manifest as irritability in children. Other symptoms include loss of interest in daily activities, diminished self-esteem, sleep and/or eating dysfunction, feelings of hopelessness, and increase in suicidal ideation. An estimated .8% to 1% of preschoolers meet the criteria for MDD, which increases to 2% in the latency childhood years and 4.5% in adolescence (Silva, Gabbay, Minami, Munoz-Silva, & Alonso, 2005). This means that more than one million youth in the U.S. are diagnosed with MDD (Silva et al.).

Although the diagnosis of MDD has been validated for children as young as 3 years old, the clinical presentation of MDD in early childhood differs slightly from that of older children (Dopheide, 2006). Similar to older children, preschoolers with MDD often manifest greater somatic complaints and unexplained irritability. In addition, they may exhibit markedly diminished interest in play; engage in suicidal, self-destructive themes in play; and report feelings of worthlessness (Dopheide). One significant difference is that preschool children often do not meet the 2-week duration criteria, and therefore this criteria needs to be adjusted to ensure that young children with MDD are not overlooked (Dopheide; Luby et al., 2003).

Luby and colleagues (2003) examined the diagnostic construct of MDD with 155 preschool children referred to a community mental health agency or a pediatrician's office through an advertisement about "emotional development." The resultant sample included 55 children with depression, 43 with attention-deficit hyperactivity disorder and obsessive compulsive disorder (ADHD/OCD), and 57 typically developing controls. Modifications were made to the *Diagnostic and Statistical Manual of Mental Disorders* (DSM-IV) diagnostic criteria for MDD to better capture early childhood manifestations of symptoms. These symptoms were compared to the clinical control (ADHD/OCD) and typical control samples to identify which symptoms, both typical and masked (nonaffective), differentiated the clinical characteristics of young children with MDD. Results indicated that a persistent sad and irritable mood (98% of children with MDD had this symptom), anhedonia, and lack of energy were the more specific and sensitive typical symptoms. Among masked symptoms, somatic complaints were the most common, although it was reported at a much lower frequency than the typical symptoms. The authors concluded that

> these findings are the first to demonstrate that the clinical picture of depression in the preschool period also manifests predominantly as 'typical symptoms' such as sadness/irritability and is associated with neurovegetative signs rather than with a predominance of 'masked' nonaffective symptoms (Luby et al., 2003, p. 347).

Table 1 presents the findings from Luby et al. (2003) regarding typical and masked symptoms in preschoolers with MDD in order of frequency.

Table 1

Symptoms of Major Depressive Disorder in Preschool Children, in Order of Frequency

Symptoms
Typical Symptoms
Sad/irritable mood
Anhedonia
Lack of energy
Change in activity
Whiny/crying often
Violent pretend play
Difficulty thinking and concentrating
Low self-esteem
Sad, scary, traumatic play
Weight/appetite and/or sleep problems
Death and/or suicide themes in play or speech
Masked Symptoms
Somatic complaints
Unexcited
Withdrawn
Afraid to leave home
Unreactive
Regression

Note. Adapted from Luby, J. L., Heffelfinger, A. K., Mrakotsky, C., Brown, K. M., Hessler, M. J., Wallis, J. M., et al. (2003). The clinical picture of depression in preschool children. *Journal of the American Academy of Child and Adolescent Psychiatry, 42*, 340-348.

This work was extended further in a more recent exploration of symptoms and clinical markers of depression among preschoolers (Luby, Belden, Pautsch, Si, & Spitznagel, 2009). Three-hundred fifty preschoolers were recruited through a depression screening checklist completed by parents, and were assessed on psychiatric symptomatology and levels of functional impairment and development. The results validate earlier findings (e.g., Luby et al., 2003) that there are distinct symptoms that differentiate children with MDD from healthy controls as well as from anxiety and disruptive disorders. The symptoms that distinguish children with MDD from healthy controls include, in order of specificity, fatigue, guilt, irritability, anhedonia, sad and tearful mood, diminished cognitive abilities, weight change, sleep problems, psychomotor agitation, and thoughts of death. The symptoms that differentiate children with MDD from children with disruptive behaviors include sleep problems, weight changes, guilt, anhedonia, and diminished cognitive abilities. Finally, the symptoms that distinguish children with MDD from children with anxiety disorders include guilt, weight changes, diminished cognitive abilities, and psychomotor agitation. The authors also note that extreme fatigue and guilt were highly specific to MDD after controlling for anxiety and disruptive behaviors, and may be particularly important clinical markers for depression in young children (Luby et al., 2009).

Further, the researchers identified depression subgroups that could be differentiated according to a statistically significant hierarchy (Luby et al., 2009). The subgroup with the highest depression levels was characterized by severe anhedonia. This finding supports earlier research supporting the role of anhedonia as a key indicator of preschool-age depression (Luby et al., 2006). In sum, these findings indicate that there are significant differences in depression symptom severity in preschool-age children such that MDD: (a) represents a unique mood disorder, (b) can be differentiated from symptoms of anxiety or an undifferentiated internalizing disorder, and (c) has clinical implications for differing treatment protocols similar to those seen with older children and adults. This is important when considering whether to prescribe antidepressant medications with young children, as research has shown that these medications have greater efficacy when used with the more severe subtypes of depression (Boylan, Romero, & Birmaher, 2007).

Complicating the clinical picture of depression in the early childhood years is the normal developmental variation and the rapid growth that occurs during this period. The preschool years represent the age when children typically leave the home, join more structured educational and play settings, expand their socialization circles, and are increasingly challenged cognitively and emotionally. All of these situations may produce stress for the young child, leading to behavioral and emotional disruptions (Stalets & Luby, 2006). To a degree, variation in emotion and behavior is developmentally appropriate and reflects the challenges faced in the course of developmental maturation. Thus, the boundary between normal variations of behavior and emotion and clinically significant symptoms can be challenging to identify (Stalets & Luby, 2006).

In addition, there is evidence for the occurrence of subsyndromal depression in early childhood. Subsyndromal depression is the presence of depressive symptoms that do not meet full diagnostic criteria for MDD. Some researchers estimate that subsyndromal depression is more prevalent than MDD and may reflect the emergent stages of a depressive disorder (Vitiello et al., 2006). The differentiation of behaviors and mood fluctuations that reflect normal developmental variations versus subsyndromal and/or emergent depression symptomatology, or other clinical mood disorders such as bipolar depression, is problematic. Additional research is needed that discriminates variations of mood and behavior that fall within normal developmental trajectories from those symptoms indicating the emergence or presence of a mood disorder.

Given the difficulties in differentiating clinical and subclinical manifestations of mood and behavior from typical development, it may make intuitive sense to wait and not treat depression until the diagnosis is confirmed beyond a reasonable doubt. However, there is growing evidence examining gene and environmental interactions that suggests there are vulnerability periods in the pathogenesis of MDD, and untreated depression may lead to deleterious effects on the central nervous system (Pruett & Luby, 2004). This may occur through recurrent and chronic activation of the neuroendocrine system in response to stress (such as abuse) that leads to alterations of the hypothalamic-pituitary-adrenal axis, causing atrophy and structural damage to brain structures like the hippocampus (Penza, Heim, & Nemeroff, 2003; Pruett & Luby). This effect is evident in adult patients, as the length of time of untreated depression correlates with the magnitude of the hippocampal volume loss (Sheline, Gado, & Kraemer, 2003). This finding suggests that antidepressant medications may have a neuroprotective effect and should be considered when weighing the potential risks and benefits of antidepressant treatment (Pruett & Luby).

In summary, research on depression in early childhood has reliably identified markers for MDD that are distinguished from other behavioral and emotional disorders, as well from normal variations of mood. This includes the presence of anhedonia, persistent sad and irritable mood, weight and sleep changes, guilt, and diminished cognitive abilities. However, additional research is needed to identify symptom patterns that are unique to MDD and predictive of exacerbation of symptoms and co-morbid disorders later in childhood. In addition, it is unclear if some subtypes of MDD in early childhood are likely to follow a milder course and perhaps lead to complete remission, including subsyndromal depression, as compared to more chronic and severe trajectories. Identification of these subtypes would help guide research that examines the neurological sequelae of depression, such as whether the more chronic and severe trajectories of depression lead to permanent neuroendocrine and structural abnormalities.

Efficacy of Antidepressant Medications in Early Childhood

Neuropsychiatric Mechanism

The most commonly prescribed antidepressant medications in early childhood are selective serotonin reuptake inhibitors (SSRI; Vitiello et al., 2006). Although each medication varies in its specific neurochemical action, they are similar in that they antagonize or block the recycling of serotonin into the transmitting and receiving neurons. This action serves to prolong the serotonin release in the synaptic cleft thus facilitating increased or enhanced interneuronal transmission. Other neurotransmitters may also be differentially enhanced (agonist) or blocked (antagonist) through the use of antidepressants, including dopamine, norepinephrine, acetylcholine, gamma-aminobutyric acid (GABA), and glutamate. Newer classes of medications are being developed that target more precisely depression symptoms. This newer class of medications includes, in addition to SSRIs, serotonin and norepinephrine reuptake inhibitors (SNRI), norepinephrine and dopamine reuptake inhibitors (NDRIs), noradrenergic and specific serotonergic antidepressants (NaSSA), and serotonin-noradrenaline-dopamine reuptake inhibitor (SNDRI; Breuer et al., 2008).

The development of new classes of antidepressant medications greatly outpaces the number of clinical trials demonstrating efficacy with young children. In fact, the U.S. Food and Drug Administration (FDA) has not approved antidepressants in children under age 6. Approval was granted for the use of fluoxetine (e.g., Prozac) for depression and obsessive compulsive disorder (OCD) in children age 7 and older, sertraline (e.g., Zoloft) for OCD in children age 6 and older, and fluvoxamine (e.g., Luvox) for OCD in children age 8 and older (Zuckerman et al., 2007). The paucity of controlled clinical studies with the early childhood population is a primary reason for the lack of approval by the FDA, citing concerns of efficacy and safety (Harvard Health Letter, 2003). Table 2 lists common antidepressants, class, and approval and therapeutic application for children.

Despite the lack of the FDA approval, off-label prescription practice is widespread, with an estimated 60% of prescriptions in the U.S. written off-label, and often prescribed to pediatric patients (Spetie & Arnold, 2007). The FDA has no authority to regulate the practice of medicine, and therefore it is incumbent upon physicians to conduct their own investigation to determine whether to prescribe off-label (Spetie & Arnold). Spetie and Arnold argue that this often places physicians in the difficult position of balancing beneficence (treating the illness according to best practices to improve health and quality of life) and nonmaleficence (protecting patients from unsafe or ineffective treatments). This is particularly true of treatments for very young children given the lack of safety and efficacy studies.

Neurodevelopment

Of critical importance to the investigation of treatment safety and efficacy is the impact of psychotropic medications on neurodevelopment in young children. Research has demonstrated the sensitivity of the developing brain. Synaptic and receptor density and cerebral metabolic rates peak at age 3 (Gleason et al., 2007), and by the age of 5 the brain has tripled in mass to almost adult weight (Nardi & Barrett, 2005). Serotonin receptors have been implicated in a variety of cognitive activities, including declarative and non-declarative memory functions, memory formation and consolidation, retrieval of aversive or emotional memories, and spatial learning. Serotonin receptors also regulate acetylcholine, dopamine, and

Table 2

Common Antidepressants, Generic and Trade Names, Antidepressant Class, and Approval Status with Younger Children.

Antidepressant Medication Trade name (generic name)	Antidepressant Class	Approved for use with young children?	Approved theraputic application(s)
Anafranil (clomipramine)	TCA	Yes, age 10 and older	OCD
Celexa (citalopram hydrobromide)	SSRI	No	Depression (adults)
Cymbalta (duloxetine)	SNRI	No	Depression (adults)
Effexor (venlafaxine)	SNRI	No	Depression (adults)
Elavil (amitriptyline)	TCA	No	Depression (adults)
Lexapro (escitalopram oxalate)	SSRI	No, age 12 and older	Depression
Luvox (fluvoxamine)	SSRI	Yes, age 8 and older	OCD
Paxil (paroxetine)	SSRI	No	Depression, Anxiety
Prozac (fluoxetine)	SSRI	Yes, age 7 and older	Depression (age 8+) OCD (age 7+)
Sinequan (trimipramine)	TCA	No, age 12 and older	Depression, Anxiety
Wellbutrin (bupropion)	NDRI	No	Depression (adults)
Zoloft (sertraline)	SSRI	Yes, age 6 and older	OCD

SSRI = Selective Serotonin Reuptake Inhibitor; SNRI = Serotonin and Norepinephrine Reuptake Inhibitor; TCA = Tricyclic Antidepressant; NDRI = Norepinephrine and Dopamine Reuptake Inhibitor

noradrenergic neural systems, all of which are involved in mechanisms of learning and memory (Ögren et al., 2008).

   Depression is characterized by a dysregulated response to stress with prolonged release of corticosterone which dominates serotonin receptors, making them less responsive to normal serotonin activity, which also impacts cholinergic, noradrenergic, and dopaminergic systems (Ögren et al., 2008). Prolonged exposure to stressful events associated with depression in early childhood can impact receptor organization and neurodevelopment (Gleason et al., 2007). Preschool children with MDD who withdraw from everyday cognitive, social, and physical experiences may be contributing to premature pruning of synaptic connections associated with normal psychological development. There is preliminary data suggesting that SSRIs and related serotonin agonists may serve a protective role in the neural development of individuals with MDD (Nardi & Barrett, 2005). For instance, serotonin activators act to lower glucocortisol levels that are triggered from stress and depression, thus helping to mitigate the harmful effects of corticosterone on learning, memory, and emotion (Nardi & Barrett, 2005). In this regard, SSRIs may help to attenuate the harmful effects of stress and potentially facilitate learning.

Conversely, research with animal models indicates that early exposure to psychotropic medications can permanently influence distribution of neurotransmitter receptors (Gleason et al., 2007). In addition, medication absorption and metabolic processes differ for young children than older children or adults, and typically indicate higher dosing to achieve comparable plasma levels (Gleason et al.). Additional adverse effects have been documented with SSRIs in the preschool population and will be discussed later in this article. Gleason and colleagues argue that, "taken together, developmental pharmacokinetic issues and sensitivity to adverse effects make dosing medications in young children a delicate balance" (2007, p. 1536).

Therapeutic Application

Antidepressant medications are used to treat a number of pediatric disorders including depression, anxiety, ADHD, selective mutism, autism, and enuresis (Vitiello et al., 2006). However, as previously mentioned, only a handful of SSRIs and tricyclic antidepressants (TCAs) have been approved by the FDA for use in pediatric populations, and none are approved for children younger than age 6. Nevertheless, off-label prescriptions are common for treating pediatric mood and behavioral disorders, and this occurs to a lesser degree in the preschool population (Vitiello et al., 2006). In one study of 120 preschool children receiving psychotropic treatment through a Health Maintenance Organization (HMO) for a behavioral and/or emotional disorder, 15 (12.5%) received an antidepressant medication either alone or in combination with a psychostimulant or an α_2–adrenergic agonist (DeBar, Lynch, Powell, & Gale, 2003). Interestingly, none of the 15 children had a specific diagnosis of mood/anxiety disorder. It is important to consider the various therapeutic applications with the use of off-label antidepressant medication in young children.

Depressive/bipolar disorders. Treatment for MDD and related mood disorders in early childhood is challenging for clinicians because of frequently comorbid disorders, psychosocial and family problems, and symptom constellations and duration that may differ from that of older children or adults. A significant number of children have recurrent syndromal or subsyndromal depressive episodes with associated psychosocial impairment, and early intervention and treatment of these symptoms can prevent exacerbation and chronicity (Boylan et al., 2007; Luby et al., 2009). However, while early intervention of depressive symptoms may prevent future problems, treatment planning should consider whether antidepressant pharmacological treatment has proven to be effective. Some researchers have reported that antidepressant use in children under age 8 does not have demonstrated efficacy (Dopheide, 2006; Emslie et al., 2002), while at least one study reported reduction of depressive symptoms with certain antidepressants (especially fluoxetine) in children as young as age 6 (Hetrick, Merry, McKenzie, Sindahl, & Proctor, 2007).

Antidepressant medications may also be prescribed to treat the depressive symptoms of an undiagnosed bipolar disorder. It is unclear if the use of antidepressant medications in the presence of subsyndromal or emerging syndromal bipolar disorder could induce mania. Luby and Mrakotsky (2003) found preschoolers with MDD had higher rates of restlessness if there was a family history of bipolar disorder, as compared to preschoolers with MDD without a family history of bipolar disorder. Similar findings have confirmed that young children with MDD with markers of risk for bipolar disorder may be vulnerable to mania induced by antidepressant medication (Pruett & Luby, 2004). In one study of 31 patients with bipolar disorder aged 2 to 5 years, 21 were previously treated with either a psychostimulant or antidepressant without a mood stabilizer (Scheffer & Apps, 2004). Of those 21 patients, 13 (62%) reported a worsening of mood symptoms. Once the appropriate diagnosis was made and treatment with a mood stabilizer was initiated (primarily valproic acid), 26 of the 31 patients (84%) showed a significant decrease in manic symptoms (Scheffer & Apps).

Accordingly, it is important to closely monitor children with a suspected mood disorder for symptoms and/or family history of mania to ensure an accurate diagnosis is made. Young children taking antidepressant medications should also be closely monitored for symptoms of activation or psychosis during the first few months of treatment, especially if there is a family predisposition for bipolar disorder (Boylan et al., 2007).

Additional research is needed examining the efficacy and safety of antidepressants prescribed to treat depressive symptoms in early childhood. Much of the extant literature is limited to chart reviews which contain limited information regarding baseline functioning, as well as studies that lack blinded experimental designs or rely on case studies. Because the treating physicians need to prescribe "off-label" to young children, there may be a concern about divulging this practice and registering patients into larger, more rigorous clinical trials. There is also the potential concern about placing a young child into a placebo condition when his or her symptoms are serious and warrant immediate intervention. Rigorous clinical trials are needed that carefully assess medication efficacy and adverse effects with young children, as well as longitudinal trials that assess medication effects later in life.

Anxiety. Although antidepressants are primarily prescribed for the treatment of depressive symptoms, there is some evidence of antidepressant off-label use, especially SSRIs, for the treatment of anxiety symptoms in preschool children. Currently, only sertraline, fluoxetine, and fluvoxamine have FDA approval for treating obsessive-compulsive symptoms in children aged 6, 7, and 8 years and older, respectively (Zuckerman et al., 2007). Nevertheless, Zuckerman et al. (2007) found in their study of 39 children below age 7 (mean age: 5.9 ± 0.8 years) who began SSRI treatment that 54% were diagnosed with an anxiety disorder and 20% were diagnosed with a combined anxiety and depressive disorder. Only 23% of study participants had a diagnosis of a depressive disorder. These findings are consistent with prevalence rates of anxiety disorders in preschool age children, which range from 0.3% to 11.5% depending on the anxiety disorder (McDonnell & Glod, 2003). When compared to a conservative prevalence rate of 1% of MDD in preschool children, anxiety disorders are significantly more widespread. This indicates that, statistically speaking, young children are more likely to be prescribed an SSRI to treat an anxiety disorder than MDD. However, with the exception of a few case studies, there is currently no research examining the efficacy or safety of SSRIs used in early childhood to treat anxiety disorders.

Selective mutism. Selective mutism, a specific form of anxiety disorder, is estimated to occur in 7 out of 1000 children (Lindsey, Piacentini, & McCracken, 2002). The disorder is often dependent on the social context, where the child is selectively silent in one or more settings while talking normally in another setting. There is a small body of evidence suggesting that SSRIs can be effective in improving symptoms. In one study, greater global improvements, speech, and functioning were noted in the 10 children who had been treated with an SSRI compared to the 7 children who were unmedicated (Manassis & Tannock, 2008). Another small study using a randomly-ordered treatment phase found improvement in speaking in four of five children within a few days of starting sertraline (Carlson, Kratochwill, & Johnston, 1999; Silva et al., 2005). Fluoxetine is the most studied SSRI with the selectively mute population, although little is known about long-term effects, optimal dosage, and duration of treatment (Kaakeh & Stumpf, 2008).

Autism. Serotonin has been implicated in the symptoms of autism and the neurodevelopment of young children with autism. Research indicates reduced brain serotonin synthesis during periods of peak synaptic growth and altered spatial patterns of serotonin synthesis in individuals with autism (Bethea & Sikich, 2007). In most individuals, serotonin synthesis is at 200% of adult levels until age 5, and then falls to adult levels several years later. However, in young children with autism, serotonin synthesis is very low until around age 9, and then increases to 120% of typical adult levels. Serotonin synthesis parallels both typical and atypical synaptogenesis patterns associated with autism, suggesting that neurodevelopment may be significantly altered in key cortical regions in the brains of children with autism (Bethea & Sikich).

Also, there is some evidence that SSRIs are effective in treating stereotypic and perseverative behaviors of autism. Not surprisingly, the SSRIs with known efficacy in reducing obsessive-compulsive behaviors have shown similar utility in treating repetitive autism behaviors (Hollander, Phillips, & Yeh, 2003). The use of citalopram with patients aged 6 to 16 years old with pervasive developmental disorder (PDD) was successful in improving PDD, anxiety, and mood scores in 73% of patients (Namerow, Thomas, Bostic, Prince, & Monuteaux, 2003). Efficacy studies examining fluoxetine, fluvoxamine, sertraline, and escitalopgram with children with PDD have found similar positive results, especially in the area of reducing anxiety and repetitive behaviors (Kolevzon, Mathewson, & Hollander, 2006; Posey, Erickson, Stigler, & McDougle, 2006). However, as with the disorders discussed above, there is limited evidence of efficacy and safety of these medications when used with children under age 6.

Enuresis. Enuresis is a troubling condition for children and affects as many as 15 to 20% of 5-year-olds (Glazener, Evans, & Peto, 2003). It is important to ascertain whether the child has progressed through the developmentally appropriate toilet training process, and despite being trained, continues to exhibit urinary incontinence. Antidepressant medications have been prescribed for children experiencing nocturnal enuresis, along with behavioral treatments and vasopressin-synthetic drugs, with some positive results. The most commonly prescribed class of antidepressant for enuresis is TCAs, such as amitriptyline, imipramine, and nortriptyline. In a study of antidepressant use in the United Kingdom, Murray, de Vries, and Wong (2004) found that in children under age 10, TCAs were used in 75% of the cases to treat nocturnal enuresis. One study found that TCAs were effective in reducing the number of wet nights while taking the medication, but most children relapsed after stopping the medication (Glazener et al., 2003). In contrast, only half the children relapsed after discontinuing the "bed-and-pad" alarm treatment. TCAs come with a host of serious adverse effects, and therefore should be considered more as a "last resort" option in treating enuresis (Nevéus, 2006).

Adverse Effects

The use of antidepressant medications with children and adolescents is associated with a number of unfavorable negative reactions, or adverse effects. Although there are few high quality, double-blind placebo research studies using the early childhood population, the available evidence suggests that adverse effects are notable in this age and must be carefully weighed against any potential benefit from medication use. For example, in the Zuckerman et al. (2007) retrospective chart review of 39 patients under age 7, 28% reported adverse effects of at least moderate severity and 18% discontinued the use of the SSRI because of adverse effects. The discontinuation rate is twice that seen in older children and adolescents, which is typically around 8 to 9% (Zuckerman et al.). Adverse effects included behavioral effects (especially behavioral activation, such as agitation, aggression, irritability, and/or increased energy) and gastrointestinal distress. The higher discontinuation rate and prevalence and severity of medication effects suggest that younger children are more vulnerable to adverse effects from SSRIs than older children and adolescents (Zuckerman et al.).

Similar rates were observed in a sample of 82 older children (mean age: 12.2 ± 3.2 years) in which 22% of the participants experienced psychiatric adverse effects (Wilens et al., 2007). Adverse effects reported by the sample, in order of frequency, include sleep disturbances, gastrointestinal complaints, mood disturbances (especially irritability, anxiety, and depression), psychotic symptoms, and tics. These effects dissipated shortly after discontinuation of the medication. Other documented adverse effects of SSRIs in children and adolescents include nausea, dry mouth, dyspepsia (i.e., indigestion), dizziness, emotional lability, hostility, tremor, pharyngitis (i.e., sore throat), respiratory distress, rhinitis, sinusitis, and flu-like symptoms (Hetrick et al., 2007).

This research highlights the importance of carefully recording younger children's responsiveness to antidepressants versus older children or adolescents, as opposed to lumping all children and adolescents together into an "under 18" category. Among other things, younger children have vastly different metabolic rates for processing medications, different hormone levels, and differential maturation of noradrenergic and serotoninergic neurotransmitter systems (Nardi & Barrett, 2005). It is likely that some adverse effects are more common among younger children than older children or adolescents, given the differences in neurodevelopment, immune system, metabolism rates, nutritional intake, and treatment adherence.

Another adverse effect of concern, particularly for young children, is stunted growth. Stunted growth may result from prolonged antidepressant use, due to the suppression effect that occurs from serotonin on growth hormone secretion (Nardi & Barrett, 2005). However, few studies have closely examined this relationship, and most have focused on exposure to antidepressants *in utero* or growth patterns in animals. One study followed four boys (aged 11.6 to 13.7) treated with SSRIs and found that all four had growth attenuation (Weintrob, Cohen, Klipper-Aurbach, Zadik, & Dickerman, 2002). Three of the boys exhibited growth retardation at puberty, and three had a reduced response to growth hormones. When SSRI therapy discontinued, normal growth patterns resumed. Work with mice examining the influence of SSRIs indicated detrimental effects on bone mineral accrual reflective of skeletal growth retardation (Warden, Robling, Sanders, Bliziotes, & Turner, 2005). Other research with mice and rats has identified troubling effects of SSRI exposure including impaired development of exploratory activity, impaired avoidance of danger, altered locomotor activity, and reduced visual discrimination and attention (Leckman & King, 2007). Additional research is needed to elucidate this important relationship further, using a larger sample and examining growth patterns of younger children.

A final and very important adverse effect of antidepressant use is reported elevations in suicide ideation and/or self-harm. In 2003 and 2004, the FDA and European regulators issued public health advisories in the form of black box warnings cautioning of the risk of suicide and self-harm with antidepressant use with children and adolescents (Leckman & King, 2007). This decision was based on analysis of 24 short-term studies of 4,400 youth in which there was a doubled risk of suicidal thinking among antidepressant users than placebo (4% vs. 2%; Silva et al., 2005). However, there were no completed suicides among the studies in the FDA review. A recent meta-analytic review of pediatric antidepressant use suggests that the benefits of antidepressant medications outweigh the likely risks for children and adolescents with MDD and anxiety disorders (Bridge et al., 2007). However, the age of the participants in these studies ranged primarily from 6 to 18, and only one study included 5-year-olds with generalized anxiety disorder. Thus, little can be said about the effect of antidepressants on suicidal thinking among very young children.

By all accounts, suicide among very young children is exceedingly rare. In fact, the Centers for Disease Control's recent Morbidity and Mortality Weekly Report only reports suicides for children age 10 and older, and those rates are quite low (1.1 deaths per 100,000 population; Centers for Disease Control [CDC], 2009). However, the suicide rate among US children aged 5 to 14 years tripled from 1979 to 1999 from 0.4 to 1.2 per 100,000 (Gould, Shaffer, & Greenberg, 2003). This trend is being observed globally as well. For example, an Austrian study found seven suicides among 5 to 9-year-olds between 1970 and 2001, all completed by hanging (thus accidental death was ruled out; Dervic et al., 2006). There were six children between the ages 5 to 11 who completed suicide in Manitoba from 1995 to 2006 (Katz et al., 2008).

Very little is known about suicidal behaviors and rates of suicide in children age 5 and under. One study compared sixteen 2.5 to 5-year-olds referred to a university psychiatric clinic for suicidal ideation to 16 behaviorally disordered non-suicidal matched peers (Rosenthal & Rosenthal, 1984). The researchers found the suicidal group to exhibit significantly more self-directed aggression, loss of interest, morbid ideas, depression, impulsivity, hyperactivity, running away behaviors and less pain after injury. They were also more likely to come from unwanted, maltreated, or neglectful parenting situations. Although younger children are less likely to attempt suicide than their older counterparts, the manifestation of suicidal ideation and other psychopathology are risk conditions that predict later suicidal attempts. For example, 3-year-old children who are under-controlled (impulsive, restless, distractible) and inhibited (shy, fearful, easily upset) are more likely to attempt suicide by age 21 (Caspi, Moffitt, Newman, & Silva, 1996). This suggests that early identification and intervention of early childhood depressive disorders is important in preventing mood symptoms and suicidality at a later age. What is unclear, however, is what role antidepressant medications should play, if any.

Efficacy of Antidepressants

A number of studies have been conducted examining the efficacy of antidepressants with children and adolescents, and most have focused on older children (e.g., age 8 and older) and on SSRIs such as fluoxetine. Bridge and colleagues (2007) examined the efficacy of antidepressants in pediatric populations as well as risk of suicidality and other adverse effects. Twenty-seven trials of pediatric MDD, OCD, and anxiety disorders were examined and pooled risk differences in rates of responding (corresponding to a number needed to treat) were calculated. Relative to placebo, the antidepressants were most effective for anxiety disorders (37.1%), moderately effective for OCD (19.8%), and modestly effective for MDD (11.0%). There was an increased risk of suicide ideation/ attempt across all trials (MDD: 3% vs. 2% placebo; OCD: 1% vs. 0.3% placebo; anxiety disorders: 1% vs. 0.2% placebo). However, the authors argued that the benefit-to-risk ratio was not significant and therefore the benefits of antidepressant treatment outweigh any potential risk of increased suicidality. Another important finding was that in children with MDD under age 12, only fluoxetine showed a significant treatment effect over placebo.

An additional meta-analysis examined both published and unpublished trial data for four SSRIs (i.e., fluoxetine, venlafaxine, nefazodone, paroxetine) to examine efficacy over placebo in patients of all ages (Kirsch et al., 2008). The authors accounted for symptom severity and drug-placebo difference scores in the meta-analysis. They found that drug-placebo differences increased as symptom severity increased, with patients with moderate depression showing almost no difference between drug and placebo groups, and severely depressed patients reaching clinical significance of drug-placebo effect. They concluded that there is little evidence that SSRI antidepressant medications should be prescribed except in the case of very severely depressed patients to whom other alternative treatments have been ineffective (Kirsch et al.).

The available evidence does not support the efficacy of antidepressant medications for treatment of depressive symptoms with children under age 12 (Dopheide, 2006). Evidence from trials with older children, adolescents, and adults indicates that fluoxetine may have limited therapeutic value especially with more severely depressed individuals. In general, treatment for younger children should not include antidepressant medications as a first-line treatment, but instead should include a multimodal treatment approach including family education, family therapy, and cognitive behavior therapy.

Research Challenges

The lack of evidence for young children's responsiveness to psychopharmacology contrasts starkly with clinician prescription practices which include off-label prescriptions of psychotropic medications without adequate safety and efficacy data (Greenhill et al., 2003). There are significant obstacles to conducting psychopharmacological research with young children, including concerns about medication effects on neurodevelopment, adverse effects, lack of animal models that mimic early childhood disorders, rapid developmental changes, and the variability of typical development. Greenhill and colleagues (2003) make a number of recommendations intended to improve the ethical, practical, and scientific value of psychopharmacological studies conducted with preschoolers. They recommend the following: (a) use only preschoolers with stable psychiatric disorders or symptom complexes; (b) use only preschoolers with severe symptoms in psychopharmacological studies; (c) gather information about symptom presentation from multiple settings and contexts; (d) monitor long-term treatment effects to assess impact on later development; and (e) involve early childhood experts to create developmentally appropriate assessments and apparatuses, and help pinpoint normal developmental variation from psychopathology.

There are important ethical considerations in terms of when and how to include young children in psychopharmacological research, as well as how to provide the best possible treatment given the symptom severity and constellation. Young children have been considered "therapeutic orphans" because researchers have heretofore avoided conducting the safety and efficacy trials necessary to validate medications (Coté, Kauffman, Troendle, & Lambert, 1996). As a result, clinicians have to decide between foregoing a medication entirely because of insufficient safety and efficacy data, or forging ahead with the medication through a downward extrapolation of adolescent and adult safety and efficacy data (Jensen, 1998).

Spetie and Arnold (2007) outline examples of ethical issues that can be applied to research conducted with child psychopharmacological research. This includes (a) respect for person, such as the autonomy needed to provide consent (which may be doubly challenging due to the vulnerability of immature age and psychiatric disturbance); (b) beneficence (including carefully considering placebo discontinuation for those children who really need treatment); and (c) justice (such as helping to build a research base of psychopharmacological treatments specifically for children). These are weighty ethical concerns when evaluating the efficacy and safety of antidepressants, which carry a risk of behavioral activation, agitation, akathisia, and mania induction in young children. Among other questions, it is unclear if the emergence of activation and mania reflects an unmasking of a subsyndromal bipolar disorder, a side effect of the medication, or an adverse effect on neurodevelopment (Spetie & Arnold).

Alternative Treatment Strategies

Although some researchers call for the "cautious and well-monitored" use of antidepressants as a first-line treatment option (Bridge et al., 2007, p. 1694), others have argued that use of antidepressants with children should only be considered in the most serious of depression cases that fail to respond to non-pharmacological interventions (Dopheide, 2006; Leckman & King, 2007; Wong, Besag, Santosh, & Murray, 2004; Zuckerman et al., 2007). This is a particularly important caution for treatment of preschool MDD as there have been no safety studies with this age (Stalets & Luby, 2006).

There is a growing body of literature supporting the efficacy of cognitive behavior therapy and interpersonal therapy with children with MDD, and the treatment options are ideally suited to children with mild or moderate depression (Wong et al., 2004). Parents and families are significant influences for young children, and interventions may be best directed at helping parents to develop supportive management skills. For example, in a study of 146 children 3 to 5-years-old with behavioral inhibition (a specific risk for social anxiety disorder, panic and depressive disorders), Hirshfeld-Becker et al. (2008) employed a cognitive behavioral intervention for parents and their behaviorally inhibited child. The intervention included hierarchical exposure, cognitive restructuring, and parent management strategies. The intervention succeeded in reducing the number of anxiety disorders in the children one year later as compared to placebo (2.1 to 0.7 in the treatment condition, 1.8 to 1.1 in the untreated condition; Rapee, Kennedy, Ingram, Edwards, & Sweeney, 2005).

Interventions directed at helping parents manage and support their child with MDD or anxiety are likely effective because they help create a therapeutic environment for the child. Bratton, Ray, Rhine, and Jones (2005) conducted a meta-analysis of play therapy interventions for children. They found that those play therapy techniques emphasizing humanistic, non-directive approaches produced a larger overall effect size than those using a non-humanistic, directive style. Also, play therapy that included a parent (filial-trained) produced a significantly larger effect size than play therapy conducted solely by the professional. Play therapy including the parent/caregiver has relevance in the early childhood population since most children spend most of their waking hours in the company of their parents, and therefore parents may be best suited to monitor and intervene when their child experiences mood relapses or related symptoms.

Interventions with a psychosocial focus may be particularly effective for young children, especially when it is apparent that the depressive symptoms are caused, in whole or part, by the child's environment (Dopheide, 2006). These interventions may include therapeutic support for depressed or overwhelmed parents. In fact, there is some evidence that cognitive behavior therapy and interpersonal therapy approaches do not have demonstrated efficacy in young children (Dopheide, 2006), and may be better directed to help parents of children with MDD to better cope with their child's symptoms.

Conclusion

The recent validation of MDD in the early childhood period has helped pave the way for earlier identification and intervention of mood disorders (Luby et al., 2009). This is important considering the rapid developmental growth during the early childhood years, as well as research suggesting that untreated depression leads to long-term neurobiological, psychiatric, and social-emotional consequences (Gleason et al., 2007; Nardi & Barrett, 2005). The efficacy of early intervention with other mental disorders (e.g., autism, conduct problems, ADHD) in early childhood is well established, and interventions targeted to alter the developmental trajectory of young children suffering chronic and relapsing depression are now possible (Luby et al., 2009). A concerted effort is needed to develop intervention strategies specifically designed for early childhood which are developmentally appropriate and sensitive (and not simply a downward extension of treatments designed for older children, adolescents, or adults). These strategies may include both psychotherapeutic and psychopharmacological treatments tailored to preschool children, although great care must be exercised to ensure that clinical trials are conducted only with those children with the most severe symptoms of depression and with close monitoring of their parents and physician (Dopheide, 2006; Leckman & King, 2007). Carefully designed studies are needed that adhere to ethical guidelines recognizing the vulnerability of young children (Spetie & Arnold, 2007), yet contribute to our understanding of how early intervention of preschool depression can significantly improve short and long-term outcomes for the child and family.

References

Bethea, T. C., & Sikich, L. (2007). Early pharmacological treatment of autism: A rational for developmental treatment. *Biological Psychiatry, 61*, 521-537.

Boylan, K., Romero, S., & Birmaher, B. (2007). Psychopharmacologic treatment of pediatric major depressive disorder. *Psychopharmacology, 191*, 27-28.

Bratton, S. C., Ray, D., Rhine, T., & Jones, L. (2005). The efficacy of play therapy with children: A meta-analytic review of treatment outcomes. *Professional Psychology: Research and Practice, 36*, 376-390.

Breuer, M. E., Chan, J. S., Oosting, R. S., Groenink, L., Korte, S. M., Campbell, U., et al. (2008). The triple monoaminergic reuptake inhibitor DOV 216,303 has antidepressant effects in the rat olfactory bulbectomy model and lacks sexual side effects. *European Neuropsychopharmacology: The Journal of the European College of Neuropsychopharmacology, 18*, 908-916.

Bridge, J. A., Iyengar, S., Salary, C. B., Barbe, R. P., Birmaher, B., Pincus, H. A., et al. (2007). Clinical response and risk for reported suicidal ideation and suicide attempts in pediatric antidepressant treatment: A meta-analysis of randomized controlled trials. *Journal of American Medical Association, 297*, 1683–1696.

Carlson, J. S., Kratochwill, T. R., & Johnston, H. F. (1999). Sertraline treatment of 5 children diagnosed with selective mutism: A single-case research trial. *Journal of Child & Adolescent Psychopharmacology, 9*, 293-306.

Caspi, A., Moffitt, T. E., Newman, D. L., & Silva, P. A. (1996). Behavioral observations at age 3 years predict adult psychiatric disorders: Longitudinal evidence from a birth cohort. *Archives of General Psychiatry, 53*, 1033-1039.

Centers for Disease Control and Prevention. (2009). *Morbidity and Mortality Weekly Report*: *Surveillance Summaries, March 20, 2009*. (MMWR Vol. 58, No. SS-1).

Coté, C. J., Kauffman, R. E., Troendle, G. J., & Lambert, G. H. (1996). Is the "therapeutic orphan" about to be adopted? *Pediatrics, 98*, 118-123.

DeBar, L. L., Lynch, F., Powell, J., & Gale, J. (2003). Use of psychotropic agents in preschool children: Associated symptoms, diagnoses, and health care services in a health maintenance organization. *Archives of Pediatrics & Adolescent Medicine, 157*, 150-157.

Delate, T., Gelenberg, A. J., Simmons, V. A., & Motheral, B. R. (2004). Trends in the use of antidepressants in a national sample of commercially insured pediatric patients, 1998 to 2002. *Psychiatric Services, 55*, 387-391.

Dervic, K., Friedrich, E., Oquendo, M. A., Voracek, M., Friedrich, M. H., & Sonneck, G. (2006). Suicide in Austrian children and young adolescents aged 14 and younger. *European Child and Adolescent Psychiatry, 15*, 427-434.

Dopheide, J. A. (2006). Recognizing and treating depression in children and adolescents. *American Journal of Health-System Pharmacy, 63*, 233-243.

Emslie, G. J., Heiligenstein, J. H., Wagner, K. D., Hoog, S. L., Ernest, D. E., Brown, E., et al. (2002). Fluoxetine for acute treatment of depression in children and adolescents: A placebo-controlled, randomized clinical trial. *Journal of the American Academy of Child and Adolescent Psychiatry, 41*, 1205-1215.

Glazener, C. M., Evans, J. H., & Peto, R. E. (2003). Tricyclic and related drugs for nocturnal enuresis in children. *Cochrane Database of Systematic Reviews, Issue 3*. (Art. No.: CD002117. DOI: 10.1002/14651858. CD002117).

Gleason, M. M., Egger, H. L., Emslie, G. J., Greenhill, L. L., Kowatch, R. A., Lieberman, A. F., et al. (2007). Psychopharmacological treatment for very young children: Contexts and guidelines. *Journal of the American Academy of Child and Adolescent Psychiatry, 46*, 1532-1572.

Gould, M. S., Shaffer, D., & Greenberg, T. (2003) The epidemiology of youth suicide. In R. A. King & A. Apter (Eds.), *Suicide in children and adolescents* (pp. 1–40). Cambridge, U.K.: Cambridge University Press.

Greenhill, L. L., Jensen, P. S., Abikoff, H., Blumer, J. L., DeVeaugh-Geiss, J., Fisher, C., et al. (2003). Developing strategies for psychopharmacological studies in preschool children. *Journal of the American Academy of Child and Adolescent Psychiatry, 42*, 406-414.

Harvard Health Letter. (2003, December). *Should children take antidepressants?* Retrieved July 20, 2009 from https://www.health.harvard.edu/newsweek/ Should_children_take_antidepressants.htm.

Hetrick, S. E., Merry, S. N., McKenzie, J., Sindahl, P., & Proctor, M. (2007). Selective serotonin reuptake inhibitors (SSRIs) for depressive disorders in children and adolescents. *Cochrane Database of Systematic Reviews 2007, Issue 3*. (Art.No.:CD004851.DOI: 10.1002/14651858.CD004851.pub2).

Hirshfeld-Becker, D. R., Micco, J., Henin, A., Bloomfield, A., Biederman, J., & Rosenbaum, J. (2008). Behavioral inhibition. *Depression and Anxiety, 25*, 357-367.

Hollander, E., Phillips, A. T., & Yeh, C. (2003). Targeted treatments for symptom domains in child and adolescent autism. *Lancet, 362*, 732-734.

Jensen, P. S. (1998). Ethical and pragmatic issues in the use of psychotropic agents in young children. *Canadian Journal of Psychiatry, 43*, 585-588.

Kaakeh, Y., & Stumpf, J. L. (2008). Treatment of selective mutism: Focus on selective serotonin reuptake inhibitors. *Pharmacotherapy, 28*, 214-224.

Katz, L. Y., Kozyrskyj, A. L., Prior, H. J., Enns, M. W., Cox, B. J., & Sareen, J. (2008). Effect of regulatory warnings on antidepressant prescription rates, use of health services and outcomes among children, adolescents and young adults. *Canadian Medical Association Journal, 178*, 1005-1011.

Kirsch, I., Deacon, B. J., Huedo-Medina, T. B., Scoboria, A., Moore, T. J., & Johnson, B. T. (2008). Initial severity and antidepressant benefits: A meta-analysis of data submitted to the Food and Drug Administration. *PLoS Medicine, 5*, 260-267.

Kolevzon, A., Mathewson, K. A., & Hollander, E. (2006). Selective serotonin reuptake inhibitors in autism: A review of efficacy and tolerability. *Journal of Clinical Psychiatry, 67*, 407-414.

Leckman, J. F., & King, R. A. (2007). A developmental perspective on the controversy surrounding the use of SSRIs to treat pediatric depression. *American Journal of Psychiatry, 164*, 1304-1306.

Lindsey, B. R., Piacentini, J., & McCracken, J. T. (2002). Prevalence and description of selective mutism in a school-based sample. *Journal of the American Academy of Child & Adolescent Psychiatry, 41*, 938-946.

Luby, J. L. (2007). Psychopharmacology of psychiatric disorders in the preschool period. *Journal of Child and Adolescent Psychopharmacology, 17*, 149-151.

Luby, J. L., Belden, A. C., Pautsch, J., Si, X., & Spitznagel, E. (2009). The clinical significance of preschool depression: Impairment in functioning and clinical markers of the disorder. *Journal of Affective Disorders, 112*, 111-119.

Luby, J. L., Heffelfinger, A. K., Mrakotsky, C., Brown, K. M., Hessler, M. J., Wallis, J. M., et al. (2003). The clinical picture of depression in preschool children. *Journal of the American Academy of Child and Adolescent Psychiatry, 42*, 340-348.

Luby, J. L., & Mrakotsky, C. (2003). Depressed preschoolers with bipolar family history: A group at high risk for later switching to mania? *Journal of Child and Adolescent Psychopharmacology, 13,* 187-197.

Luby, J. L., Sullivan, J., Belden, A., Stalets, M., Blankenship, S., & Spitznagel, E. (2006). An observational analysis of behavior in depressed preschoolers: Further validation of early-onset depression. *Journal of the American Academy of Child and Adolescent Psychiatry, 45,* 203-212.

Manassis, K., & Tannock, R. (2008). Comparing interventions for selective mutism: A pilot study. *The Canadian Journal of Psychiatry, 53*, 700-703.

McDonnell, M. A., & Glod, C. (2003). Prevalence of psychopathology in preschool-age children. *Journal of Child and Adolescent Psychiatric Nursing, 16*, 141–152.

Murray, M. L., de Vries, C. S., & Wong, C. K. (2004). A drug utilisation study of antidepressants in children and adolescents using the General Practice Research Database. *Archives of Disease in Childhood, 89*, 1098-1102.

Namerow, L. B., Thomas, P., Bostic, J. Q., Prince, J., & Monuteaux, M. C. (2003). Use of citalopram in pervasive developmental disorders. *Journal of Developmental & Behavioral Pediatrics, 24(2)*, 104-108.

Nardi, D. A., & Barrett, S. (2005). Potential effects of antidepressant agents on the growth and development of children and adolescents. *Journal of Psychosocial Nursing, 43*, 22-35.

Nevéus, T. (2006). The evaluation and treatment of therapy-resistant enuresis: A review. *Upsala Journal of Medical Sciences, 111*, 61-71.

Ögren, S. O., Eriksson, T. M., Elvander-Tottie, E., D'Addario, C., Ekström, J. C., Svenningsson, P., et al. (2008). The role of 5-HT1A receptors in learning and memory. *Behavioural Brain Research, 195*, 54-77.

Penza, K. M., Heim, C., & Nemeroff, C. B. (2003). Neurobiological effects of childhood abuse: Implications for the pathophysiology of depression and anxiety. *Archives of Women's Mental Health, 6*, 15-22.

Posey, D. J., Erickson, C. A., Stigler, K. A., & McDougle, C. J. (2006). The use of selective serotonin reuptake inhibitors in autism and related disorders. *Journal of Child and Adolescent Psychopharmacology, 16*, 181-186.

Pruett, J. R., & Luby, J. L. (2004). Recent advances in prepubertal mood disorders: Phenomenology and treatment. *Current Opinions in Psychiatry, 17*, 31-36.

Rapee, R. M., Kennedy, S., Ingram, M., Edwards, S., & Sweeney, L. (2005). Prevention and early intervention of anxiety disorders in inhibited preschool children. *Journal of Consulting and Clinical Psychology, 73*, 488-497.

Rosenthal, P. A., & Rosenthal, S. (1984). Suicidal behavior by preschool children. *The American Journal of Psychiatry, 141*, 520-525.

Scheffer, R. E., & Niskala Apps, J. A. (2004). The diagnosis of preschool bipolar disorder presenting with mania: open pharmacological treatment. *Journal of Affective Disorders, S82*, S25-S34.

Sheline, Y. I., Gado, M. H., & Kraemer, H. C. (2003). Untreated depression and hippocampal volume loss. *American Journal of Psychiatry, 160*, 1516-1518.

Silva, R. R., Gabbay, V., Minami, H., Munoz-Silva, D., & Alonso, C. (2005). When to use antidepressant medication in youths. *Primary Psychiatry, 12(9)*, 42-50.

Spetie, L., & Arnold, L. E. (2007). Ethical issues in child psychopharmacology research and practice: Emphasis on preschoolers. *Psychopharmacology, 191*, 15-26.

Stalets, M. M., & Luby, J. L. (2006). Preschool depression. *Child and Adolescent Psychiatric Clinics of North America, 15*, 899-917.

Vitiello, B., Zuvekas, S. H., & Norquist, G. S. (2006). National estimates of antidepressant medication use among U.S. children, 1997-2002. *Journal of the American Academy of Child and Adolescent Psychiatry, 45*, 271-279.

Warden, S. J., Robling, A. G., Sanders, M. S., Bliziotes, M. M., & Turner, C. H. (2005). Inhibition of the serotonin (5-hydroxytryptamine) transporter reduces bone accrual during growth. *Endocrinology, 146*, 685-693.

Weintrob, N., Cohen, D., Klipper-Aurbach, Y., Zadik, Z., & Dickerman, Z. (2002). Decreased growth during therapy with selective serotonin reuptake inhibitors. *Archives of Pediatrics & Adolescent Medicine, 156*, 696-701.

Wilens, T. E., Biederman, J., Kwon, A., Chase, R., Greenberg, L., Mick, E., et al. (2007). A systematic chart review of the nature of psychiatric adverse events in children and adolescents treated with selective serotonin reuptake inhibitors. *Journal of Child and Adolescent Psychopharmacology, 13*, 143-152.

Wong, I. C., Besag, F. M., Santosh, P. J., & Murray, M. L. (2004). Use of selective serotonin reuptake inhibitors in children and adolescents. *Drug Safety, 27*, 991-1000.

Zito, J. M., Safer, D. J., DosReis, S., Gardner, J. F., Boles, M., & Lynch, F. (2000). Trends in the prescribing of psychotropic medications to preschoolers. *Journal of the American Medical Association, 283*, 1025-1030.

Zito, J. M., Safer, D. J., DosReis, S., Gardner, J. F., Magder, L., Soeken K., et al. (2003). Psychotropic practice patterns for youth: A 10-year perspective. *Archives of Pediatrics & Adolescent Medicine, 157*, 17–25.

Zito, J. M., Safer, D. J., Valluri, S., Gardner, J. F., Korelitz, J. J., & Mattison, D. R. (2007). Psychotherapeutic medication prevalence in Medicaid-insured preschoolers. *Journal of Child and Adolescent Psychopharmacology, 17*, 195-203.

Zuckerman, M. L., Vaughan, B. L., Whitney, J., Dodds, A., Yakhkind, A., MacMillan, C., et al. (2007). Tolerability of selective serotonin reuptake inhibitors in thirty-nine children under age seven: A retrospective chart review. *Journal of Child and Adolescent Psychopharmacology, 17*, 165-174.

Young Children with Developmental Disabilities and Atypical Antipsychotic Medications: Dual Diagnosis, Direction, and Debate

Steven R. Shaw, Jennifer Bruce, Tia Ouimet, Akanksha Sharma, & Sarah Glaser
McGill University

Intensive early behavioral interventions are the consensus treatment of choice for children with autism and many other developmental disabilities. Developing and implementing the earliest possible intervention is the common assumption for addressing the behavioral and medical needs of young children with developmental disabilities and severe mental health problems. Yet, whether early intervention with a powerful class of psychotropic medications is effective, safe, and desirable remains unclear. This paper reviews the evolution of the prescription of atypical antipsychotic medications for children with developmental disabilities and the effectiveness and side effects of this class of medication. In addition, contrasts are made between treatment options for youngsters with developmental disabilities and those with a dual diagnosis. Finally, the controversies and ethical considerations in prescribing this class of medications to young children with developmental disabilities will be discussed.

Intensive early behavioral interventions are the treatment of choice for children with autism and many other developmental disabilities, as these children demonstrate symptoms such as aggression, hyperactivity/impulsivity, self-injurious behaviors, and irritability (Aman, Crisman, Francis, King, & Rojan, 2004). Providing effective treatments as early as possible is a primary goal of professionals working with children with developmental disabilities (Horner, Carr, Strain, Todd, & Reed, 2002). In keeping with this goal, physicians are increasingly prescribing atypical antipsychotic medications to children with autism and many other developmental disabilities (Dinca, Paul, & Spencer, 2005). However, the early prescription of psychotropic medications for children is controversial. This is especially so in the case of powerful medications such as

All correspondence should be addressed to Steven Shaw, 3700 McTavish St, Rm 517, McGill University, Montreal, Canada, H3A 1YA. Electronic mail may be sent to steven.shaw@mcgill.ca atypical antipsychotic medications, which have significant and fairly common short-term side effects and unknown long-term effects.

Atypical antipsychotic medications are approved for use in older children and adolescents with bipolar disorder and early onset psychotic symptoms (Collins, 2008). One atypical antipsychotic (i.e., Risperdal) is also approved to treat irritability, aggression, and self-injurious behaviors in children ages 5 to 18 who have been diagnosed with autism (Chavez, Chavez-Brown, & Rey, 2006). Atypical antipsychotic medications are frequently prescribed off label (i.e., in a manner not approved by the US Food and Drug Administration [FDA]) for preschool aged children diagnosed with attention deficit hyperactivity disorder (ADHD), autism, bipolar disorder, early onset schizophrenia, intellectual disabilities, psychotic disorders, and other developmental disabilities (American Academy of Pediatrics Committee on Drugs, 1996; Antochi, Stavrakaki, & Emory, 2003; Findling & McNamara, 2004; Konstantinos, Fountoulakis, Nimatoudis, Iacovides, & Kaprins, 2004).

Although early administration of psychotropic medication may be as important as early behavioral interventions, administering medications in the effort to control the problem behaviors among young children points to special problems (Harris, 2008; Lilienfeld, 2005; Tyrer & Kendall, 2009). Among these issues or controversies are difficulties in making accurate diagnoses of mental health issues for young children, the increase in prescription practices, and the possible side effects of these medications. Indeed, the long-term effects in children younger than 5 years of age are unknown (Correll, 2008; Scahill, 2008). Given the potentially severe side effects of atypical antipsychotic medications (e.g., sedation, enuresis, seizures, decrease in white blood cells, constipation, dizziness, nausea, weight gain, excessive salivation), there is a tension between the need to implement earliest possible interventions and the vulnerability of young children to the potential side effects. In order to consider this issue, the physiological mechanisms of action, the evidence of effectiveness and side effects, and the medication debate are discussed.

Mechanisms of Action and Review of Evidence

Rationale

The general effectiveness and relative safety of atypical antipsychotic medication among adults with schizophrenia has recently caused many practitioners to begin prescribing these medications to children and adolescents (Findling, Steiner, & Weller, 2005). Despite the widespread popularity of these medications, surprisingly little research has been conducted regarding their efficacy, side effects, and mechanisms with children, especially young children

(Aman et al., 2005; Harrison-Woolrych, Garcia-Quiroga, Ashton, & Herbison, 2007). In general, studies evaluating the use of atypical antipsychotics are lacking and the majority are confounded by methodological flaws (Aman & Madrid, 1999; Matson & Dempsey, 2008). A review of the existing literature suggests that although antipsychotic medications benefit children and adolescents with developmental disabilities and mental illness, careful consideration regarding their mechanism of action and effectiveness as compared to use among adults is crucial in the safe treatment of these individuals (Biederman et al., 2005; Fedorowicz & Fombonne, 2005).

The Evolution of Antipsychotic Medications

The consensus among practitioners is that atypical antipsychotic medications are less dangerous, more effective, and produce fewer side effects than the older, traditional class of antipsychotic medications (Jensen, Buitelaar, Pandima, Binder, & Haas, 2006; McDougle, Stigler, Erickson, & Posey, 2008). Clozapine (Clozaril) was the first atypical antipsychotic medication introduced in the United States (Masi, 2004). The drug was classified as atypical because of its effectiveness in treating the negative symptoms of schizophrenia (e.g., antisocial behavior and flat affect) without causing many of the serious motor side effects, including tardive dyskinesia frequently associated with the first generation of antipsychotic medications (e.g., Thorazine, Haldol; Wonodi et al., 2007).

The effectiveness of the first atypical antipsychotic medication (Clozapine) among patients with schizophrenia spawned the creation of similar atypical antipsychotic medications, including risperidone (Risperdal), quetiapine (Seroquel), ziprasidone (Geodon), and olanzapine (Zyprexa). All of these medications were approved by the FDA in 2001 for use in adults with psychotic disorders (Gardner, Baldessarini, & Waraich, 2005). Atypical antipsychotic medications are increasingly being used for the treatment of young children with schizophrenia, bipolar disorder, and Autism Spectrum Disorders (ASD) (Chavez et al., 2006); however, a thorough examination of their mechanisms of action, safety, and efficacy is necessary when evaluating appropriateness for children (DuBois, 2005).

Mechanisms of Action

The mechanisms of action of atypical antipsychotic drugs vary greatly, with little evidence for a unifying theory of antipsychotic activity or of drug design (Gardner et al., 2005). Although it is well established that antipsychotics generally act as antagonists of various types of neurotransmitter receptors, there are several underlying mechanisms of action that have been proposed for the differences between typical and atypical antipsychotic drugs. Dopamine and serotonin-blocking effects have been of primary interest in understanding how antipsychotic medications work. Most theories have been based on the observation that atypical antipsychotics have higher affinities and greater selectivity for dopamine and serotonin receptor subtypes (Aman & Madrid, 1999).

The dopamine hypothesis. When typical antipsychotics were first introduced, they produced many major Parkinson-like side effects such as tremor, akinesia, and rigidity. As Parkinson's disease was known to be a disease of insufficient dopamine neurotransmission, these findings of Parksinson-like side effects led researchers and clinicians to hypothesize that antipsychotics interfered with dopamine pathways in the brain (Seeman, 2004). These important clinical observations led to the dopamine hypothesis of antipsychotic drug action.

Current evidence supports the dopamine pathway as the primary target for antipsychotic medications (Seeman, 2004). Five dopamine receptor subtypes have been identified in humans. Types 1 and 5 are similar in structure and drug sensitivity and are referred to as the "D1-like" group or class of receptors (Seeman, 2004). Dopamine receptor types 2, 3, and 4 are also similar in structure and are grouped together as the "D2-like" group, although they have significantly different sensitivities to antipsychotic drugs (Seeman, 2004). The D2-like family has been of particular interest in understanding the mechanism of action of antipsychotic drugs, as all antipsychotics seem to have relevant affinities for the dopamine D2 receptor (Aman & Madrid, 1999; Kapur & Remington, 2001).

One of the unifying characteristics of classic and atypical antipsychotics is that they both block dopamine D2 receptors (Aman & Madrid, 1999). However, the specific affinity to the D2 receptor is also what distinguishes one class from the other, as it is the single most important discriminator between classic and atypical drugs (Aman & Madrid, 1999; Kapur & Mamo, 2003; Kapur & Seeman, 2001; Seeman, Chau-Wong, Tedesco, & Wong, 1975). The role of D1-like receptors in psychosis and its mechanisms of action are unclear, and much less is known about the role of D3 and D4 receptors in antipsychotic activity. However, certain atypical antipsychotics demonstrate a significant affinity for these D3 and D4 receptor subtypes, thus generating interest in their potential functional relevance (Aman & Madrid, 1999).

The serotonin-dopamine hypothesis. The interaction between serotonin (5-HT) and dopamine systems may play a critical role in the mechanism of action of atypical antipsychotic drugs (Kuroki, Nagao, & Nakaha, 2008). The major 5-HT receptors implicated in the action of some atypical antipsychotics are of potential value for developing more effective medications include 5-HT_{1a}, 5-HT_{2a}, 5-HT_{2c}, 5-HT_{3}, 5-HT_{6}, and 5-HT_{7} receptors (Meltzer, 1999).The serotonin-dopamine hypothesis proposes that the unique feature of the atypical antipsychotics is its greater affinity to bind to the serotonin 5-HT2 than the dopamine D2 receptors

(Kapur & Remington, 2001; Meltzer, 1999). A certain ratio of serotonin 5-HT2 to dopamine D2 affinity is believed to be the critical mechanism behind several of the new atypical antipsychotics (Kapur & Mamo, 2003; Meltzer). In fact, a relatively potent blockade of 5-HT2A receptors coupled with the weaker antagonism of the dopamine D2 receptors is the only pharmacological feature that most atypical antipsychotic drugs share (Kuroki, Nagao, & Nakaha, 2008). There is strong evidence for the role of 5-HT$_{2a}$ receptors and suggestive evidence for the roles of the 5-HT$_{1a}$ and 5-HT$_{2c}$ receptors in the antipsychotic effects and ability to improve cognition of various actions of clozapine, risperidone, olanzapine, quetiapine, ziprasidone, iloperidone, and sertindole (Meltzer, 1999).

However, some researchers argue against this hypothesis, asserting that there has been no direct demonstration that the addition of 5-HT2 antagonism to ongoing treatment through D2 blockade leads to an atypical profile of antipsychotic effects. In addition, several typical antipsychotic medications have a very high affinity at the 5-HT2 receptor. Finally, drugs that have a very high affinity for the 5-HT2 receptor alone, without any affinity for the D2 receptor do not show a typical or atypical antipsychotic effect. Thus, while most of the current atypical antipsychotic medications have a higher affinity for 5-HT2 than D2 receptors, evidence suggests that the action at the 5-HT2 receptor by itself is neither necessary nor sufficient for atypical antipsychotic activity (Kapur & Mamo, 2003).

"Fast-off" hypothesis. In light of the mounting evidence against the dopamine-serotonin hypothesis, Kapur and Seeman (2001) hypothesized that the difference between typical and atypical antipsychotic drugs may be explained by the physical action of the medications (i.e., pharmacokinetics) with the D2 receptor alone. The "fast-off" hypothesis of atypical antipsychotic action proposes that atypical antipsychotics have low affinities for the dopamine D2 receptor and are bound loosely and released rapidly from these receptors (Kapur & Seeman, 2001; Seeman, 2004). Typical and atypical antipsychotics differ because atypical psychotic medications bind more loosely to the D2 receptor than dopamine itself, while typical antipsychotic medications bind more tightly to D2 than dopamine (Kapur & Seeman, 2001; Seeman, 2004).

This "fast-off" hypothesis also accounts for the reduced extrapyramidal side effects (EPS) caused by atypical antipsychotics when compared to EPS caused by typical antipsychotics (Seeman, 2005). EPS are neurological symptoms that include tremor, slurred speech, poor movement regulation, distress, paranoia, and slowing of thought. As the typical psychotic medications are tightly bound to D2, they are more likely to produce EPS (Seeman, 2004). Other atypical antipsychotics (e.g., olanzapine) bind more tightly to the D2 receptor when compared with many other atypical antipsychotic medications, which may explain its association to dose-dependent incidence of EPS in some patients. Other atypical antipsychotics such as clozapine, remoxipride, quetiapine, and melperone have extremely loose binding which may explain the low incidence of EPS (Seeman, 2004). This hypothesis also explains the very low rates of tardive dyskenesia in patients who take atypical antipsychotic medications. Typical drugs remain attached to D2 and thus accumulate in brain tissue which can lead to tardive dyskenesia, whereas atypical antipsychotic drugs are loosely bound to D2 and do not accumulate in the brain in the same fashion, thus greatly reducing the risk of tardive dyskenesia (Seeman, 2004).

The combination of a fast dissociation and transient D2 occupancy is believed to be sufficient to provide an atypical antipsychotic effect, with activity at other receptors not necessary for the drugs to work (Kapur & Seeman, 2001). This hypothesis does not infer an explicit difference between the typical and atypical antipsychotic medications, but rather a continuum of difference, whereby antipsychotics become increasingly more atypical as their binding to the D2 receptor becomes looser and they are released more quickly (Seeman, 2004). Despite the research that has been conducted, no unified theory of the mechanism of action has been determined (Fedorowicz & Fonbonne, 2005; Kapur & Mamo, 2003). In addition, the review of evidence regarding the effectiveness of antipsychotics also lacks consensus (Jerrell & McIntyre, 2008; Lilienfeld, 2005).

Review of Evidence

Use of atypical antipsychotics in children with autism spectrum disorders. The use of atypical antipsychotic medications among children with ASD is widespread. Researchers have found that the behavioral symptoms common to ASD such as aggression, hyperactivity/impulsivity, and self-injurious behaviors are reduced with atypical antipsychotics (Cheng-Shannon, McGough, Pataki, & McCracken, 2004). A reduction in depressed or anxious mood has also been reported in some case studies of children with autism (Findling et al., 2004; Hardan, Jou, & Handen, 2005). However, studies regarding the effectiveness of atypical antipsychotics in improving the core features of ASD, such as social interaction, communication, and stereotyped behaviors are lacking and inconsistent (Potenza, Holms, Kanes, & McDougle, 1999; Toren, Ratner, Laor, & Weitzman, 2004).

The use of risperidone may reduce stereotypic behaviors among children with ASD (McDougle et al., 1997). Improvements in communication and social relatedness are also reported in children diagnosed with ASD who are treated with risperidone or olanzapine, but findings remain inconsistent (Dinca et al., 2005; Fishman & Steele, 1996; Potenza et al., 1999; Troost et al., 2005). Researchers often fail to find improvements in language ability in children with ASD who are prescribed atypical antipsychotics. In some studies, a decrease in verbal perseveration and stereotypic use of language was observed in children with ASD (Biederman et al., 2005; Findling et al., 2004; Fishman & Steele,

1996). Even though language ability may not improve with the use of atypical antipsychotics among this population, reductions in stereotyped language and in verbal perseveration may lead to improved communication.

Although the use of atypical antipsychotic medication in children with ASD often leads to the reduction of symptoms, the potential for serious side effects is a cause for concern (Jerrell & McIntyre, 2008). Relatively common adverse events associated with use of clozapine, olanzapine, risperidone, quetiapine, and ziprasidone in children with ASD include sedation, enuresis, seizures, decrease in white blood cells, constipation, increased appetite, dizziness, nausea, weight gain, and excessive salivation (Correll, 2008; DuBois, 2005; McDougle et al., 1997; Potenza et al., 1999). Although these side effects are sometimes serious, they appear to be less adverse than the side effects associated with treatment via traditional typical agents such as haloperidol (Findling et al., 2005). Despite the fact that some children with ASD benefit from treatment with antipsychotic medications, it is not clear whether existing findings generalize to children with all subtypes of ASD (Hardan et al., 2005; Matson & Dempsey, 2008).

Considerations for Children Younger than 5 Years of Age

An extremely limited amount of research has been conducted thus far regarding the use of atypical antipsychotics among young children (Yan, 2007). Double-blind, placebo-controlled, randomized studies are necessary in order to provide evidence for their safety and tolerability. Much of the existing empirical evidence is flawed due to small sample sizes, heterogeneity of clinical profiles among participants, lack of consistent measures across cases, and complications due to interactions between multiple medications (Dinca et al., 2005; McDougle et al., 1997). It is also clear that the gap between research and clinical practice is widening. Rather than being prescribed by child psychiatrists, antipsychotics are now frequently dispensed by pediatricians and general practitioners, who may be less familiar with the clinical characteristics of developmental disabilities and mental disorders (Patel, Crimson, Hoagwood, & Jensen, 2005). Despite the potential for positive outcomes, the limited research base and side effects may not justify the rapid increase in the number of prescriptions for atypical antipsychotic medications (Cheng-Shannon et al., 2004; Curtis et al., 2005; Findling & McNamara, 2004).

There has been a significant increase in the prescription of atypical antipsychotics to children and youth in the United States (Olfson, Blanco, Liu, Moreno, & Laje, 2006). From 1997 to 2000, prescriptions for atypical antipsychotics rose from 2.4% to 5.1% of the pediatric population (Martin & Leslie, 2003). Even more striking was that from 1996 to 2000 there was an increase in the prescription of atypical antipsychotic medication among children (160%) and adolescents (496%) in the Texas Medicaid system (Curtis et al., 2005).

One quarter of children and youth with private insurance prescribed atypical antipsychotic medications were children under the age of 10, 80% being boys (Curtis et al.). More specifically, almost 10% of children under the age of 7 with ASD were treated with antipsychotic medications in 2004 (Witwer & Lecavalier, 2005). This dramatic increase is likely due to growing evidence of the efficacy of these medications (Luby, Mrakotsky, Stalets, Belden, & Heffelfinger, 2006; McCracken et al., 2002).

There remains a lack of long-term studies reporting efficacy and side effects in the pediatric population. A recent study investigated the safety of risperidone in preschool children with ASD over a 6-month treatment period. They observed no significant serious adverse effects over this time frame (Luby et al., 2006). Although these positive results seem warranted, it is important to recognize that a 6-month period of time is not long enough to observe the long-term side effects that may occur. Many children that are prescribed atypical antipsychotics will remain on the drug for longer than 6 months depending on co-morbid psychopathology, resistance to previous interventions, type and dose of medication, and many other factors (Matson & Dempsey, 2008). Given the chronic nature of the disorders for which atypical antipsychotics are prescribed, longitudinal data is essential. Furthermore, children may experience long-term side effects even after the drug is discontinued (Stachnik & Nunn-Thompson, 2007; Troost et al., 2005). Further clinical research is needed to support the rationale of prescribing these medications to young children.

Dual Diagnosis

Although atypical antipsychotic medications are used widely for children with developmental disabilities, this class of medications is most closely associated with the treatment of severe mental health problems (Cheng-Shannon et al., 2004). However, developmental disabilities and severe mental health issues commonly co-occur, making atypical antipsychotic medications an efficient treatment option for both issues (Cooper, Melville, & Einfeld, 2003). Dual diagnosis is the co-occurrence of mental health problems among individuals with developmental disabilities (Cooper-Smiley, Morrison, Williamson, & Allan, 2007; Reiss, 1990). Compared to typically developing populations, children with developmental disabilities are at an elevated risk for psychopathology (Bregman, 1991; Cooper et al., 2007). Although children with developmental disabilities are at a higher risk of psychopathology, there are issues and controversies in determining prevalence rates, with estimates ranging from 30 to 70% (Cooper et al., 2007; Mason & Scior, 2004; Reiss, 1990).

Issues in Dual Diagnosis

Assessing psychiatric conditions is complicated because psychiatric conditions in children with developmental disabilities may be "masked" or manifested in altered clusters of symptoms (Mason & Scior, 2004; Rush & Francis, 2000; Sovner, 1986). Because of this, the presentation of mental health problems in children with developmental disabilities is difficult to diagnose. For many of these children, communication of emotions is difficult and feelings of grandeur or paranoia may be prevalent due to lower levels of self-awareness and impaired communication skills. For example, behavioral shifts from baseline states can be indicative of psychopathology (Reiss, 1994). Children who develop extreme levels of aggression or withdrawal without apparent antecedents or history of consequences may be experiencing the onset of mental health issues. Furthermore, there is a tendency among mental health professionals to overlook mental health problems for children with developmental disabilities (Cooper et al., 2007; Mason & Scior). This bias is known as diagnostic overshadowing and refers to mental health problems becoming less salient and significant when accompanied by developmental disabilities (Mason & Scior). These issues complicate the diagnosis of mental health issues among children with developmental disabilities and hinder the process of providing them the resources and treatment that they require.

Current Developments

Currently, there are movements within the mental health field that can guide the decision making process regarding the use of atypical antipsychotics in children with developmental disabilities. First, the National Association for the Dually Diagnosed, in collaboration with the American Psychiatric Association, released a clinical guide for the diagnosis of mental disorders in persons with a developmental disability. *The Diagnostic Manual-Intellectual Disability Clinical Guide* (DM-ID; Fletcher, Loschen, Stavrakaki, & First, 2007) corresponds closely with the *Diagnostic and Statistical Manual of Mental Disorders (*DSM-IV-TR; American Psychiatric Association, 2000) classification system, while at the same time adapting the criteria for mental health diagnosis to persons with developmental disabilities. This document can facilitate an increase in the accurate diagnosis of mental health problems among individuals with developmental disabilities, thereby reducing the chances of overlooking a child in need of treatment.

The Use of Atypical Antipsychotics in Children with Developmental Disabilities

Because individuals with developmental disabilities are restricted in the expression of their psychiatric symptoms, psychiatric diagnoses among this population are usually made based on behavioral symptoms (Antochi et al., 2003;

Cooper et al., 2003; Reiss, Levitan & Szysko, 1982). This diagnostic method indicates that problematic behavior exhibited by a child with developmental disabilities may or may not be a symptom of an underlying psychiatric disorder. In such a situation, the use of atypical antipsychotic medications could address target behaviors or symptoms associated with a psychiatric diagnosis. Therefore, the relationship between antipsychotic medication and dual diagnosis is complex (Findling & McNamara, 2004).

Dual diagnosis guidelines can be found in the expert consensus guidelines for treatment of psychiatric and behavioral problems common in children with developmental disabilities (Rush & Frances, 2000). The guidelines were developed based on surveys completed by 48 experts on psychosocial treatment and 45 experts on psychopharmacology. Aman and colleagues (2004) revised this document, emphasizing the importance of assessing behavioral symptoms even when a diagnosis is available and acknowledging that making a diagnosis becomes more challenging as the level of developmental impairment increases. In discussing preferred medications for specific diagnoses and behavioral problems, Aman and colleagues (2004) stated that the experts preferred atypical antipsychotics for schizophrenia, other psychotic symptoms, and for self-injurious and aggressive behaviors. Thus, physicians tend to prescribe atypical antipsychotic medications for a variety of behaviors rather than using the atypical antipsychotics only for a specific diagnosis.

Debate and Controversy

Controversies of Prescribing Atypical Antipsychotic Medications to Young Children

Despite their increasingly widespread use, the prescription of atypical antipsychotic medications in the pediatric population continues to be a controversial issue (Elias, 2006; Harris, 2008; Lilienfeld, 2005). Parents, mental health professionals, and physicians have yet to reach a consensus on the safety of these medications. There are many reasons to be wary of these medications and of the doctors who are prescribing them. These reasons include a lack of evidence to determine side effects, the freedom of doctors to prescribe medication without approval, the suspicion that monitoring prescribed medications may not be done carefully and thoroughly, and serious case reports illustrating danger of atypical antipsychotic use in the treatment of young children (Tyrer & Kendall, 2009; Witwer & Lacavelier, 2005). Furthermore, non-intrusive behavioral interventions without medications may be as effective and without the potentially harmful side effects (Horner et al., 2002).

Off-label Prescriptions

Despite its common occurrence, off-label prescriptions pose many side effects and dangers to children with developmental disabilities. In October of 2006, the US FDA approved the use of Risperidone in children and adolescents aged 5 to 16 who suffered from symptoms of irritability associated with ASD (Yan, 2007). There are currently no atypical antipsychotics approved for prescription in children younger than 5 years. Nevertheless, general practitioners, pediatricians, and psychiatrists prescribe these medications off-label to infants and young children. Off-label prescription is a common practice that occurs in approximately 80% of all medication prescriptions. Although this practice is legal, this does not mean that it is without danger (Konstantinos et al., 2004). The FDA has not yet approved atypical antipsychotics in children under the age of 5 due to the lack of scientific evidence. Therefore, off-label prescribing to young children involves serious risks, as doctors extrapolate doses from clinical trials outside the age range without knowing the safety, efficacy, and long-term side effects within the population they are prescribing (McCracken et al., 2002; Olfson et al., 2006; Rappley, 2006).

Best Practices and Current Practices

Despite consensus among physicians on the best practices of prescribing atypical antipsychotics, not all doctors follow these recommendations (Pappadopulos et al., 2002). Physicians were interviewed in an inpatient setting to investigate their beliefs concerning optimal practices in prescribing atypical antipsychotic medication. Following the interviews, charts were tracked to determine whether these practices were carried out in real world settings. Surprisingly, none of the patients' target symptoms were tracked regularly and systematically and only 14% of patients' side effects were monitored on a regular basis. This discrepancy is a concern given the serious nature of side effects of atypical antipsychotic medications. Children prescribed such medications need to be monitored closely, and best practices must be followed by all physicians prescribing antipsychotics. The failure to follow these precautions and a lack of understanding regarding the powerful nature of antipsychotic medications often results in various side effects (e.g., weight gain and sedation) among these patients.

Common Side Effects of Atypical Antipsychotics

The common rationalization that atypical antipsychotic medications are safe and effective for use in young children simply because their efficacy has repeatedly been demonstrated in older children, adolescents, and adults is inherently flawed

(Cheng-Shannon et al., 2004; Correll, 2008; DuBois, 2005). Adults are generally more tolerant to medications and are less likely to develop serious side effects associated with antipsychotics (Cooper et al., 2006; McConville & Sorter, 2004). Sedation and extreme lethargy among children prescribed atypical antipsychotic medication are of particular concern, as fatigue and drowsiness have the potential to impair academic performance, efficacy of therapy, and social interaction (McCracken et al., 2002; McDougle et al., 2008). Weight gain, one of the most common adverse side effects associated with atypical antipsychotic treatment, can also pose negative effects on the physical, social, and emotional health of young children (McConville & Sorter).

Little is known regarding the neurobiological effects of these drugs on the developing brains of children (Rappley, 2006). Most studies focus on immediate or short-term response and side effects, leaving unknown the effect of atypical antipsychotics on the developing brain over the most critical years of cognitive, physical, emotional, and linguistic development (Troost et al., 2005). Age-related dosage and titration guidelines for many atypical antipsychotics remain largely untested (Findling et al., 2005). Developmental issues among children and adolescents also suggest that the pharmacokinetics of these medications may be different depending upon maturity. For example, children possess larger livers relative to body weight and often metabolize drugs faster than adults (DuBois, 2005; Fedorowicz & Fombonne, 2005). These factors increase the risk of toxicity of the liver and other major organ systems among younger individuals (Harrison-Woolrych et al., 2007). Of equal concern is that atypical antipsychotics are frequently prescribed in combination with other psychotropic drugs, including mood stabilizers and selective serotonin reuptake inhibitors ([SSRIs]; McConville & Sorter, 2004). Little is known about the additive and interactive effects of these medications or their long-term effects in young children (Jerrell & McIntyre, 2008).

Severe Adverse Reactions

With the increase in atypical antipsychotic prescriptions and the prevalence of off-label prescribing, children are at risk for drug-induced side effects and long-term dangers that may even result in death. According to a recent report from the US FDA, from 1993 through the first 3 months of 2008, 1,207 children prescribed Risperdal experienced side effects serious enough to warrant medical attention. Further, 31 out of 1,215,000 prescriptions for patients aged birth through 12 years resulted in death (Collins, 2008). Of these deaths, 10 were related to nervous system disorders, 9 were cardiac related, 8 were miscellaneous causes, and 4 had an indeterminate cause of death. Other warnings and precautions include hyperglycemia, diabetes, weight gain, EPS, and development of breast tissue in males and females. Although this report identified no new safety concerns, the

FDA panel expressed concern with the rise in the use of atypical antipsychotic medications, especially for children with ADHD, ASD, and other developmental disabilities (Collins).

Efficacious Behavioral Interventions with No Harmful Risks or Side Effects

No evidence is available to suggest the superiority of pharmacological treatment versus non-pharmacological treatment, or vice-versa (Jensen et al., 2006). A meta-analysis of problem behavior interventions for children with ASD determined an efficacy rate of 80 to 90% in the reduction of problem behaviors (Horner et al., 2002). These methods, unlike medications, are not biologically intrusive and contain minimal risk. Techniques include interventions such as stimulus-based procedures (e.g., altering antecedent events), instruction-based procedures (e.g., instruction of appropriate behaviors), extinction-based procedures (e.g., withhold or minimize presumed reinforcers), reinforcement-based procedures (e.g., increase desired behaviors), punishment-based procedures (e.g., reduce behavior by delivering a contingent event), and systems change procedures (e.g., alter structural features of environment) (Horner et al.). Scahill (2008) recommends exposing children to these low-risk therapies prior to medication use. A thorough clinical assessment should be conducted to determine which therapies have been tried or are currently in place before prescribing atypical antipsychotic medications to young children with ASD. Atypical antipsychotics are best considered as a last resort for children with moderate to high levels of aggression, tantrums or self-injury, and only when behavioral therapy is ineffective (Scahill). Although the earliest possible interventions are recommended, extreme caution is to be exercised with prescribing atypical antipsychotic medications to children with developmental disabilities.

Conclusions

Early intervention for children with developmental disabilities is a common refrain. However, there is significant hesitation in many quarters when early intervention involves medications that are included in the treatment plan. Atypical antipsychotic medications represent important improvements over the first generation of antipsychotics. Nonetheless, such improvement does not mean that atypical antipsychotic medications are without risks. Although off-label prescription practices are common for psychopharmaceutical use with young children, atypical antipsychotics may have severe short-term side effects and the long-term effects are unknown. The unintended cognitive and behavioral effects of atypical antipsychotics have not been studied in sufficient detail to make broad statements concerning efficacy. Given that one in five visits to a pediatric psychiatrist results in the prescription of atypical antipsychotic medications, the number of children experiencing unintended effects is potentially high (Curtis et al., 2005). Moreover, many of the side effects are severe, with significant neurological side effects and even deaths being reported (Collins, 2008). The popular press continues to report and publicize the dangerous side effects of atypical antipsychotic medications (Couric, 2007; Harris, 2008). Despite these concerns, prescription of atypical antipsychotics among young children remains a popular practice.

For many children with developmental disabilities, atypical antipsychotic medications lead to considerable improvement of symptoms such as hallucinations, aggression, fear, overactivity, and self-injurious behaviors. This class of medications has the potential to greatly improve the quality of life for children with ASD and their families. Moreover, the earliest possible administration, which requires early diagnosis, has potential to prevent or ameliorate severe behaviors and other mental health issues. Yet, the current state of the scientific knowledge suggests that the use of atypical antipsychotic medications for young children carries significant risk to some individuals. For this reason, early behavioral treatments remain the first line of treatment for children with developmental disabilities with severe and difficult to manage behaviors.

References

Aman, M. G., Arnold, L. E., McDougle, C. J., Vitello, B., Scahill, L., Davies, M., et al. (2005). Acute and long-term safety and tolerability of risperidone in children with autism. *Journal of Child and Adolescent Psychopharmacology, 15*, 869-884.

Aman, M. G., Crismon, M. L., Frances, A., King, B. H., & Rojahn, J. (Eds.) (2004). *Treatment of psychiatric and behavior problems in individuals with mental retardation: An update of the Expert Consensus Guidelines® for mental retardation/developmental disability populations.* Englewood, CO: Postgraduate Institute for Medicine.

Aman, M. G., & Madrid, A. (1999). Atypical antipsychotics in persons with developmental disabilities. *Mental Retardation and Developmental Disabilities Research Reviews, 5*, 253-263.

American Academy of Pediatrics Committee on Drugs. (1996). Unapproved uses of approved drugs: The physician, the package insert, and the Food and Drug Administration: Subject review. *Pediatrics, 98*, 143–145.

American Psychiatric Association. (2000). *Diagnostic and Statistical Manual of Mental Disorders* (4th ed., Text Rev.). Washington, DC: Author.

Antochi, R., Stavrakaki, C., & Emery, P. C. (2003). Psychopharmacological treatments in persons with dual diagnosis of psychiatric disorders and developmental disabilities. *Postgraduate Medical Journal, 79*, 139-146.

Biederman, J., Mick, E., Hammerness, P., Harpold, T., Aleardi, M., Dougherty, M., et al. (2005). Open-label, 8-week trial of olanzapine and risperidone for the treatment of bipolar disorder in preschool-age children. *Biological Psychiatry, 58*, 589-594.

Bregman, J. D. (1991). Current developments in the understanding of mental retardation part II: Psychopathology. *Journal of the American Academy of Child and Adolescent Psychiatry, 30*, 861-872.

Chavez, B., Chavez-Brown, M., & Rey, J. A. (2006). Role of risperidone in children with autism spectrum disorder. *The Annals of Pharmacotherapy, 40*, 909-916.

Cheng-Shannon, J., McGrough, J. J., Pataki, C., & McCracken, J. T. (2004). Second-generation antipsychotic medications in children and adolescents. *Journal of Child and Adolescent Psychopharmacology, 14*, 372-394.

Collins, F. (2008, November 18). *One year post-exclusivity adverse event review: Risperidone*. Washington, DC: FDA Pediatric Advisory Committee.

Cooper, S. A., Melville, C. A., & Einfeld, S. L. (2003). Psychiatric diagnosis, intellectual disabilities and diagnostic criteria for psychiatric disorders for use with adults with learning disabilities/mental retardation. *Journal of Intellectual Disability Research, 47*, 3-15.

Cooper, S. A., Smiley, E., Morrison, J., Williamson, A., & Allan, L. (2007). Mental ill-health in adults with intellectual disabilities: Prevalence and associated factors. *The British Journal of Psychiatry, 190*, 27-35.

Cooper, W., Arbogast, H., Ding, G., Hickson, D., Fuchs, D., & Ray, W. (2006). Trends in prescribing antipsychotic medications for US children. *Ambulatory Pediatrics, 6*, 79-83.

Correll, C. U. (2008). Antipsychotic use in children and adolscents. *Journal of the American Academy of Child and Adolescent Psychiatry, 47*, 9-20.

Couric, K. (2007, September 30). What killed Rebecca Riley? *CBS News*, Retrieved March 25, 2009, from http://www.cbsnews.com

Curtis, L. H., Masselink, L. E., Østbye, T., Hutchison, S., Dans, P. E., Wright, A., et al. (2005). Prevalence of atypical antipsychotic drug use among commercially insured youths in the United States. *Archives of Pediatric and Adolescent Medicine, 159*, 362-366.

Dinca, O., Paul, M., & Spencer, N. J. (2005). Systematic review of randomized controlled trials of atypical antipsychotics and selective serotonin reuptake inhibitors for behavioral problems associated with pervasive developmental disorders. *Journal of Psychopharmocology, 19*, 521-532.

DuBois, D. (2005). Toxicology and overdose of atypical antipsychotic medications in children: Does newer necessarily mean safer? *Current Opinion in Pediatrics, 17*, 227-233.

Elias, M. (2006, May 2). New antipsychotic drugs carry risks for children. *USA Today*. Retrieved June 20, 2009, from http://www.usatoday.com/news/health/2006-05-01-atypical-drugs_x.htm

Fedorowicz, V. J., & Fombonne, E. (2005). Metabolic side effects of atypical antipsychotics in children: A literature review. *Journal of Psychopharmacology, 19*, 533-550.

Findling, R. L., & McNamara, N. K. (2004). Atypical antipsychotics in the treatment of children and adolescents: Clinical applications. *Journal of Clinical Psychiatry, 65 Supplement 6*, 30-44.

Findling, R. L., McNamara, N. K., Gracious, B. L., O'Riordan, M. A., Reed, M. D., Demeter, C., et al. (2004). Quetiapine in nine youths with autistic disorder. *Journal of Child and Adolescent Psychopharmacology, 14*, 287-294.

Findling, R. L., Steiner, H., & Weller, E. B. (2005). Use of antipsychotics in children and adolescents. *Journal of Clinical Psychiatry, 66*, 29-40.

Fisman, S., & Steele, M. (1996). Use of risperidone in pervasive developmental disorders: A case series. *Journal of Child and Adolescent Psychopharmacology, 6*, 177-190.

Fletcher, R., Loschen, E., Stavrakaki, C., & First, M. (Eds.). (2007). *Diagnostic manual -- intellectual disability (DM-ID): A clinical guide for diagnosis of mental disorders in persons with intellectual disability.* Kingston, NY: National Association for the Dually Diagnosed Press.

Gardner, D. M., Baldessarini, R. J., & Waraich, P. (2005). Modern antipsychotic drugs: A critical overview. *Canadian Medical Association Journal, 172*, 1703-1711.

Hardan, A. Y., Jou, R. J., & Handen, B. L. (2005). Retrospective study of quetiapine in children and adolescents with pervasive developmental disorder. *Journal of Autism and Developmental Disorders, 35*, 387-391.

Harris, G. (2008, November 17). Use of antipsychotics in children is criticized. *The New York Times*. Retrieved June 20, 2009 from http://www.nytimes.com/2008/11/19/health/policy/19fda.html?_r=1&scp=2&sq=Gardiner%20Harris%20antipsychotics&st=cse

Harrison-Woolruch, M., Garcia-Quiroga, J., Ashton, J., & Herbison, P. (2007). Safety and usage of atypical medicines in children. *Drug Safety, 30*, 569-579.

Horner, R. H., Carr, E. G., Strain, P. S., Todd, A. W., & Reed, H. K. (2002). Problem behavior interventions for young children with autism: A research synthesis. *Journal of Autism and Developmental Disorders, 32*, 423-446.

Jensen, P. S., Buitelaar, J., Pandima, G. J., Binder, C., & Haas, M. (2006). Management of psychiatric disorders in children and adolescents with atypical antipsychotics. *European Child & Adolescent Psychiatry, 16*, 104-120.

Jerrell, J. M., & McIntyre, R. S. (2008). Adverse events in children and adolescents treated with antipsychotic medications. *Human Psychopharmacology: Clinical and Experimental, 23*, 283-290.

Kapur, S., & Mamo, D. (2003). Half a century of antipsychotics and still a central role for dopamine D2 receptors. *Progress in Neuro-Psychopharmacology & Biological Psychiatry, 27,* 1081–1090.

Kapur, S., & Remington, G. (2001). Dopamine D2 receptors and their role in atypical antipsychotic action: Still necessary and may even be sufficient. *Biological Psychiatry, 50,* 873–883.

Kapur, S., & Seeman, P. (2001). Does fast dissociation from the dopamine D2 receptors explain atypical antipsychotic action? A new hypothesis. *American Journal of Psychiatry, 158,* 360–369.

Konstantinos, N., Fountoulakis, N., Nimatoudis, I., Iacovides, A., & Kaprins, G. (2004). Off-label indications for atypical antipsychotics: A systematic review. *Annals of General Hospital Psychiatry, 3*, 4.

Kuroki, T., Nagao, N., & Nakaha, T. (2008). Neuropharmacology of second-generation antipsychotic drugs: A validity of the serotonin–dopamine hypothesis. *Progress in Brain Research, 172, 199-212.*

Lilienfeld, S. O. (2005). Scientifically unsupported and supported interventions for childhood psychopathology: A summary. *Pediatrics, 115*, 761-764.

Luby, J., Mrakotsky, C., Stalets, M. M., Belden, A., & Heffelfinger, A. (2006). Risperidone in preschool children with autistic spectrum disorders: An investigation of safety and efficacy. *Journal of Child and Adolescent Psychopharmacology, 16*, 575-587.

Martin, A., & Leslie, D. (2003). Trends in psychotropic medication costs for children and adolescents. *Archives of Pediatrics & Adolescent Medicine, 157,* 997-1004.

Masi, G. (2004). Pharmacotherapy of pervasive developmental disorders in children and adolescents. *CNS Drugs, 18*, 1031-1052.

Mason, J., & Scior, K. (2004). 'Diagnostic overshadowing' amongst clinicians working with people with intellectual disabilities in the UK. *Journal of Applied Research in Intellectual Disabilities, 17,* 85-90.

Matson, J. L., & Dempsey, T. (2008). Autism spectrum disorders: Pharmacotherapy for challenging behaviors. *Journal of Developmental and Physical Disabilities, 20,* 175-191.

McConville, B. J., & Sorter, M. T. (2004). Treatment challenges and safety considerations for antipsychotic use in children and adolescents with psychoses. *Journal of Clinical Psychiatry, 65,* 20-29.

McCracken, J. T., McGough, J., Shah, B., Cronin, P., Hong, D., Aman, M. G., et al. (2002). Risperidone in children with autism and serious behavioral problems. *New England Journal of Medicine, 347,* 314-321.

McDougle, C. J., Holmes, J. P., Bronson, M. R., Anderson, G. M., Volkmar, F. R., Price, L. H., et al. (1997). Risperidone treatment of children and adolescents with pervasive developmental disorders: A prospective open-label study. *Journal of the American Academy of Child & Adolescent Psychiatry, 36,* 685-693.

McDougle, C. J., Stigler, K. A., Erickson, C. A., & Posey, D. J. (2008). Atypical antipsychotics in children and adolescents with autistic and other pervasive developmental disorders. *Journal of Clinical Psychiatry, 69 Supplement 4,* 15-20.

Meltzer, H. Y. (1999). The role of serotonin in antipsychotic drug action. *Neuropsychopharmocology, 21,* 106-115.

Olfson, M., Blanco, C., Liu, L., Moreno, C., & Laje, G. (2006). National trends in the outpatient treatment of children and adolescents with antipsychotic drugs. *Archives of General Psychiatry, 63,* 679-685.

Pappadopulos, E., Jensen, P. S., Schur, S. B., MacIntyre II, J. C., Ketner, S., Van Orden, K., et al. (2002). "Real world" atypical antipsychotic prescribing practices in public child and adolescent inpatient settings. *Schizophrenia Bulletin, 28,* 111-121.

Patel, N. C., Crismon, L., Hoagwood, K., Johnsrud, M. T., Rascati, K. L., Wilson, J. P., et al. (2005). Trends in the use of typical and atypical antipsychotics in children and adolescents. *Journal of the American Academy of Child & Adolescent Psychiatry, 44,* 548-556.

Potenza, M. N., Holmes, J. P., Kanes, S. J., & McDougle, C. J. (1999). Olanzapine treatment of children, adolescents, and adults with pervasive developmental disorders: An open-label pilot study. *Journal of Clinical Psychopharmacology, 19,* 37-44.

Rappley, M. D. (2006). Actual psychotropic medication use in preschool children. *Infants & Young Children, 19,* 154-163.

Reiss, S. (1990). Prevalence of dual diagnosis in community based day programs in the Chicago metropolitan area. *American Journal on Mental Retardation, 94, 578-588.*

Reiss, S. (1994*). Handbook of challenging behavior: Mental health aspects of mental retardation.* Worthington, OH: IDS Publishing.

Reiss, S., Levitan, G., & Szysko, J. (1982). Emotional disturbance and mental retardation: Diagnostic overshadowing. *American Journal of Mental Deficiency, 86,* 567-574.

Rush, A. J., & Frances, A. (2000). The expert consensus guidelines: Treatment of psychiatric and behavioral problems in mental retardation. *American Journal on Mental Retardation, 105,* 159-228.

Scahill, L. (2008). How do I decide whether or not to use medication for my child with autism? Should I try behavioral therapy first? *Journal of Autism and Developmental Disorders, 38,* 1197-1198.

Seeman, P. (2004). Atypical antipsychotics: Mechanism of action. *The Journal of Lifelong Learning in Psychiatry, 2,* 48-58.

Seeman, P. (2005). An update on fast-off dopamine D2 atypical antipsychotics. *American Journal of Psychiatry, 162,* 1984-1985.

Seeman, P., Chau-Wong, M., Tedesco, J., & Wong, K. (1975). Brain receptors for antipsychotic drugs and dopamine: Direct binding assays. *Proceeding from the National Academy of Sciences, 72,* 4376–4380.

Sovner, R. (1986). Limiting factors in the use of DSM-III criteria with mentally ill/ mentally retarded persons. *Psychopharmacology Bulletin, 22,* 1055-1059.

Stachnik, J., M., & Nunn-Thompson, C. (2007). Use of atypical antipsychotics in the treatment of autistic disorder. *The Annals of Pharmacotherapy, 41,* 626-634.

Toren, P., Ratner, S., Laor, N., & Weitzman, A. (2004). Benefit-risk assessment of atypical antipsychotics in the treatment of schizophrenia and comorbid disorders in children and adolescents. *Drug Safety, 27,* 1135-1156.

Troost, P., Lahuis, B., Steenhuis, M.-P., Ketelaars, C. E., Buitelaar, J., van Engeland, H., et al. (2005). Long-term effects of risperidone in children with autism spectrum disorders: A placebo discontinuation study. *Journal of the American Academy of Child and Adolescent Psychiatry, 44,* 1137-1144.

Tyrer, P., & Kendall, T. (2009). The spurious advance of antipsychotic drug therapy. *The Lancet, 373,* 4-5.

Witwer, A., & Lecavelier, L. (2005). Treatment incidence and patterns in children and adolescents with autism spectrum disorders. *Journal of Child and Adolescent Psychopharmacology, 15,* 671-681.

Wonodi, I., Reeves, G., Carmichael, D., Verosky, I., Avila, M. T., Elliot, A., et al. (2007). Tardive dyskinesia in children treated with atypical antipsychotic medications. *Movement Disorders, 22,* 1777-1782.

Yan, J. (2007). Risperidone approved to treat schizophrenia in children. *American Psychiatric News, 42,*18.

Author Note

Steven R. Shaw is Assistant Professor in the Department of Educational and Counselling Psychology, McGill University. Jennifer Bruce, Tia Ouimet, Akanksha Sharma, and Sarah Glaser are graduate students at McGill University.

Preschool ADHD and Medication…More Study Needed?!

W. Mark Posey, Sarah A. Bassin, & Ashley Lewis
University of South Carolina School of Medicine

The purpose of this work is to provide an examination of the diagnosis of ADHD, the efficacy of the medication use for controlling ADHD symptoms, and the concerns with medication use for ADHD in preschool populations. Thus, the perceived validity of the ADHD diagnosis in preschool children is reviewed. The evidence base to support efficacy of medication use for ADHD in preschoolers is discussed. Consideration is given to arguments for and against medication use in this population. Suggestions for future research are presented.

More than 70 years ago, Bradley (1937) reported on the behavioral effects of stimulants. These medications produced a calming effect and also improved compliance and academic performance. Bradley continued to publish studies showing positive outcomes for children using this type of treatment (e.g., Bradley & Bowen, 1941). Since that time Swanson et al. (1993) noted that there have been 250 reviews and more than 3,000 articles on stimulant effects. For example, Jensen and colleagues (1999) have reported that only one-eighth of the children who met the criteria of attention deficit hyperactivity disorder (ADHD) received adequate stimulant treatment. In contrast, 72% of school-aged children prescribed stimulants in rural North Carolina did not meet criteria for ADHD (Angold, Erkanli, Egger, & Costello, 2000). Still, the stability and validity of the ADHD diagnosis is high from 4 years of age throughout elementary school (Lahey et al., 2004). While discussing how ADHD manifests itself differently in school-age children and preschoolers, Döpfner and colleagues state that "on the basis of this data one can start to make an argument about the utility of the preschool ADHD construct" (Döpfner, Rothenberger, & Sonuga-Barke, 2004, p. 132). The Preschoolers with Attention-Deficit/Hyperactivity Disorder Treatment Study (PATS) was sponsored by the National Institute of Mental Health (NIMH) and several universities (i.e., University of California, Irvine; Duke University Medical Center; Columbia University; New York University Child Study Center;

All correspondence should be addressed to Dr. W. Mark Posey, 9 Medical Park, Suite 200, Department of Pediatrics, University of South Carolina School of Medicine, Columbia, SC 29203. Electronic mail may be sent to Mark.Posey@uscmed.sc.edu.

University of California, Los Angeles; and Johns Hopkins University). The PATS was not designed to look at whether ADHD is a valid diagnosis, but rather to address the efficacy and safety of short-term use of methylphenidate (MPH). The PATS included preschoolers aged 3 to 5 years who were diagnosed with ADHD. Several studies have been published based on the PATS data (e.g., Greenhill et al., 2006; Kollins et al., 2006).

The focus of the PATS suggests that the notion of whether ADHD is a valid diagnosis in early childhood is more settled than what to do when the diagnosis is obtained. The present paper begins with reasons why diagnosing ADHD in the preschool child has been challenging. Second, it reviews medication and the preschool child. Third, it addresses issues related to medication efficacy in the treatment of ADHD. Focus is given specifically to medication concerns resulting from the use of stimulant and nonstimulant psychotropic drugs on preschool children. The goal is to identify research trends while describing areas where additional research is warranted.

Diagnosing ADHD in Preschoolers and Children

Two mainstream scientific consensus statements address the diagnosis and treatment of ADHD: one organized by Russell Barkley (Barkley et al., 2002) and one sponsored by the National Institutes of Health (NIH, 1998). The statement organized by Barkley (and 74 other prominent scientists) addresses misinformation about ADHD covered in the mainstream media. Barkley et al. state that the American Medical Association (AMA), the American Psychiatric Association (APA), the American Academy of Child and Adolescent Psychiatry (AACAP), and the American Academy of Pediatrics (AAP), among others, all recognize ADHD as a valid disorder that can be diagnosed in children as young as 3 years of age. To provide evidence that ADHD is a disorder Barkley et al. (2002) assert that "...there must be scientifically established evidence that those suffering the condition have a serious deficiency in or failure of a physical or psychological mechanism that is universal to humans" (p. 89). There must be some type of harm to the individual. Harm is established through evidence of increased "mortality, morbidity, or impairment in the major life activities required of one's developmental stage in life" (Barkley et al., 2002, p. 89). They report on brain imaging studies that show "as a group, those with ADHD have less brain activity and show less reactivity to stimulation" (Barkley et al., 2002, p. 90) in different parts of the brain. They assert that there are hundreds of studies on the effectiveness of medication, and acknowledge the importance of educational, family, and other social accommodations. Barkley et al. conclude that ADHD is not a benign disorder and that ADHD can cause devastating problems.

The NIH (1998) Consensus Statement noted the need for treatment strategies that use combined behavioral and medication approaches. The NIH also reported research underway to evaluate treatment strategies thoroughly. However, conclusive recommendations concerning long-term treatment could not be made easily. Specifically, regarding stimulant medication usage for the treatment of ADHD, the NIH concluded that "substantial evidence exists of wide variations in the use of psychostimulants across communities and physicians, suggesting no consensus among practitioners regarding which ADHD patients should be treated with psychostimulants" (NIH, 1998, p. 10). Furthermore, the NIH asserted that there were benefits to the use of the medication, but there was no evidence regarding an ADHD diagnostic threshold where the benefits outweighed the risks of taking the stimulant medication. A need for improved awareness by the health service sector concerning appropriate assessment, treatment, and follow-up, as well as a need for a more consistent set of diagnostic procedures and practice guidelines was proposed by the NIH.

The NIH (1998) and Barkley et al. (2002) statements suggest credible evidence exists for the diagnosis of ADHD. The characteristics of ADHD are similar to age appropriate behaviors of normal preschool-aged children and are often difficult to differentiate (Blackman, 1999). The ADHD core symptoms of inattention, hyperactivity, and impulsivity are also symptoms associated with other mental disorders, learning disorders, developmental issues, differences in personality/temperament, or even parent and societal expectations (Furman & Berman, 2004). As with most mental disorders, the ADHD diagnosis is made from subjective observation, interview, and/or other non-medical type tests.

Teachers are often the initial source when beginning the diagnostic process (Sax & Kautz, 2003), and they are usually the primary sources of diagnostic information (Havey, Olson, McCormack, & Cates, 2005). Norvilitis and Fang (2005) reported that 82% of teachers in the United States consider ADHD to be over-diagnosed. Pediatric and family practice physicians play an important role in ADHD diagnosis. Parents bring their children into the physician's office and only a small portion of children will exhibit the overt symptoms of ADHD during the office visit (Johnson, 1997). In a study by Williams, Klinepeter, Palmes, Pulley, and Meschan (2004), pediatricians estimated that the average percentage of children in their practices with a behavioral health disorder was 15%. Williams et al. report that 45 of 47 pediatricians reported ADHD as their most common diagnosis. Wasserman et al. (1999) report that almost 19% of all patient visits for children between the ages 4 and 15 involved children with behavioral problems; 9% of all patient visits were related to attention and/or hyperactivity.

In discussing the diagnosis of ADHD for young children, Terjesen and Kurasaki (2009) correctly point out several considerations in the assessment of young children in this area. It is important to consider "the appropriateness of the current *Diagnostic and Statistical Manual: 4th Edition – Text Revision* ([DSM-IV-TR]; APA, 2000) diagnostic criteria for this age group" (Terjesen & Kurasaki, 2009, p. 354). One must also consider the context in which these behaviors occur; different settings may elicit different behaviors with this age group. Thus, multiple informants are required. As with many of the diagnoses within the DSM-IV, there are overlaps with other classifications. The issue of comorbidity has been addressed by many researchers (e.g., Posner et al., 2007; Schatz & Rostain, 2006; Wilens et al., 2002). Finally, Terjesen and Kurasaki discuss how the expectations of different referral sources affect reporting accuracy. There may be parent issues (e.g., parenting styles, family dynamics), medical issues (e.g., asthma, seasonal allergies), and early school issues (e.g., peer socialization, learning differences), all of which may influence an observer's report of the behavior. A recent article by Tobin, Schneider, Reck, and Landau (2008) discusses how assessment of children for ADHD should be connected to the child's ability to function within the domains of family, peers, and school. Thus the importance of culture, academics, sensory motor skills, peers, and family cannot be neglected when assessing for a possible diagnosis. Timimi and Taylor (2004) and Conrad (2005) discuss that ADHD could be a product of a social construct. Researchers who take this view question whether ADHD is a biologically based illness, in whole or in part.

As Gordon et al. (2006) suggest, the DSM-IV emphasizes the symptoms of ADHD more than the impairment. Cormier (2008) suggests over-diagnosis, the use of stimulant medications in children, and the ways in which children are diagnosed with ADHD are some of the main reasons for the controversies surrounding ADHD in children. Cosgrove, Krimsky, Vijayaraghavan, and Schneider (2006) discuss the problem of the ties between many professionals on the panel who constructed the most recent version of the DSM-IV diagnostic criteria for ADHD and the pharmaceutical companies. Mayes, Bagwell, and Erkulwater (2009) discuss many controversies, including whether ADHD is over-diagnosed, the subjectivity of the diagnosis, the evolution of the diagnosis, the use of stimulant medication to treat ADHD, the potential side effects of the medication, and the possible relationship between the physician and the pharmaceutical companies.

ADHD Treatment and Medication

The AMA agrees that ADHD is a valid diagnosis. Once diagnosed, however, the treatment is less clear and continues to be subject to controversy and political issues. Since the Multimodal Treatment Study of Children with ADHD (MTA Cooperative Group, 1999) gave stronger validity to possible treatment effects of medication over behavioral methods alone, more studies with preschool children have emerged. The MTA study involved 579 children between 7 and 9.9 years of age, in first through fourth grade at six different sites. The results of the study indicated that long-term combination treatments (i.e., combining pharmaceutical and behavioral treatments) and the medication-managed treatments were superior to intensive behavioral treatment and routine community treatment.

A few years after the MTA study, Greenhill et al. (2006) addressed medication dosages for preschool children. The PATS became the most rigorous evaluation, thus far, of the effects of stimulant medication on ADHD symptoms in preschoolers. Children aged 3 to 5 years participated at six different sites. First, parents participated in behavioral training, and only those children who did not respond to this less invasive treatment were invited to continue participation. The study occurred in the following eight phases over 70 weeks: (a) screening and enrollment; (b) parent training; (c) baseline; (d) open-label safety lead-in; (e) 5-week double-blind, placebo-controlled, crossover titration study; (f) 4-week double-blind, placebo-controlled parallel study; (g) open-label maintenance; and (h) discontinuation (Kollins & Greenhill, 2006). Initially, 303 children were enrolled in the PATS (Kollins et al., 2006). However, the exact number of participants varied depending on the phase of the study, in part because parents were re-consented at the beginning of each phase. Still, the number of participants in each phase was much higher than any previous study. Parent and teacher ratings across doses during Phase E were combined to create the primary outcome measure (Kollins & Greenhill, 2006). In Phase F, children began taking either their best dose or a placebo. In the next phase, open-label maintenance continued for 10 months to measure long-term treatment effects.

The PATS was prompted, in part, by the findings of Zito et al. (2000) who addressed the disturbing trend to prescribe psychotropic medications for preschoolers. Zito et al. (2000) showed that between 1991 and 1995 the use of stimulants in this age group tripled. Many of the drugs used had not even been approved for the 2- to 4-year-olds who were receiving them. Many other studies also show this increase in medication treatment for preschool children (e.g., Gleason et al., 2007; Kaplan, 2008). Zito et al. (2007) reported that in a 7-state Medicaid study, the actual prevalence rates for receiving one or more psychotherapeutic medications in 2001 were 0.96% for 2-year-olds, 2.08% for 3-year-olds, and 3.99% for 4-year-olds.

Coyle (2000) commented on the ethical issues relevant to prescribing these medications to children given the rapid changes in brain development during this time. There were also concerns expressed about the long-term effects of this medication on development (Kuehn, 2007). A story in the New York Times (Goode, 2003) discussed many concerns about giving such medication to young children without more knowledge of the correct dosage, side effects, and long-term effects. The AMA (2007) considers that stimulants are generally safe and are the most effective treatment to reduce the core symptoms of ADHD when they are administered and used in the way they are intended. Furthermore, "the FDA has recently taken actions to strengthen warnings on the product labeling for medications approved to treat ADHD, some disagreement continues about the risks of these medications" (Summary/Conclusion section, para. 3). Finally, the AMA-developed policy statement H-60.950 encouraged "further research on the relative risks and benefits of medication used to treat ADHD, including evaluation of the impact of labeling changes on access to treatment and physician prescribing" (Recommendations section, para. 3).

In summary, psychotropic medications are being prescribed more and more to address behavioral issues in the preschool population. Psychostimulants are the most common medications prescribed to address issues related to ADHD. Many studies have been published in the last 10 years to help explore the efficacy and concerns regarding use of psychostimulants among children (e.g., Debar, Lynch, Powell, & Gale, 2003; Gleason et al., 2007; Luby, Stalets, & Belden, 2007). The PATS is the first study to include multi-site locations and many phases to address different screening, ethical, parent training, and treatment concerns. Given the increased use of psychostimulant medications, it is logical to ask how effective these types of medications are.

Medication Efficacy

The beneficial effects of psychostimulant medication on ADHD symptoms have been noted in the literature. Preschoolers in studies reviewed by Greenhill (1998) ranged in age from 3 to 6 years, and the number of children taking stimulants varied from 14 to 31. Five of the six studies reviewed were double-blind placebo studies, while one used an open-label design. Dosage differed across studies and the length of the studies varied from 1 week on each treatment to 6 weeks. According to Greenhill (1998), four out of the six studies reported improvements in ADHD-related behaviors, such as decreased hyperactivity, decreased impulsivity, improved attention, and improved compliance. However, two studies found side effects to be more common in preschoolers compared to the school-age population. Side effects included decreased socialization, appetite suppression, fatigue, sleep problems, and mood dysregulation, with difficulties such as dysphoria and irritability. The small number of child participants and the variation in dosage and effects across studies limits the generalizability of these studies.

Since the time of Greenhill's (1998) review additional studies have examined the efficacy of stimulants for treating ADHD symptoms in preschool-age children. Byrne, Bawden, DeWolfe, and Beattie (1998) completed a matched control study of eight children with ADHD and eight comparison children. Results suggested improved behavior with stimulant medication based on parent report, as well as decreased errors of omission and commission on visual and auditory vigilance tasks.

Handen, Feldman, Lurier, and Murray (1999) carried out a double-blind placebo study with 11 children for 4 weeks, with stimulant medication administered at 0.3 mg/kg and 0.6 mg/kg for 7 consecutive days, one to three times per day. Because these stimulant medications are quickly metabolized and lose their effectiveness, the number of times the medication is administered may not be as relevant as the dosage of the medication. Although 8 of 11 children demonstrated improvements based on teacher ratings of behavior, almost half experienced significant side effects, including social withdrawal, increased crying, and irritability, particularly at high doses. The rate of side effects is concerning. However, the current cognitive abilities (IQ range 40-78) of the participating children may have limited the children's ability to cope with medication side effects.

Short, Manos, Findling, and Schubel (2004) explored the efficacy of psychostimulants among 28 preschool children (age 4.0 - 5.9 years) with ADHD in a naturalistic setting. Both parent and teacher behavior ratings were obtained to evaluate the efficacy of personal best dose of stimulant. Behavior ratings improved by at least one standard deviation for 82% of participating children. Ghuman and associates (2001) conducted a chart review of 27 preschool children using ratings from helping professionals (i.e., psychologists, psychiatrists, nurses) to examine the children's long-term response to stimulant medication at 3, 12, and 24 months. A 74% positive response rate at 3 months and a 70% positive response rate at 12 and 24 months was reported. Interestingly, the number of children experiencing side effects decreased over time.

More recent studies have included measurement of additional constructs related to ADHD, as well as multiple forms of measurement. For example, one group found that MPH led to improvements in four social behaviors and two areas of academic functioning for 36 preschool children attending a treatment program (Chacko et al., 2005). These social behaviors included rule following, rates of non-compliance, conduct problems, and negative statements made by children in recreation settings. The areas of academic functioning included following classroom rules and completion of seatwork.

The PATS results suggest that the MPH stimulant medication contributed to improvements in children's ADHD-related behaviors. The children's best dose varied, but it was smaller on average than doses generally used with older children (Abikoff et al., 2007). Initially, reported effect sizes were between 0.4 to 0.8 for Cohen's d. Yet, later analyses indicated that when data from children with zero or one co-morbid conditions were examined alone, effect sizes rose to a level similar to school-age children (Ghuman et al., 2001; Greenhill et al., 2006). In addition, improvement appeared to continue during the 10-month open-label maintenance phase (Vitiello et al., 2007). About 11% of children withdrew from the study due to side effects, which suggests that younger children may be more sensitive to medication side effects (Greenhill et al., 2006). However, investigators for the PATS indicate that they were limited somewhat in their findings due to the amount of necessary precautions (e.g., multiple consents, explanations to the parents), and all of the other safety checks that were required. Thus, there is the concern that these precautions may have had a systematic effect on those who chose to leave the study at different points. Although providing appropriate safety precautions is essential, this effort necessarily limited findings.

Heriot, Evans, and Foster (2007) conducted a study comparing MPH with parent training to MPH with a parent support group, as well as placebo comparison groups. Multiple methods of evaluation were used, including clinical observations, parent and teacher rating scales, and measures of parenting and family factors. Results indicated improvements in attention and decreased hyperactivity-impulsivity for the stimulant medication and parent training group, with more consistent improvements reported across teacher ratings. However, only four children participated in each experimental group.

The studies reviewed above generally suggest improvements in ADHD-related behaviors due to stimulant medication. Unfortunately, generalizing from these studies is limited due to variations in study design, medication dosage, and outcomes across studies, as well as a limited number of child participants. Some of the differences in effects may be accounted for by the many different measures used to determine the child's response to the medication. Such measures included parent, teacher, and helping professionals' behavior ratings, observations of *in vivo* behavior, and errors on continuous performance tasks.

Research to this point has clearly focused on determining the efficacy of stimulant medication, although physicians prescribe other nonstimulant medications, such as atomoxetine (Strattera) and clonidine, to treat ADHD symptoms in very young children. Although some articles have commented on recommended prescription guidelines and use of these alternative medications, only one article to date has been published on the efficacy of atomoxetine in treating preschool-age children with ADHD (Kratochvil et al., 2007). Twenty-two 5- and 6-year-old boys participated in this open-label study for 8 weeks. Based on pre- and post-study clinical interviews with the parents, the children demonstrated significant improvements greater than one standard deviation in inattention, as well as hyperactivity and impulsivity. Improvements in ratings completed by helping professionals also were significant and consistent with findings from parent interviews. Yet, there were still some side effects similar in type and rate to stimulant medications. Although these results provide initial evidence for the efficacy of atomoxetine for treating ADHD in preschool children, these findings should be viewed as preliminary and interpreted with caution.

Medication Concerns

A pervasive issue found in the use of both stimulant and nonstimulant medications to treat ADHD has focused upon psychological and/or physiological side effects. Left untreated a child diagnosed with ADHD will likely experience some negative psycho-social problems that impact both the family and those who provide services to the child (Posner et al., 2007). However, negative physiological issues may occur with medication. A suitable balance between these issues is challenging.

Schleifer et al. (1975) reported unwanted side effects that made MPH less useful for preschool children than older hyperactive children. These side effects included clinginess, melancholy, irritability, increased withdrawal in play, limited appetite, and difficulty sleeping. Rosenberg (1987) found negative side effects to be common in 5 of 6 studies looking at preschool children and stimulant medication (MPH). In follow-up, many parents chose to discontinue the medication even though there were positive behavioral effects. Similarly, Handen and colleagues (1999) reported preschool children with developmental disabilities and ADHD respond to MPH at rates similar to those of school-age children with mental retardation and ADHD. Preschool children, however, were more susceptible to adverse drug side effects.

In contrast, Firestone, Musten, Pisterman, Mercer, and Bennet (1998) reported that MPH had relatively low toxicity in the first 7 to 10 days. Some of the side effects seen were thought to be normal behaviors or behaviors related to ADHD types of behaviors in preschool children, such as effects on the child's sociability. They also concluded that the side effect behaviors were more common for preschool-aged children compared to school-aged children. In addition, some side effects were correlated with decreased ADHD behaviors. Finally, preschool-aged and school-aged children experienced different side effects related to MPH use. Preschool children in this study were more prone to be irritable, worried, tearful, and to experience sleep problems.

Zito and associates (2000) began a flurry of activity on many fronts when reporting the high number of preschool children, ages 2 to 4 years, who were taking psychiatric medication. They reported that as many as 150,000 children (1.5% of all preschool children) were taking stimulants, tranquilizers, antidepressants, or antipsychotic drugs. Two subsequent studies by Zito's group (Zito et al., 2003; Zito et al., 2007) not only showed the continuing trend of preschoolers taking these medications, but they also found that they were taking psychotropic medications for longer periods of time. Several studies commented on the possible negative effects of taking these on the brain (Coyle, 2000; Good, 1997; Gray et al., 2007). Greenhill, a child psychiatrist and an author on the PATS, was met with criticism for even proposing to examine the effects of medication on the preschool child's developing brain (Stohlberg, 2002). Much of the criticism focused on the trials proposed in these studies, especially after the research by Zito and his colleagues on the side effects of stimulant medication in preschool children (Zito et al., 2000; Zito et al., 2003).

The PATS, funded by the NIH partially in response to concerns that had surfaced stemming from the Zito et al. (2000) study, involved medication trials with MPH at six different sites. One finding from the PATS was the fact that there was a higher degree of discontinuation of the medication due to the adverse side effects in preschool children than in school-aged children. Significant side effects included irritability, sadness, anxiety, nightmares, limited appetite, sleepiness, decreased verbal interactions, and being uninterested in socializing. Interestingly, even when a nonstimulant medication was used to treat ADHD, mood lability was the most commonly reported adverse event, but there was also appetite suppression and weight loss (Kratochvil et al., 2007).

In the MTA study's 14- and 24-month follow-up, initial findings confirmed that medication, as well as medication and behavioral treatment, were much better than behavioral treatment alone for addressing ADHD symptoms in preschool children (MTA Cooperative Group, 2004). However, there was a surprising finding at the 24-month follow-up in that the relative advantage of drug therapy began to fade. At the 36-month follow-up it had completely disappeared. Still, the MTA study concluded that medication provided the best outcome for about one-third of the children. The most common side effects of the stimulant medications in the MTA study were loss of appetite, insomnia, headaches, and weight loss.

The effect of ADHD medications on growth is unresolved, and there has been some discussion as to whether long-term stimulant medication use causes growth retardation. One of the studies from the PATS revealed significant declines in height and increases in rate of weight gain in preschoolers (Swanson et al., 2006). These are consistent with the findings that occurred with school-aged children in the MTA study (MTA Cooperative Group, 2004).

Additional issues have been reported in the literature concerning the use of stimulant medications for treating ADHD in small children. Ghuman, Arnold, and Anthony (2008) discuss the difficulty of having to balance exposing preschool-aged children's rapidly developing brains to psychopharmacological agents against the potentially damaging consequences of not treating or under-treating the disorder. The review acknowledges the relative lack of studies that address this issue in preschool-aged children compared to school-aged children. Ghuman et al. (2008) reference the PATS finding that increased rates of social withdrawal and lethargy were seen in preschoolers taking higher doses of the medication. Ghuman and associates suggest that many healthcare providers and families would rather use the psychosocial methods of intervention for children's behavioral difficulties. However, there is the acknowledgement of the time-consuming nature of this option, which will probably lead to less treatment compliance. Ghuman and colleagues (2008) add their own note of caution about the lack of data on the long-term effects of medication intervention on the developing brains of preschoolers. In terms of prescribing medications, they recommend, "start low, go slow" and "at the same time, care should be taken to avoid under-treatment with lower doses" (Ghuman et al., 2008, p. 440).

Greenhill et al. (2006) discuss various theories of brain functioning in those diagnosed with ADHD. They comment on the "relative absence" of information on preschool children relative to school-age children in several important areas:

MPH, pharmacokinetics, pharmacodynamics, peak and duration of behavioral effects, interaction between drugs and the developing brain, guidelines for dosage response, and side effects related to short- and long-term exposure to stimulants. They report the following two challenges in prescribing medication for preschoolers: (a) the starting dose and (b) the "treatment challenge" of teaching preschoolers to swallow pills using behavioral training, as identified by the AACAP (2002).

Gleason et al. (2007), as well as Gleason and Froehlich (2008), report that even very young children can demonstrate significant psychiatric illness. Consequently, there may still be severe, impairing, and sometimes dangerous, symptoms of ADHD, even after an adequate course of an evidence-based psychosocial treatment. Kessler, Foster, Saunders, and Stang (1995) also suggest that untreated mental health issues may place children at higher risk for more severe problems later. Clinicians and families must therefore balance the potential adverse consequences of the ineffectively treated disorder with the known and unknown risks of preschool psychopharmacological treatment.

Gleason et al. (2007) report a dearth of statistical evidence on the effects of early exposure to psychopharmacological agents on the developing brain. Rey, Walter, and Hazell (2000) also express the concern of how much pressure from outside sources affect the medical professional's practice, including the parents and childcare services. Systemic issues are complex: There is the lack of FDA indications for preschool psychotropic use and limited insurance coverage of psychosocial treatment, yet childcare needs may increase the pressure to prescribe (Gleason et al., 2007).

Gleason and Froehlich (2008) present some unique preschool factors that need to be considered and what could be done to accommodate each of these issues. These preschool factors are important because they are the most concerning to parents and those prescribing the medications, as well as individuals doing research in this area. Gleason's group (2008, p. 3) describes the following factors to consider in ADHD diagnosis and treatment in preschool children: (a) rapid central nervous system development, (b) higher rates of adverse effects, (c) easily affected emotional and cognitive development, (d) language and developmental level, (e) the parent-child relationship, (f) the lack of focus on young children in the current DSM-IV criteria, (g) nearly all medications for ADHD are not FDA-approved for children under 5 and are considered to be "off-label," (h) limited access to evidence-based psychosocial treatment, and (i) limited mental health consultation available to childcare settings.

Mayes et al. (2009) attempted:

> …to pull together different research traditions and academic disciplines to produce a single study of how and why ADHD and stimulants have evolved over time to become the most commonly diagnosed disorder

and form of pharmacology among children and adolescents, as well as one of the most controversial (p. 10).

Representing the fields of public policy, psychology, and political science Mayes et al. did not receive any funding from pharmaceutical companies. This is in contrast "to so many other clinical researchers who publish their findings on ADHD and stimulants in academic journals" (Mayes et al., 2009, p. 12). Campbell (2007) suggests a link between physicians and pharmaceutical companies that may impact drug development initiatives, provision of free sample medications, enrollment of participants into clinical trials, and provision of "perks," such as free meals, vacations, or fees for consultation.

Discussion

Terjesen and Kurasaki (2009) indicate the need for more research regarding assessment and intervention with younger children who present with ADHD or ADHD-related behaviors. They recognize that the "means for identifying, measuring, and intervening with ADHD behaviors, in an evidenced-based manner, is still developing" (Terjesen & Kurasaki, 2009, p. 371). Anderson and Phelps (2009) stated, "Needless to say, there is work to be done before we can safely study the effectiveness of, much less safely administer, psychotropic medication in preschool children" (p. 580). Clinicians, researchers, and others continue to voice their concerns with prescribing ADHD medications while physicians working with children continue to observe the efficacy of medication in addressing the behavioral issues of the preschool child with ADHD. In some ways, researchers addressing the efficacy issues are moving slowly to determine the best dosage because one still has to consider the negative side effects of loss of appetite, growth suppression (perhaps related to the appetite suppression issue), sleep disturbances, and the still unknown effect of the medications on the preschool child's developing brain.

Beginning with the PATS there is a stronger research trend towards investigating and developing practice parameters for prescribing ADHD medications to preschoolers. Gupta states "The question with regard to psychotropic medications should not be whether to use them or not, but how to use them judiciously" (2000, p. 391). Gupta also commented that psychostimulants are useful in preschool children with ADHD, but only after careful consideration and not as a "knee-jerk" response. Kollins and others (2006) note that the PATS adds to a limited literature and improves our understanding of the safety and efficacy of MPH in the treatment of preschoolers with ADHD. However, research design and implementation problems with the

PATS impose some specific limitations. For example, the risks involved in including young children in clinical research invite intense scrutiny for both ethical and safety reasons. The PATS showed this scrutiny creates limitations. Future research must address these weaknesses. This is particularly important given the increasing use of MPH in preschool-age children that persists in spite of the lack of FDA approval (Medco Health Solutions, 2004).

One new avenue of exploration may lie in the pharmacogenetics of drug efficacy and response in preschool children with ADHD. McGough et al. (2006) present an emerging body of evidence that supports a potential for understanding the individual response to and side effects of ADHD medications from the study of genetics. More research is certainly warranted in the area before practical application of this new finding can be applied.

As referenced earlier, Gleason and Froehlich (2008) listed many unique factors that need to be addressed by those prescribing medication to the preschool child. For example, due to rapid central nervous system development, medications may affect the child's developmental course; thus, frequent assessments of social, emotional, and cognitive functioning should be conducted. Preschool children may also require different dosing than older children and different intervals between doses because they have different absorption, distribution, and metabolism processes. Due to the higher rates of adverse effects, starting doses should be lower and monitored closely. Because of emotional, cognitive, and language developmental levels, multiple areas should be assessed. Measures should include multiple respondents, information from multiple contexts, and interaction with the child, as well as observations, in structured and informal settings.

The importance of the parent-child relationship must also be addressed because of its impact on the child's mental health. In addition, the DSM-IV TR needs to be more relevant to the preschool-age child. There is hope for improvement in this area with development of the DSM-V. Furthermore, physicians need to discuss the FDA status of treatment in the informed consent process. Children should also participate in evidence-based psychosocial intervention, and there needs to be more access to non-pharmacological interventions, which may require further legislative and insurer advocacy. Additionally, there is limited mental health consultation available in childcare settings; thus, parents may perceive pressure to find a "quick fix" (Gleason & Froehlich, 2008).

Vitiello (1997) concluded that three things needed to happen in working with children and medication issues. First, it must be clearly understood that adult data on the effects of medication seldom translate to children. Second, more research is needed to support the use of psychotropic medication with children, especially with regard to the ethical issues. Third, in doing research a concerted effort must be made to include all stakeholders in this process. Progress in these areas is being made. However, more research is needed as we work in developing improved knowledge, algorithms, testing, assessment, and understanding of ADHD diagnosis and treatment as it applies to the preschool child.

The final issue associated with preschool children diagnosed with ADHD and receiving treatment with medication is the social and political one. There continues to be those who disagree with the validity of the diagnosis of ADHD and even more with the administration of psychotropic medication to children, much less preschoolers (Angold et al., 2000; Zwillich, 2005). The long-term effects of stimulants on the developing brain of the preschool child will probably only slowly be discovered. There will continue to be discussions on the merits of the disorder itself, its biological or environmental extent, best treatment options, and where to put the emphasis in intervention. There have been problems with schools requiring medication before a child with behavioral problems returns to school, as well as having children use drugs merely to enhance cognitive performance (Greely et al., 2008; Zwillich, 2005). Zwillich (2005) reports that Congress has enacted legislation that prohibits schools from excluding children from attending unless they are put on medication. The cognitive enhancement aspect of medication use for children may increase the voices of those who are opposed to psychotropic medications for children.

Unique responses to medication observed in older children make a definitive answer to the preschool child medication controversy even more challenging and elusive. For the preschool child who has ADHD and is prescribed medication, the continual mantra of clinicians, either researcher or prescriber, should be "more study needed." Longitudinal studies are needed that investigate the impact of both stimulant and nonstimulant medication upon brain development. Additional long-term studies should probe if a link exists between growth retardation and the use of medications for ADHD. Such work would have to consider the complex interplay between the previously observed side effects of appetite suppression, sleep disturbance, and growth difficulties.

Balancing side effects, both the known and the potential (i.e., developing brain effects), is necessary for each child. Mayes et al. (2009) draw an interesting conclusion in their recent book on ADHD medication and children,

> Despite the fact that scientific research can inform our choices, where the boundary between ADHD and typical childhood behavior is located is ultimately a political and social choice, not a scientific one. No amount of clinical research, therefore, can resolve this question for us (p. 172).

Anderson and Phelps (2009) note in their conclusion "the practice of preschool psychopharmacology is in its infancy; there is no doubt that more evidence is needed for the development of confident, empirically driven, scientist practitioners" (pp. 584-585). There is an acknowledgement that although more study is needed in this area, practitioners should not preclude helping these preschoolers and their families. The ethical issues in this developing field may need to be shared with the families who are receiving the medications for their preschoolers. Is more study needed? This is an area in which most researchers agree in the affirmative.

References

Abikoff, H., Vitiello, B., Riddle, M., Cunningham, C., Greenhill, L., Swanson, J., et al. (2007). Methylphenidate effects on functional outcomes in the Preschoolers with Attention-Deficit/Hyperactivity Disorder Treatment Study (PATS). *Journal of Child and Adolescent Psychopharmacology, 17,* 581-592.

American Academy of Child and Adolescent Psychiatry. (2002). Practice parameter for the use of stimulant medications in the treatment of children, adolescents, and adults. *Journal of the American Academy of Child & Adolescent Psychiatry, 41,* 26S-49S.

American Medical Association. (2007, June). *Report 10 of the Council on Science and Public Health: Attention Deficit Hyperactivity Disorder (A-07).* Retrieved August 20, 2009, from http://www.ama-assn.org/ama/no-index/about-ama/18470.shtml

American Psychiatric Association. (2000). *The Diagnostic and Statistical Manual of Mental Disorders (4th edition – text revision).* Washington, DC: Author.

Anderson, L., & Phelps, L. (2009). Psychopharmacology. In B. Mowder, F. Rubinson, & A.Yasik (Eds.), *Evidence-based practice in infant and early childhood psychology* (pp. 575-588). Hoboken, NJ: John Wiley and Sons.

Angold, A., Erkanli, A., Egger, H., & Costello, E. (2000). Stimulant treatment for children: A community perspective. *Journal of the American Academy of Child and Adolescent Psychiatry, 39,* 975- 984.

Barkley, R., Cook, E., Diamond, A., Zametkin, A., Thapar, A., Teeter, A., et al. (2002). International consensus statement on ADHD. *Clinical Child and Family Psychology Review, 5,* 89-111.

Blackman, J. A. (1999). Attention-deficit hyperactivity disorder in preschoolers. Does it exist and should we treat it? *Pediatric Clinics of North America, 46,* 1011-1025.

Bradley, C. (1937). The behavior of children receiving Benzedrine. *American Journal of Psychiatry*, *94,* 577-585.

Bradley, C., & Bowen, M. (1941). Amphetamine (Benzedrine) therapy of children's behavior disorders. *American Journal of Orthopsychiatry*, *11,* 92-103.

Byrne, J., Bawden, H., DeWolfe, N., & Beattie, T. (1998). Clinical assessment of psychopharmacological treatment of preschoolers with ADHD. *Journal of Clinical and Experimental Neuropsychology, 20,* 613-627.

Campbell, E. (2007). Doctors and drug companies – scrutinizing influential relationships. *New England Journal of Medicine, 357,* 1796-1787.

Chacko, A., Pelham, W., Gnagy, E., Greiner, A., Vallano, G., Bukstein, O., et al. (2005). Stimulant medication effects in a summer treatment program among young children with attention-deficit/hyperactivity disorder. *Journal of the American Academy of Child & Adolescent Psychiatry, 44,* 249-257.

Conrad, P. (2005). The shifting engines of medicalization. *Journal of Health and Social Behavior, 46,* 3-14.

Cormier, E. (2008). Attention deficit/hyperactivity disorder: A review and update. *Journal of Pediatric Nursing, 23,* 345-357.

Cosgrove, L., Krimsky, S., Vijayaraghavan, M., & Schneider, L. (2006). Financial ties between DSM-IV panel members and pharmaceutical industry. *Psychotherapy and Psychosomatics, 75,* 154-160.

Coyle, J. T. (2000). Psychotropic drug use in very young children. *Journal of the American Medical Association, 283,* 1059-1060.

Debar, L. L., Lynch, F., Powell, J., & Gale, J. (2003). Use of psychotropic agents in preschool children: Associated symptoms, diagnoses, and health care services in a health maintenance organization. *Archives of Pediatrics & Adolescent Medicine, 157,* 150-157.

Döpfner, M., Rothenberger, A., & Sonuga-Barke, E. (2004). Areas for future investment in the field of ADHD: Preschoolers and clinical networks. *European Child and Adolescent Psychiatry (Supplement 1), 13,* 130-135.

Firestone, P., Musten, L., Pisterman, S., Mercer, J., & Bennet, S. (1998). Short-term side effects of stimulant medication are increased in preschool children with attention-deficit/hyperactivity disorder: A double-blind placebo controlled study. *Journal of Child and Adolescent Psychopharmacology, 8,* 13-25.

Furman, L., & Berman, B. (2004). Rethinking the AAP attention deficit/ hyperactivity disorder guidelines. *Clinical Pediatrics, 43,* 601-603.

Ghuman, J. K., Arnold, L. E., & Anthony, B. J. (2008). Psychopharmacological and other treatments in preschool children with attention-deficit/ hyperactivity disorder: Current evidence and practice. *Journal of Child and Adolescent Psychopharmacology, 18,* 413-447.

Ghuman, J. K., Ginsburg, G. S., Subramaniam, G., Ghuman, H. S., Kau, A. S. M., & Riddle, M. A. (2001). Psychostimulants in preschool children with attention-deficit/hyperactivity disorder: Clinical evidence from a developmental disorders institution. *Journal of the American Academy of Child & Adolescent Psychiatry, 40,* 516-524.

Gleason, M. M., Egger, H. L., Emslie, G. J., Greenhill, L. L., Kowatch, R. A., Lieberman, A. F., et al. (2007). Psychopharmacological treatment for very young children: Contexts and guidelines. *Journal of the American Academy of Child and Adolescent Psychiatry, 46,* 1532-1572.

Gleason, M. M., & Froehlich, W. (2008). Preschoolers and psychopharmacological interventions. *Child and Adolescent Psychopharmacology News, 13,* 1-5.

Good, B. (1997). Studying mental illness in context: Local, global or universal? *Ethos, 25,* 230-248.

Goode, E. (2003, January 14). Study finds jump in children taking psychiatric drugs. *New York Times,* p. A21.

Gordon, M., Antshel, K., Faraone, S., Barkley, R., Lewandowski, J., Hudziak, J. J., et al. (2006). Symptoms versus impairment: The case for respecting DSM-IV's criterion D. *Journal of Attention Disorders, 9,* 465-475.

Gray, J., Punsoni, M., Tabori, N., Melton, J., Fanslow, V., Ward, M., et al. (2007). Methylphenidate administration to juvenile rats alters brain areas involved in cognition, motivated behaviors, appetite, and stress. *Journal of Neuroscience, 27,* 7196-7207.

Greely, H., Sahakian, B., Harris, J., Kessler, R., Gazzaniga, M., Campbell, P., et al. (2008). Towards responsible use of cognitive-enhancing drugs by the healthy. *Nature, 456,* 702-705.

Greenhill, L. L. (1998). The use of psychotropic medication in preschoolers: Indication, safety, and efficacy. *Canadian Journal of Psychiatry, 43,* 576-581.

Greenhill, L. L., Kollins, S., Abikoff, H., McCracken, J., Riddle, M., Swanson, J., et al. (2006). Efficacy and safety of immediate-release methylphenidate treatment for preschoolers with ADHD. *Journal of the American Academy of Child & Adolescent Psychiatry, 45,* 1284-1293.

Gupta, V. B. (2000). The escalating use of psychotropic medications to treat behavior problems in preschoolers. *Developmental and Behavioral Pediatrics, 21,* 391.

Handen, B. L., Feldman, H. M., Lurier, A. M., & Murray, P. J. H. (1999). Efficacy of methylphenidate among preschool children with developmental disabilities and ADHD. *Journal of the American Academy of Child & Adolescent Psychiatry, 38,* 805-812.

Havey, J., Olson, J., McCormack, C., & Cates, G. (2005). Teachers' perceptions of the incidence and management of attention deficit/hyperactivity disorder. *Applied Neuropsychology, 12,* 120-127.

Heriot, S. A., Evans, I. M., & Foster, T. M. (2007). Critical influences affecting response to various treatments in young children with ADHD: A case series. *Child: Care, Health and Development, 34,* 121-133.

Jensen, P. S., Kettle, L., Roper, M. T., Sloan, M., Dulcan, M. K., Hoven, C., et al. (1999). Are stimulants overprescribed? Treatment of ADHD in four US communities. *Journal of the American Academy of Child & Adolescent Psychiatry, 38,* 797-804.

Johnson, T. (1997). Evaluating the hyperactive child in your office: Is it ADHD? *American Family Physician, 56,* 155-160, 168-170.

Kaplan, A. (2008). Psychiatric medication guidelines set for preschoolers. *Psychiatric Times, 25(3),* 1-2.

Kessler, R. C., Foster, C. L., Saunders, W. B., & Stang, P. E. (1995). Social consequences of psychiatric disorders. I: Educational attainment. *American Journal of Psychiatry, 152,* 1026-1032.

Kollins, S. H., & Greenhill, L. (2006). Evidence base for the use of stimulant medication in preschool children with ADHD. *Infants and Young Children, 19,* 132-141.

Kollins, S., Greenhill, L., Swanson, J., Wigal, S., Abikoff, H., McCracken, J., et al. (2006). Rationale, design, and methods of the Preschool ADHD Treatment Study (PATS). *Journal of the American Academy of Child & Adolescent Psychiatry, 45,* 1275-1283.

Kratochvil, C. J., Vaughan, B. S., Mayfield-Jorgensen, M. L., March, J. S., Kollins, S. H., Murray, D. W., et al. (2007). A pilot study of atomoxetine in young children with attention-deficit/hyperactivity disorder. *Journal of Child and Adolescent Psychopharmacology, 17,* 175-185.

Kuehn, B. M. (2007). Scientists examine benefits, risks of treating preschoolers with ADHD drugs. *Journal of the American Medical Association, 298,* 1747-1749.

Lahey, B. B., Pelham, W. E., Loney, J., Kipp, H., Ehrhardt, A., Lee, S. S., et al. (2004). Three-year predictive validity of DSM-IV attention deficit hyperactivity disorder in children diagnosed at 4-6 years of age. *American Journal of Psychiatry, 161,* 2014-2020.

Luby, J., Stalets, M., & Belden, A. (2007). Psychotropic prescriptions in a sample including both healthy and mood and disruptive disordered preschoolers: Relationships to diagnosis, impairment, prescriber type, and assessment methods. *Journal of Child and Adolescent Psychopharmacology, 17,* 205-215.

Mayes, R., Bagwell, C., & Erkulwater, J. (2009). *Medicating children: ADHD and pediatric mental health.* Cambridge, MA: Harvard University Press.

McGough, J., McCracken, J., Swanson, J., Riddle, M., Kollins, S., Greenhill, L., et al. (2006). Pharmacogenetics of methylphenidate response in preschoolers with ADHD. *Journal of the American Academy of Child & Adolescent Psychiatry, 45,* 1314-1322.

Medco Health Solutions. (2004). *2004 Drug Trend Report.* Retrieved September 29, 2009, from http://www.medcohealth.com

MTA Cooperative Group. (1999). A 14-month randomized clinical trial of treatment strategies for attention-deficit/hyperactivity disorder. *Archives of General Psychiatry*, 56, 1073-1086.

MTA Cooperative Group. (2004). National Institute of Mental Health multimodal treatment study of ADHD follow-up: Changes in effectiveness and growth after the end of treatment. *Pediatrics, 113*, 762-769.

National Institute of Health. (1998 Nov 16-18). Diagnosis and treatment of attention deficit hyperactivity disorder. *NIH Consensus Statement Online, 16(2)*, 1-37. Retrieved August 18, 2009, from http://consensus.nih.gov/199 8/1998AttentionDeficitHyperactivityDisorder110html.htm

Norvilitis, J., & Fang, P. (2005). Perceptions of ADHD in China and the United States: A preliminary study. *Journal of Attention Disorders, 9(2),* 413-24.

Posner, K, Melvin, G., Murray, D, Gugga, S., Fisher, P., Skrobala, A., et al. (2007). Clinical presentation of attention-deficit/hyperactivity disorder in preschool children: The Preschoolers with Attention deficit/ hyperactivity Treatment Study (PATS). *Journal of Child and Adolescent Psychopharmacology, 17*, 547-562.

Rey, J. M, Walter, G., & Hazell, P. L. (2000). Psychotropic drugs and preschoolers. *Medical Journal of Australia, 173,* 172-173.

Rosenberg, M. S. (1987). Psychopharmacological interventions with young hyperactive children. *Topics in Early Childhood Special Education, 6*, 62-74.

Safer, D. J., Zito, J. M., & Fine, E. M. (1996). Increased methylphenidate usage for attention deficit disorder in the 1990s. *Pediatrics, 98,* 1084-1088.

Sax, L., & Kautz, K. (2003, September - October). Who first suggests the diagnosis of attention deficit/hyperactivity disorder? *Annals of Family Medicine 1*, 171-174.

Schatz, D., & Rostain, A. (2006). ADHD with comorbid anxiety: A review of the current literature. *Journal of Attention Disorders, 10*, 141-149.

Schleifer, N., Weiss, G., Cohen, N., Elman, M., Cvejic, H., & Kruger, E. (1975). Hyperactivity in preschoolers and the effect of methylphenidate. *American Journal of Orthopsychiatry, 45,* 38-50.

Short, E. J., Manos, M. J., Findling, R. L., & Schubel, E. A. (2004). A prospective study of stimulant response in preschool children: Insights from ROC analyses. *Journal of the American Academy of Child & Adolescent Psychiatry, 43,* 251-259.

Stohlberg, S. (2002, November 17). Preschool meds. *New York Times*, E58.

Swanson, J., Greenhill, L., Wigal, T., Kollins, S., Stehli, A., Davies, M., et al. (2006). Stimulant-related reductions of growth rates in the PATS. *Journal of the American Academy of Child & Adolescent Psychiatry, 45,* 1304-1313.

Swanson, J. M., McBurnett, K., Wigal, T., Pfiffner, L. J., Lerner, M. A., Williams, L., et al. (1993). Effect of stimulant medication on children with attention deficit disorder: A "review of reviews." *Exceptional Children, 60,* 154-162.

Terjesen, M., & Kurasaki, R. (2009). Attention deficit hyperactivity disorder. In B. Mowder, F. Rubinson, & A.Yasik (Eds.), *Evidence-based practice in infant and early childhood psychology* (pp. 351-380). Hoboken, NJ: John Wiley and Sons.

Timimi, S., & Taylor, E. (2004). ADHD is best understood as a cultural construct. *The British Journal of Psychiatry, 184,* 8-9.

Tobin, R., Schneider, W., Reck, S., & Landau, S. (2008). Best practices in the assessment of children with attention deficit hyperactivity disorder: Linking assessment to response to intervention. In A. Thomas & J. Grimes (Eds.), *Best Practices in School Psychology V* (pp. 617-631). Bethesda, MD: National Association of School Psychologists.

Vitiello, B. (1997, September). Medication development and testing in children and adolescents. *Archives of General Psychiatry*, 54, 871-876.

Vitiello, B., Abikoff, H. B., Chuang, S. Z., Kollins, S. H., McCracken, J. T., Riddle, M. A., et al. (2007). Effectiveness of methylphenidate in the 10-month continuation phase of the Preschoolers with ADHD Treatment Study (PATS). *Journal of Child and Adolescent Psychopharmacology, 17,* 593-603.

Wasserman, R. C., Kelleher, K. J., Bocian, A., Baker, A., Childs, G. E., Indacochea, F., et al. (1999). Identification of attention and hyperactivity problems in primary care: A report from pediatric research in office settings and the ambulatory sentinel practice network. *Pediatrics, 103*(3), e38.

Wilens, T., Biederman, J., Brown, S., Tanguay, S., Monuteaux, M. C., Blake, C., et al. (2002). Psychiatric comorbidity and functioning in clinically referred preschool children and school-age youths with ADHD. *American Academy of Child and Adolescent Psychiatry. 4,* 262-268.

Williams, J., Klinepeter, K., Palmes, G., Pulley, A., & Meschan, J. (2004). Diagnosis and treatment of behavioral health disorders in pediatric practice. *Pediatrics, 114 (3),* 601-606.

Zito, J. M., Safer, D. J., dosReis, S., Gardner, J. F., Boles, M., & Lynch, F. (2000). Trends in the prescribing of psychotropic medication to preschoolers. *Journal of the American Medical Association, 283,* 1025-1030.

Zito, J., Safer, D., dosReis, J., Gardner, J., Magder, L., Soeken, K., et al. (2003). Psychotropic practice patterns for youth: A 10-year perspective. *Archives of Pediatric and Adolescent Medicine, 157,* 17-25.

Zito, J. M., Safer, D. J., Valluri, S., Gardner, J. F., Korelitz, J. J., & Mattison, D. R. (2007). Psychotherapeutic medication prevalence in Medicaid-insured preschoolers. *Journal of Child and Adolescent Psychopharmacology, 17,* 195-203.

Zwillich, T. (2005). Schools can't require ADHD drugs. *WebMD Health News.* Retrieved August 21, 2009, from http://www.webmd.com/add-adhd/ news/20051116/schools-cant-require-adhd-drugs

Author Note

W. Mark Posey, Ph.D. is the Associate Director of the Developmental Pediatric Clinic and the Program Director of the Dunbar ADHD Program at the University of South Carolina School of Medicine. Sarah A. Bassin, Ph.D. is working as a school psychologist in Richland School District Two in Columbia, South Carolina. Ashley Lewis, M.A. is a school psychology doctoral student at the University of South Carolina; she is completing her pre-doctoral internship in school psychology with Guilford County Schools, Greensboro, North Carolina.

Double Jeopardy in the Low-income Child:
The Case of Antibiotic Use

Anita L. Kozyrskyj
University of Alberta & University of Manitoba

Peter J. Gill, Terry P. Klassen, & Sarah E. D. Forgie
University of Alberta

Inappropriate prescribing of antibiotics to children is not uncommon despite public availability of good quality evidence and clinical practice guidelines. Low-income children are frequently treated by physicians who do not practice evidence-based medicine, and whose parents are more likely to believe that antibiotics are needed. Because respiratory tract infections are more common in low-income children to begin with, this combination of physician and parent factors places low-income children at double jeopardy. They continue to be the recipients of inappropriate antibiotic prescribing, even though antibiotic use has declined among higher income children over the last 20 years. The consequences of this inappropriate use are the development of antibiotic resistance and chronic conditions, such as asthma. Recognizing the complexity of physician-parent interactions and the challenges that low-income families face, we propose that proven-effective, multi-faceted strategies be aimed at physicians caring for children from low-income neighborhoods.

Children are generally healthy, but societal investment to optimize the health of children is a key public health strategy to prevent many chronic conditions in adulthood. Children are not little adults. They differ from adults with respect to disease pathophysiology and pharmacologic response to medications, such that the safety and efficacy profiles of medications frequently vary between children and adults (Kearns et al., 2003). Despite this well-known fact, over half of the medication treatments for children are for drugs which are not licensed for use in children, often resulting in child health care providers relying on evidence that has been generated on adult populations (Conroy et al., 2000; Cramer et al., 2005). This practice results in failure to use medications that are effective or

All correspondence should be addressed to Anita Kozyrskyj, Department of Pediatrics, Faculty of Medicine, University of Alberta, Rm 8226a, Aberhart Centre One, 11402 University Ave, Edmonton, AB, Canada, T6G 2J3. Electronic mail may be sent to kozyrsky@ualberta.ca.

in the continued use of ineffective medications, even those causing unintended harm (Johnson, 2003). As a result, there are calls for better quality trials to test interventions in children (Klassen, Hartling, Craig, & Offringa, 2008).

Moreover, even in countries with universal health insurance, not all children enjoy the same level of health or quality of care. It would not be an over generalization to state that children from low-income families are not like children living in more affluent households. They are more likely to suffer from poor health and development, including a higher prevalence of respiratory tract infections and chronic conditions, such as asthma (Aber, Bennett, Conley, & Li, 1997; Kozyrskyj, Kendall, Jacoby, Sly, & Zubrick, in press; Seguin, Nikiema, Gauvin, Zunzunegui, & Xu, 2007). Low-income children are also less likely to receive quality health care and subsequently, do less well when they have a chronic condition (Newacheck, Hughes, & Stoddard, 1996). For example, fewer low-income children with asthma receive prophylaxis medications (Kozyrskyj, Mustard, & Simons, 2003). Hence, low-income children are at double jeopardy of being in poorer health and receiving less optimal health care. To illustrate our point further, this paper will draw on antibiotic use in children as a case study. The case study will summarize current trends and concerns around antibiotic use, identify determinants of antibiotic prescribing and propose strategies for improving antibiotic use in low-income children. Under each topic, low-income children will be discussed separately.

Trends in Antibiotic Use in North America

Children were subject to increasing exposure to antibiotics throughout the 1980s (McCaig & Hughes, 1995). Concerns over increasing inappropriate prescribing and antibiotic resistance led to several community-wide campaigns in the 1990s that were successful in decreasing antibiotic use (Finkelstein et al., 2001; Perz et al., 2002). On a population basis, antibiotic use among US children fell during the 1990s (Finkelstein et al., 2003; McCaig, Besser, & Hughes, 2002). Decreasing antibiotic consumption also occurred in Canada. In 1995, half of the children in the province of Manitoba had received at least one antibiotic prescription, yielding an average of 1.2 antibiotic prescriptions per child (Kozyrskyj, Carrie, et al., 2004). Antibiotic use declined by almost one-third in 2001. The use of older-generation antibiotics, such as the "sulfa" suspensions, declined by 70%. Infants and preschool children experienced the greatest reduction in antibiotic use. These rates of decline continued in Manitoba from 2001 to 2005 (Manitoba Centre for Health Policy, 2008). In 2001, 45% of children received at least one antibiotic prescription for an average of 0.93 prescriptions per child. Four years later, this dropped to 39% of children and an average of 0.75 prescriptions. Reductions in use indicated physician adherence to clinical practice guidelines to not prescribe antibiotics for bronchitis and the common cold (O'Brien et al., 1998; Rosenstein et al., 1998). Compared to 1995, children less often received an antibiotic prescription following a physician visit for these infections in 2001 (Finkelstein, Stille, Rifas-Shiman, & Goldmann, 2005; Kozyrskyj et al., 2004; McCaig et al., 2002).

Despite these improvements in physician prescribing, non-evidence-based prescribing of antibiotics continues to occur (Arnold, Allen, Al-Zahrani, Tan, & Wang, 1999; Le Saux, Bjornson, & Pitters, 1999; Nyquist, Gonzales, Steiner, & Sande, 1998; Pennie, 1998; Wang, Einarson, Kellner, & Conly, 1999). Although systematic reviews show little benefit in treating acute otitis media (AOM; ear infections) with a 7-day course of antibiotics (Kozyrskyj et al., 1998) or any antibiotics for that matter (Glasziou, Del Mar, Sanders, & Hayem, 2004; Shaikh & Harvey, 2009), reductions in antibiotic use for AOM are the result of a reduction in physician visits rather than a change in physician prescribing (Finkelstein et al., 2003; Kozyrskyj et al., 2004; McCaig et al., 2002). Among 20,000 Manitoba children in the late 1990s, almost half of physician visits for viral respiratory tract infections (VRTI) had resulted in an antibiotic prescription and second-line antibiotics were prescribed in 20% of visits for common childhood infections (Kozyrskyj, Dahl et al., 2004). Non-evidence-based antibiotic treatment is more common in children with a chronic condition. Sixty-four percent of physician visits for wheezing in asthmatic children in 2001 resulted in an antibiotic prescription within 7 days of the episode (Kozyrskyj, Dahl, Ungar, Becker, & Law, 2006).

Low-income children are more likely to be treated with antibiotics (Kozyrskyj, 2002; Petersson & Hakansson, 1996). In the late 1990s, Manitoba children living in low-income neighborhoods in urban centers had the highest rates of antibiotic use and were less likely to experience a decline in use over time (see Figure 1; Kozyrskyj et al., 2004). While it is true that respiratory tract infections are more prevalent in low-income children, many of these are viral infections for which antibiotics are not needed (Margolis et al., 1992; O'Brien et al., 1998). On the other hand, broad-spectrum (BS) antibiotics are prescribed less often in low-income children (Henricson et al., 1998). Throughout the 1990s, low-income Manitoba children did not experience the same increases in use of BS macrolide antibiotics as did high-income children. Inability of low-income families to pay out-of-pocket for antibiotics not reimbursed by drug insurance plans was a likely contributing factor (Reuveni et al., 2002).

Concerns About Antibiotic Use

Immediate hazards of antibiotic use are increased side effects and costs of therapy (Berman, Byrns, Bondy, Smith, & Lezotte, 1997; Slama et al., 2005). Common side effects, such as diarrhea, are related to the antibiotic effect on

Figure 1
Antibiotic Prescriptions per Population by Urban Income Quintile (Q1-Q5)
Neighborhood, 1995-2001.

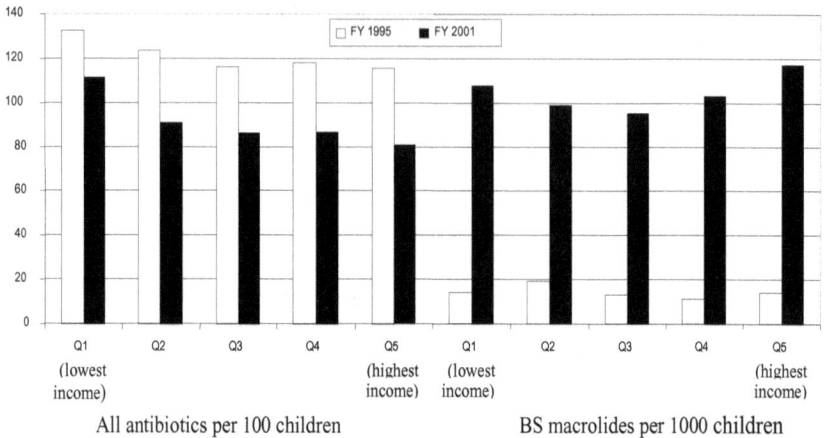

"good" bacteria in the gastrointestinal tract, known as the intestinal microbiota. The intestinal microbiota is required for the absorption of nutrients and protection against pathogenic bacteria. In the adult, the intestinal microbiota is home to as many as 400 different species of bacteria acquired after birth (Mackie, Sghir, & Gaskins, 1999).

All antibiotics alter intestinal microbiota in humans, but have a greater suppressive effect in the newborn, especially if they are BS antibiotics (Edlund & Nord, 2000). During the treatment of infants with penicillins or cephalosporins, important intestinal bacteria are suppressed to undetectable levels (Adlerberth et al., 2007; Bennet, Eriksson, & Nord, 2002; Penders et al., 2006). Suppression of the intestinal microbiota can lead to the overgrowth of bacteria that are resistant to the administered antibiotic. For example, ampicillin is associated with overgrowth of clostridia and yeasts in infants (Sakata, Fujita, & Yoshioka, 1986). Following triplicate antibiotic therapy, the biodiversity of the intestinal microbiota in infants has been found to be low, with rapid growth of staphylococci and yeasts (Bonnemaison et al., 2003). The emergence of resistant bacteria in intestinal microbiota or elsewhere in the body can result in difficult to treat infections. Long-term consequences of the disruption of microbiota include the development of asthma (Farooqi & Hopkin, 1998; Kozyrskyj, Ernst, & Becker, 2007; McKeever et al., 2002) or inflammatory bowel disease (Hildebrand, Malmborg, Askling, Ekbom, & Montgomery, 2008). The rest of the discussion will focus on the development of antibiotic resistance, and asthma and allergic disease in children.

Antibiotic Resistance and Difficult to Treat Infection

The emergence of bacteria that become resistant to an antibiotic has been emerging since the discovery of penicillin. Resistance to an antibiotic can occur through alterations in the genetic makeup of bacteria (Mulvey & Simor, 2009; Neu, 1992). Antibiotic resistant bacteria emerge wherever antibiotics are used, both in a hospital setting or the community (McGowan, 1983; Seppala et al., 1997). Following treatment with an antibiotic, most susceptible bacteria will be inhibited or killed. However, subsequent to natural selection, bacteria that are resistant to the drug will continue to grow and reproduce, and become dominant within a short time frame.

The risk of a resistant bacterial infection correlates strongly with recent use of an antibiotic (Boken, Chartrand, Goering, Kruger, & Harrison, 1995; Guillemot et al., 1998; Hillier et al., 2007; Nasrin et al., 2002; Seppala et al., 1997). Once an individual is infected, resistant bacteria can be transmitted to others. Once an organism is introduced into a community, spread occurs rapidly (Smith, Manges, & Riley, 2008). Resistance patterns in communities mirror patterns of antibiotic use (Arason et al., 1996; Manninen, Huovinen, & Nissinen, 1997; Seppala et al., 1997). In fact, antibiotic resistance has been reported among children not receiving antibiotics when community use of antibiotics is high (Boken et al., 1995; Guillemot et al., 1998).

Penicillin resistance to *Streptococcus pneumoniae,* a bacterium that causes AOM, has been on the rise in Canadian children, leveling off to 16% in the last few years (Canadian Bacterial Surveillance Network, 2009; Greenberg et al., 2002; Scheifele et al., 2000). The latter has been attributed to the introduction of the pneumococcal vaccine and declining antibiotic use (Marra et al., 2007; Winters et al., 2008). At the same time, *Streptococcus pneumoniae* is becoming less sensitive to macrolide antibiotics such as erythromycin, especially in child care centers (Boken et al., 1995; Hyde et al., 2001; Whitney et al., 2000). Soon, cloxacillin, the first line therapy for *Staphylococcus aureus*, will no longer be effective (Hawkes et al., 2007). Cloxacillin resistance is over 70% in parts of the United States. Similar trends are expected in Canada (Chambers, 2005; Kaplan et al., 2005; King et al., 2006). A UK study found that prescribing amoxicillin in children doubled the risk of haemophilus bacterial resistance (Chung et al., 2007). The increase was transitory in individual children, but sufficient to sustain a high level of antibiotic resistance in the population.

Antibiotic Resistance is More Common in Low-income Children

Certain adult populations such as military recruits, Native Americans and prisoners, have been identified at high risk for antibiotic resistance (Centers for Disease Control and Prevention, 2005). The results of a surveillance study found that low socioeconomic status played a major role in the rising rates of resistant staphyloccocus infection in the US during 1991-2004 (Herman, Kee, Moores, & Ross, 2008). Antibiotic use patterns in low-income children put them at greater risk for resistance (Kozyrskyj et al., 2004). Data is emerging to support this notion. A recent study of 884 preschool children found that colonization of intestinal microbiota with resistant *Escherichia coli* was greater in households where the mother had a lower level of education (Lietzau, Raum, von Baum, Marre, & Brenner, 2007).

Development of Asthma and Allergic Disease

To date, epidemiologic studies have both supported and refuted an association between antibiotic treatment in early life and the development of childhood asthma (Marra et al., 2006). A database study of 14,000 children born in Manitoba, Canada found that the risk of asthma was increased by 50% in children receiving more than four courses of antibiotics during the first year of life (Kozyrskyj et al., 2007). These findings have been confirmed in a similar database study of 250,000 children in British Columbia, Canada (Marra et al., 2009).

Disruption of the normal composition of intestinal microbiota in the infant has been proposed as the mechanism for the development of allergic disease. Lower levels of intestinal lactobacilli and bifidobacteria, and higher concentrations of *Clostridium difficile* have been observed in infants who show signs of developing allergies (Gore et al., 2008; Murray et al., 2005; Penders et al., 2006). The evidence to support the connection with antibiotic use is more limited (Murray et al., 2005; Penders et al., 2007). In a three-center European study, infants receiving antibiotics before 6 months of age were more likely to become colonized with *Clostridium* species and had reduced ratios of strict to facultative anaerobes (Adlerberth et al., 2007). Both scenarios increased the risk of allergic disease, although associations were not statistically significant. A study is underway in Manitoba to study the link between antibiotic use, infant microbiota, and childhood asthma.

Asthma is More Common in Low-income Children

Children living in chronically low-income families are more likely to develop asthma (Kozyrskyj et al., in press; Seguin et al., 2007). It is plausible, but remains to be determined, that the increased prevalence of asthma is due to disruption of infant microbiota during infancy from more frequent use of antibiotics (Kozyrskyj et al., 2004).

Determinants of Antibiotic Use

Physician Prescribing

Antibiotic resistance has been promoted by multiple courses of antibiotics, long duration of antibiotic treatment, treatment with BS antibiotics and antibiotic treatment of VRTI (Arason et al., 1996; Block et al., 1995; Guillemot et al., 1998; Nasrin et al., 2002; Seppala et al., 1997). Canadian and US studies show that antibiotic prescribing is influenced by physician characteristics, such as location of medical training, physician specialty, years in practice, hospital affiliation, and private or clinic practice (Berman et al., 1997; Cadieux, Tamblyn, Dauphinee, & Libman, 2007; Davy, Dick, & Munk, 1998; Mainous, Hueston, & Love, 1998; Pennie, 1998; Watson et al., 1999). In Manitoba, pediatricians were 50% less likely than family physicians to prescribe an antibiotic for a VRTI, but 1.3 times more likely to prescribe second-line (BS) antibiotics for infections, such as AOM (Kozyrskyj, Dahl et al., 2004). Canadian or United States trained physicians were 40% less likely than those trained elsewhere to prescribe an antibiotic for a VRTI and to provide a prescription for a second-line agent. Finally, an evaluation of antibiotic use in Manitoba children with asthma found that family physicians were twice as likely to prescribe antibiotics for wheeze when compared with pediatricians (Kozyrskyj et al., 2006).

Physician characteristics such as specialty of practice or location of training have been found to account for 20-30% of neighborhood variation in antibiotic prescribing for a VRTI (see Table 1). Collectively, almost half of the neighborhood variation ($r^2 = 0.45$) in antibiotic prescribing for a VRTI in Winnipeg in 1999 was attributed to these characteristics. Viral respiratory infections remain the second most common reason for antibiotic use in children (Kozyrskyj et al., 2004). As such, physician determinants of prescribing can drastically affect antibiotic use and resistance at the community level (Roark, Petrofski, Berson, & Berman, 1995).

Physician-parent interactions play an important role in the continued inappropriate prescribing of antibiotics. The most predictive behavior of antibiotic prescribing is physician perception that parents expect a prescription, especially when prompted by parent communication such as the suggestion of a diagnosis (Mangione-Smith, McGlynn, Elliott, Krogstad, & Brook, 1999; Palmer & Bauchner, 1997; Stivers, 2002b; Vinson & Lutz, 1993). Numerous studies have proven that physicians are not accurate in their perceptions (Lundkvist, Akerlind,Borgquist, & Molstad, 2002; Mangione-Smith et al., 1999; Ong et al., 2007). Parents who expect to receive an antibiotic prescription for their child may simply be seeking reassurance that their child is not seriously ill or that they were correct to obtain medical care (Stivers, Mangione-Smith, Elliott, McDonald, & Heritage, 2003).

Table 1

Physician Predictors of Regional Variation in Antibiotic Prescriptions for Viral Respiratory Tract Infections (VRTI) in 55 Winnipeg Income Neighborhoods, 1999

Physician (MD) Variable	Univariate Regression			Multivariate Linear Regression		
	Coefficient	*p*-value	R2	Coefficient	*p*-value	R2
Income Quintile[a]						
1		NS	0.14			
2	0.036	0.04				
3		NS				
4		NS				
5		NS				
% VRTI in children < 5 years old		NS				
% VRTI treated by:						
Hospital-affiliated MD	-0.096	.05	0.17			
Pediatricians[b]	-0.182	0.008	0.22	-0.205	0.002	
Specialists[b]	-0.918	0.24		-0.666	0.32	
Non-NA trained MD	0.155	0.0005	0.29	0.214	0.0001	
MD > 50 years	0.175	0.014	0.20			
Male MD		NS		-0.317	0.006	
MD practicing < 20 years		NS				
Solo practitioners	0.243	0.0025	0.25			
All Variables						0.45

Note. Physician variable adjusted for 1/number of VRTI episodes; NS = non-significant; NA = North America.

[a] Income quintile 5 = Highest. [b]Reference: % treated by family MD

Less Optimal Prescribing in Low-income Children

Physician determinants of antibiotic prescribing have particular relevance to low-income children. In 1999, 22% of Manitoba children in low-income, urban neighborhoods had received an antibiotic for a VRTI, compared with 16% of children living in the highest income neighborhoods (see Table 2). An antibiotic was prescribed more often following a physician visit for a VRTI in low-income children. One third of physician visits for VRTIs among children living in low-income neighborhoods were to a pediatrician, in comparison to 41% for children in the highest income neighborhoods. A hospital-affiliated physician provided care in two-thirds of visits by children in low-income neighborhoods, compared with 80% in higher income children. Finally, approximately half of VRTI visits by low-income children were to non North American trained physicians, compared with 36% in the highest income neighborhood children. Similar income variations in physician characteristics for VRTI visits were observed among children living in rural neighborhoods. However, the majority of VRTIs in low-income children were treated by a non North American trained physician and only 6% by a pediatrician. Almost half of VRTI visits in rural children had resulted in an antibiotic prescription.

Table 2
Percentage of Child Physician Visits for Viral Respiratory Tract Infections by Physician Characteristics and Urban income Neighborhood, 1999

Physician Characteristics	Urban Neighborhood Income Quintile[a]				
	1	2	3	4	5
Pediatrician	32%	35%	37%	39%	41%
Non-NA trained	51%	48%	43%	40%	36%
Age > 50 years	48%	49%	45%	46%	43%
Male	82%	81%	80%	79%	78%
Practiced > 20 years	30%	32%	30%	31%	29%
Hospital affiliation	67%	74%	77%	80%	80%
Solo practitioner	17%	14%	13%	11%	9%
Total antibiotics per visit	39%	40%	37%	37%	37%
Total antibiotics per child population	22%	19%	18%	17%	16%

Note. NA = North America.
[a] Income quintile 5 = Highest.

Parental Influences on Prescribing

Parents can influence physician prescribing of an antibiotic for their child (Watson et al., 1999), an effect that is mediated through their level of knowledge and ability to pay for the prescription (Bondy, Berman, Glazner, & Lezotte, 2000; Henricson et al., 1998). Studies document that 48% to 65% of parents expect antibiotics for viral illnesses (Hamm, Hicks, & Bemben, 1996; Mangione-Smith et al., 1999). However, it is uncommon for parents to overtly request an antibiotic prescription (Lundkvist et al., 2002; Mangione-Smith et al., 2001; Stivers, 2002a).

The expectation for an antibiotic prescription arises from the complex interaction of social, economic, cultural and personal factors. Parents face economic pressures to take time off work to care for their sick children and meet infection control policies at daycare centers that prohibit sick children (Barden, Dowell, Schwartz, & Lackey, 1998; Pichichero, 1999). They are also dependent on the availability of accurate information on the appropriate use of antibiotics, information that often is too generalized or relies on basic assumptions that unintentionally exclude low-income or ethnic populations. Widespread education and awareness campaigns have reduced parental expectations for the need of antibiotics (Schwartz, Bell, & Hughes, 1997). Despite these campaigns, some parents believe that antibiotics will decrease the likelihood of a secondary bacterial infection or shorten the duration of a viral illness (Belongia, Naimi, Gale, & Besser, 2002; Collett, Pappas, Evans, & Hayden, 1999). Previous inappropriate antibiotic prescribing for viral illnesses may also enhance these beliefs and reinforce that the standard of care is treatment with antibiotics.

Low-income Family Barriers to Optimal Antibiotic Use

Lack of evidence-based antibiotic use is more common in children whose parents have a low household income or level of education (Mangione-Smith et al., 1999; Thrane, Olesen, Schonheyder, & Sorensen, 2003). Independent of physician factors, Manitoba children in the highest household incomes are significantly less likely to receive an antibiotic prescription for a VRTI than children in middle- and low-income households (Kozyrskyj, Dahl et al., 2004). On the other hand, as noted earlier, low-income children are less likely to receive more expensive, BS antibiotics. Aside from prescription cost, several explanations have been proposed for household income differences in antibiotic use among children.

Firstly, parents from low-income families have less flexibility in taking time off work for a return visit to a physician if the child's symptoms do not resolve. They also face the economic cost of missing work to stay home with a sick child due to daycare infection control policies (Belongia et al., 2002). Secondly, lower-income parents may be less informed about appropriate antibiotic therapy through limited access to published literature and material from educational campaigns (Pichichero, 1999). Finally, their belief systems may favor antibiotic use. Parental expectations for an antibiotic prescription are noted to be higher in ethnic groups, such as Latino and Asian Americans (Mangione-Smith et al., 2004). Palmer et al. reported that 22% of parents attending a clinic in a low-income neighborhood believed that antibiotics were essential to treat childhood infections versus 12% of higher-income parents from a private clinic (Palmer & Bauchner, 1997).

Strategies to Improve Antibiotic Use

As we have argued in this paper, whether a child receives an antibiotic may have little bearing on the nature of the illness and more to do with where they live and receive care. Clinical practice guidelines (CPGs) created through "formal consensus development [that] uses a systematic approach to assess expert opinion and to reach agreement on recommendations" have been developed to address physician practice variations (Woolf, 1992, p. 946). CPGs for antibiotic treatment in children are well established (Dowell, Marcy, Phillips, Gerber, & Schwartz, 1998; O'Brien et al., 1998; Rosenstein et al., 1998).The American Academy of Pediatrics (2009) currently has six CPGs for antibiotic prescribing. The Canadian Pediatric Society has several CPGs as well, including one for AOM that offers concise information on the diagnosis of AOM, the best choice of an antibiotic and the "watchful waiting" approach for antibiotic use.

While the aim of CPGs is to optimize the quality of patient care, many physicians do not incorporate CPGs in their daily practice. In a random survey of general pediatricians in the US, only 35% reported adopting CPGs (19% used the AOM CPG; Flores, Lee, Bauchner, & Kastner, 2000). Failure to allow for clinical judgment, concern about their use in litigation and limitation of autonomy, were cited as reasons for not using CPGs. In this paper, we have provided Canadian examples of physician non-compliance with CPGs for antibiotic prescribing in children. In an excellent systematic review of interventions that improve antibiotic prescribing practices, Arnold and Strauss (2005) found that, with one exception, CPGs produced small changes in antibiotic prescribing.

Multi-faceted strategies for changing physician prescribing, such as interactive workshops (but not lectures) on appropriate antibiotic use, personal visits to physicians by educators and physician reminders about appropriate use in general or feedback on their own prescribing, have been reported to be the most effective in changing physician prescribing of antibiotics in children (Arnold & Straus, 2005). Some of the successful programs have incorporated parent involvement. One example is the "watchful waiting" management approach for AOM, which instructs parents to avoid filling a prescription written for an antibiotic unless the child's symptoms do not resolve. As the majority of AOM cases are of viral etiology and self-limited, many parents do not end up filling antibiotic prescriptions (Arnold & Straus, 2005). The use of delayed prescriptions has resulted in fewer antibiotics being used in children without increasing the risk of serious complications of AOM. Non-compliance with this approach may become an issue in low-income parents subsequent to their belief systems, or daycare and sick-leave policies at work (Finkelstein, Stille, Rifas-Shiman, & Goldmann, 2005; Ronsaville & Hakim, 2000). It is therefore encouraging that the "watchful waiting" intervention has been tested in low-income settings (McCormick et al., 2005).

In summary, we have identified several challenges to the appropriate prescribing of antibiotics to children, despite the availability of CPGs and systematic reviews. These challenges are exacerbated in low-income children, who are frequently treated by physicians less likely to practice evidence-based medicine, and whose parents are more likely to believe that antibiotic prescriptions are always needed. As respiratory tract infections are more common in low-income children to begin with, this observed combination of physician and parent factors places low-income children at double jeopardy. They continue to be the recipients of inappropriate antibiotic prescribing, even though antibiotic use has declined in higher income children.

Recognizing that physician-parent interactions are complex and that low-income families may have limited access to reliable information resources, we propose that the proven-effective, multi-faceted strategies as described above, be aimed at physicians serving children from low-income neighborhoods. It is hoped that this manuscript will serve as a starting point for physician education on the extent and consequences of overuse of antibiotics in low-income children. To disregard solutions for inappropriate antibiotic prescribing in low-income children is to ignore opportunities to improve their short- and long-term health.

References

Aber, J. L., Bennett, N. G., Conley, D. C., & Li, J. (1997). The effects of poverty on child health and development. *Annual Review of Public Health, 18*, 463-483.

Adlerberth, I., Strachan, D. P., Matricardi, P. M., Ahrne, S., Orfei, L., Aberg, N., et al. (2007). Gut microbiota and development of atopic eczema in 3 European birth cohorts. *The Journal of Allergy and Clinical Immunology, 120*, 343-350.

American Academy of Pediatrics. (2009). *Clinical practice guidelines.* Retrieved March 25, 2009, from http://aappolicy.aappublications.org/practice_ guidelines/index.dtl

Arason, V. A., Kristinsson, K. G., Sigurdsson, J. A., Stefansdottir, G., Molstad, S., & Gudmundsson, S. (1996). Do antimicrobials increase the carriage rate of penicillin resistant pneumococci in children? Cross sectional prevalence study. *British Medical Journal (Clinical Research Ed.), 313*, 387-391.

Arnold, S. R., Allen, U. D., Al-Zahrani, M., Tan, D. H., & Wang, E. E. (1999). Antibiotic prescribing by pediatricians for respiratory tract infection in children. *Clinical Infectious Diseases: An Official Publication of the Infectious Diseases Society of America, 29*, 312-317.

Arnold, S. R., & Straus, S. E. (2005). Interventions to improve antibiotic prescribing practices in ambulatory care. *Cochrane Database of Systematic Reviews (Online), 4*, CD003539.

Barden, L. S., Dowell, S. F., Schwartz, B., & Lackey, C. (1998). Current attitudes regarding use of antimicrobial agents: Results from physician's and parents' focus group discussions. *Clinical Pediatrics, 37*, 665-671.

Belongia, E. A., Naimi, T. S., Gale, C. M., & Besser, R. E. (2002). Antibiotic use and upper respiratory infections: A survey of knowledge, attitudes, and experience in Wisconsin and Minnesota. *Preventive Medicine, 34*, 346-352.

Bennet, R., Eriksson, M., & Nord, C. E. (2002). The fecal microflora of 1-3-month-old infants during treatment with eight oral antibiotics. *Infection, 30,* 158-160.

Berman, S., Byrns, P. J., Bondy, J., Smith, P. J., & Lezotte, D. (1997). Otitis media-related antibiotic prescribing patterns, outcomes, and expenditures in a pediatric medicaid population. *Pediatrics, 100,* 585-592.

Block, S. L., Harrison, C. J., Hedrick, J. A., Tyler, R. D., Smith, R. A., Keegan, E., et al. (1995). Penicillin-resistant streptococcus pneumoniae in acute otitis media: Risk factors, susceptibility patterns and antimicrobial management. *The Pediatric Infectious Disease Journal, 14,* 751-759.

Boken, D. J., Chartrand, S. A., Goering, R. V., Kruger, R., & Harrison, C. J. (1995). Colonization with penicillin-resistant streptococcus pneumoniae in a child-care center. *The Pediatric Infectious Disease Journal, 14,* 879-884.

Bondy, J., Berman, S., Glazner, J., & Lezotte, D. (2000). Direct expenditures related to otitis media diagnoses: Extrapolations from a pediatric Medicaid cohort. *Pediatrics, 105,* E72.

Bonnemaison, E., Lanotte, P., Cantagrel, S., Thionois, S., Quentin, R., Chamboux, C., et al. (2003). Comparison of fecal flora following administration of two antibiotic protocols for suspected maternofetal infection. *Biology of the Neonate, 84,* 304-310.

Cadieux, G., Tamblyn, R., Dauphinee, D., & Libman, M. (2007). Predictors of inappropriate antibiotic prescribing among primary care physicians. *Canadian Medical Association Journal, 177,* 877-883.

Canadian Bacterial Surveillance Network. (2009). *Percentage of penicillin non-susceptible S.pneumoniae in Canada: 1988-2008.* Retrieved April 6, 2009, from http://microbiology.mtsinai.on.ca/data/sp/sp_2008.shtml#figure1

Centers for Disease Control and Prevention. (2005). *Community-associated MRSA information for clinicians.* Retrieved April 9, 2009, from http://www.cdc.gov/ncidod/dhqp/ar_mrsa_ca_clinicians.html

Chambers, H. F. (2005). Community-associated MRSA--resistance and virulence converge. *The New England Journal of Medicine, 352,* 1485-1487.

Chung, A., Perera, R., Brueggemann, A. B., Elamin, A. E., Harnden, A., Mayon-White, R., et al. (2007). Effect of antibiotic prescribing on antibiotic resistance in individual children in primary care: Prospective cohort study. *British Medical Journal (Clinical Research Ed.), 335,* 429.

Collett, C. A., Pappas, D. E., Evans, B. A., & Hayden, G. F. (1999). Parental knowledge about common respiratory infections and antibiotic therapy in children. *Southern Medical Journal, 92,* 971-976.

Conroy, S., Choonara, I., Impicciatore, P., Mohn, A., Arnell, H., Rane, A., et al. (2000). Survey of unlicensed and off label drug use in paediatric wards in european countries. European network for drug investigation in children. *British Medical Journal (Clinical Research Ed.), 320,* 79-82.

Cramer, K., Wiebe, N., Moyer, V., Hartling, L., Williams, K., Swingler, G., et al. (2005). Children in reviews: Methodological issues in child-relevant evidence syntheses. *BMC Pediatrics, 5*, 38.

Davy, T., Dick, P. T., & Munk, P. (1998). Self-reported prescribing of antibiotics for children with undifferentiated acute respiratory tract infections with cough. *The Pediatric Infectious Disease Journal, 17*, 457-462.

Dowell, S. F., Marcy, S. M., Phillips, W. R., Gerber, M. A., & Schwartz, B. (1998). Otitis media-principles of judicious use of antimicrobial agents. *Pediatrics, 101*, 165-171.

Edlund, C., & Nord, C. E. (2000). Effect on the human normal microflora of oral antibiotics for treatment of urinary tract infections. *The Journal of Antimicrobial Chemotherapy, 46 Suppl 1*, 41-48, 63-65.

Farooqi, I. S., & Hopkin, J. M. (1998). Early childhood infection and atopic disorder. *Thorax, 53*, 927-932.

Field, M. J., & Lohr, K. N. (1990). *Clinical practice guidelines: Directions for a new program*. Washington, D.C.: National Academy Press.

Finkelstein, J. A., Davis, R. L., Dowell, S. F., Metlay, J. P., Soumerai, S. B., Rifas-Shiman, S. L., et al. (2001). Reducing antibiotic use in children: A randomized trial in 12 practices. *Pediatrics, 108*, 1-7.

Finkelstein, J. A., Stille, C., Nordin, J., Davis, R., Raebel, M. A., Roblin, D., et al. (2003). Reduction in antibiotic use among US children, 1996-2000. *Pediatrics, 112(3 Pt 1)*, 620-627.

Finkelstein, J. A., Stille, C. J., Rifas-Shiman, S. L., & Goldmann, D. (2005). Watchful waiting for acute otitis media: Are parents and physicians ready? *Pediatrics, 115(6)*, 1466-1473.

Flores, G., Lee, M., Bauchner, H., & Kastner, B. (2000). Pediatricians' attitudes, beliefs, and practices regarding clinical practice guidelines: A national survey. *Pediatrics, 105(3 Pt 1)*, 496-501.

Glasziou, P. P., Del Mar, C. B., Sanders, S. L., & Hayem, M. (2004). Antibiotics for acute otitis media in children. *Cochrane Database of Systematic Reviews (Online), 1*, CD000219.

Gore, C., Munro, K., Lay, C., Bibiloni, R., Morris, J., Woodcock, A., et al. (2008). Bifidobacterium pseudocatenulatum is associated with atopic eczema: A nested case-control study investigating the fecal microbiota of infants. *The Journal of Allergy and Clinical Immunology, 121*, 135-140.

Greenberg, D., Speert, D. P., Mahenthiralingam, E., Henry, D. A., Campbell, M. E., Scheifele, D. W., et al. (2002). Emergence of penicillin-nonsusceptible streptococcus pneumoniae invasive clones in Canada. *Journal of Clinical Microbiology, 40*, 68-74.

Guillemot, D., Carbon, C., Balkau, B., Geslin, P., Lecoeur, H., Vauzelle-Kervroedan, F., et al. (1998). Low dosage and long treatment duration of beta-lactam: Risk factors for carriage of penicillin-resistant streptococcus pneumoniae. *The Journal of the American Medical Association, 279*, 365-370.

Hamm, R. M., Hicks, R. J., & Bemben, D. A. (1996). Antibiotics and respiratory infections: Are patients more satisfied when expectations are met? *The Journal of Family Practice, 43*, 56-62.

Hawkes, M., Barton, M., Conly, J., Nicolle, L., Barry, C., & Ford-Jones, E. L. (2007). Community-associated MRSA: Superbug at our doorstep. *Canadian Medical Association Journal, 176*, 54-56.

Henricson, K., Melander, E., Molstad, S., Ranstam, J., Hanson, B. S., Rametsteiner, G., et al. (1998). Intra-urban variation of antibiotic utilization in children: Influence of socio-economic factors. *European Journal of Clinical Pharmacology, 54*, 653-657.

Herman, R. A., Kee, V. R., Moores, K. G., & Ross, M. B. (2008). Etiology and treatment of community-associated methicillin-resistant staphylococcus aureus. *American Journal of Health Systems and Pharmacology, 65*, 219-225.

Hildebrand, H., Malmborg, P., Askling, J., Ekbom, A., & Montgomery, S. M. (2008). Early-life exposures associated with antibiotic use and risk of subsequent Crohn's disease. *Scandinavian Journal of Gastroenterology, 43*, 961-966.

Hillier, S., Roberts, Z., Dunstan, F., Butler, C., Howard, A., & Palmer, S. (2007). Prior antibiotics and risk of antibiotic-resistant community-acquired urinary tract infection: A case-control study. *The Journal of Antimicrobial Chemotherapy, 60*, 92-99.

Hyde, T. B., Gay, K., Stephens, D. S., Vugia, D. J., Pass, M., Johnson, S., et al. (2001). Macrolide resistance among invasive streptococcus pneumoniae isolates. *The Journal of the American Medical Association, 286*, 1857-1862.

Johnson, T. N. (2003). The development of drug metabolising enzymes and their influence on the susceptibility to adverse drug reactions in children. *Toxicology, 192*, 37-48.

Kaplan, S. L., Hulten, K. G., Gonzalez, B. E., Hammerman, W. A., Lamberth, L., Versalovic, J., et al. (2005). Three-year surveillance of community-acquired staphylococcus aureus infections in children. *Clinical Infectious Diseases: An Official Publication of the Infectious Diseases Society of America, 40*, 1785-1791.

Kearns, G. L., Abdel-Rahman, S. M., Alander, S. W., Blowey, D. L., Leeder, J. S., & Kauffman, R. E. (2003). Developmental pharmacology--drug disposition, action, and therapy in infants and children. *The New England Journal of Medicine, 349*, 1157-1167.

King, M. D., Humphrey, B. J., Wang, Y. F., Kourbatova, E. V., Ray, S. M., & Blumberg, H. M. (2006). Emergence of community-acquired methicillin-resistant staphylococcus aureus USA 300 clone as the predominant cause of skin and soft-tissue infections. *Annals of Internal Medicine, 144*, 309-317.

Klassen, T. P., Hartling, L., Craig, J. C., & Offringa, M. (2008). Children are not just small adults: The urgent need for high-quality trial evidence in children. *PLoS Medicine, 5*, e172.

Kozyrskyj, A. L. (2002). Prescription medications in Manitoba children: Are there regional differences? *Canadian Journal of Public Health, 93 Suppl 2*, S63-9.

Kozyrskyj, A. L., Carrie, A. G., Mazowita, G. B., Lix, L. M., Klassen, T. P., & Law, B. J. (2004). Decrease in antibiotic use among children in the 1990s: Not all antibiotics, not all children. *Canadian Medical Association Journal, 171*, 133-138.

Kozyrskyj, A. L., Dahl, M. E., Chateau, D. G., Mazowita, G. B., Klassen, T. P., & Law, B. J. (2004). Evidence-based prescribing of antibiotics for children: Role of socioeconomic status and physician characteristics. *Canadian Medical Association Journal, 171*, 139-145.

Kozyrskyj, A. L., Dahl, M. E., Ungar, W. J., Becker, A. B., & Law, B. J. (2006). Antibiotic treatment of wheezing in children with asthma: What is the practice? *Pediatrics, 117*, e1104-10.

Kozyrskyj, A. L., Ernst, P., & Becker, A. B. (2007). Increased risk of childhood asthma from antibiotic use in early life. *Chest, 131*, 1753-1759.

Kozyrskyj, A. L., Hildes-Ripstein, G. E., Longstaffe, S. E., Wincott, J. L., Sitar, D. S., Klassen, T. P., et al. (1998). Treatment of acute otitis media with a shortened course of antibiotics: A meta-analysis. *The Journal of the American Medical Association, 279*, 1736-1742.

Kozyrskyj, A. L., Kendall, G. E., Jacoby, P., Sly, P. D., & Zubrick, S. R. (in press). Complexity of the association between socioeconomic status and the development of asthma as revealed by trajectory analyses. *American Journal of Public Health.*

Kozyrskyj, A. L., Mustard, C. A., & Simons, F. E. (2003). Inhaled corticosteroids in childhood asthma: Income differences in use. *Pediatric Pulmonology, 36*, 241-247.

Le Saux, N., Bjornson, C., & Pitters, C. (1999). Antimicrobial use in febrile children diagnosed with respiratory tract illness in an emergency department. *The Pediatric Infectious Disease Journal, 18*, 1078-1080.

Lietzau, S., Raum, E., von Baum, H., Marre, R., & Brenner, H. (2007). Household contacts were key factor for children's colonization with resistant escherichia coli in community setting. *Journal of Clinical Epidemiology, 60*, 1149-1155.

Lundkvist, J., Akerlind, I., Borgquist, L., & Molstad, S. (2002). The more time spent on listening, the less time spent on prescribing antibiotics in general practice. *Family Practice, 19*, 638-640.

Mackie, R. I., Sghir, A., & Gaskins, H. R. (1999). Developmental microbial ecology of the neonatal gastrointestinal tract. *The American Journal of Clinical Nutrition, 69*, 1035S-1045S.

Mainous, A. G., III, Hueston, W. J., & Love, M. M. (1998). Antibiotics for colds in children: Who are the high prescribers? *Archives of Pediatrics & Adolescent Medicine, 152*, 349-352.

Mangione-Smith, R., Elliott, M. N., Stivers, T., McDonald, L., Heritage, J., & McGlynn, E. A. (2004). Racial/ethnic variation in parent expectations for antibiotics: Implications for public health campaigns. *Pediatrics, 113*, e385-94.

Mangione-Smith, R., McGlynn, E. A., Elliott, M. N., Krogstad, P., & Brook, R. H. (1999). The relationship between perceived parental expectations and pediatrician antimicrobial prescribing behavior. *Pediatrics, 103(4 Pt 1)*, 711-718.

Mangione-Smith, R., McGlynn, E. A., Elliott, M. N., McDonald, L., Franz, C. E., & Kravitz, R. L. (2001). Parent expectations for antibiotics, physician-parent communication, and satisfaction. *Archives of Pediatrics & Adolescent Medicine, 155*, 800-806.

Manitoba Centre for Health Policy. (2008). *Annual report 2007/2008.* Retrieved April 9, 2009, from http://umanitoba.ca/faculties/medicine/units/mchp/media_room/media/Annual_report_Aug25_complete_revised.pdf

Manninen, R., Huovinen, P., & Nissinen, A. (1997). Increasing antimicrobial resistance in streptococcus pneumoniae, haemophilus influenzae and moraxella catarrhalis in Finland. *The Journal of Antimicrobial Chemotherapy, 40*, 387-392.

Margolis, P. A., Greenberg, R. A., Keyes, L. L., LaVange, L. M., Chapman, R. S., Denny, F. W., et al. (1992). Lower respiratory illness in infants and low socioeconomic status. *American Journal of Public Health, 82*, 1119-1126.

Marra, F., Lynd, L., Coombes, M., Richardson, K., Legal, M., Fitzgerald, J. M., et al. (2006). Does antibiotic exposure during infancy lead to development of asthma?: A systematic review and metaanalysis. *Chest, 129*, 610-618.

Marra, F., Marra, C. A., Richardson, K., Lynd, L. D., Kozyrskyj, A., Patrick, D. M., et al. (2009). Antibiotic use in children is associated with increased risk of asthma. *Pediatrics, 123*, 1003-1010.

Marra, F., Monnet, D. L., Patrick, D. M., Chong, M., Brandt, C. T., Winters, M., et al. (2007). A comparison of antibiotic use in children between Canada and Denmark. *The Annals of Pharmacotherapy, 41*, 659-666.

McCaig, L. F., Besser, R. E., & Hughes, J. M. (2002). Trends in antimicrobial prescribing rates for children and adolescents. *The Journal of the American Medical Association, 287*, 3096-3102.

McCaig, L. F., & Hughes, J. M. (1995). Trends in antimicrobial drug prescribing among office-based physicians in the United States. *The Journal of the American Medical Association, 273*, 214-219.

McCormick, D. P., Chonmaitree, T., Pittman, C., Saeed, K., Friedman, N. R., Uchida, T., et al. (2005). Nonsevere acute otitis media: A clinical trial comparing outcomes of watchful waiting versus immediate antibiotic treatment. *Pediatrics, 115*, 1455-1465.

McGowan, J. E., Jr. (1983). Antimicrobial resistance in hospital organisms and its relation to antibiotic use. *Reviews of Infectious Diseases, 5*, 1033-1048.

McKeever, T. M., Lewis, S. A., Smith, C., Collins, J., Heatlie, H., Frischer, M., et al. (2002). Early exposure to infections and antibiotics and the incidence of allergic disease: A birth cohort study with the West Midlands General Practice Research Database. *The Journal of Allergy and Clinical Immunology, 109*, 43-50.

Mulvey, M. R., & Simor, A. E. (2009). Antimicrobial resistance in hospitals: How concerned should we be? *Canadian Medical Association Journal, 180*, 408-415.

Murray, C. S., Tannock, G. W., Simon, M. A., Harmsen, H. J., Welling, G. W., Custovic, A., et al. (2005). Fecal microbiota in sensitized wheezy and non-sensitized non-wheezy children: A nested case-control study. *Clinical and Experimental Allergy: Journal of the British Society for Allergy and Clinical Immunology, 35*, 741-745.

Nasrin, D., Collignon, P. J., Roberts, L., Wilson, E. J., Pilotto, L. S., & Douglas, R. M. (2002). Effect of beta lactam antibiotic use in children on pneumococcal resistance to penicillin: Prospective cohort study. *British Medical Journal (Clinical Research Ed.), 324*, 28-30.

Neu, H. C. (1992). The crisis in antibiotic resistance. *Science, 257*, 1064-1073.

Newacheck, P. W., Hughes, D. C., & Stoddard, J. J. (1996). Children's access to primary care: Differences by race, income, and insurance status. *Pediatrics, 97*, 26-32.

Nyquist, A. C., Gonzales, R., Steiner, J. F., & Sande, M. A. (1998). Antibiotic prescribing for children with colds, upper respiratory tract infections, and bronchitis. *The Journal of the American Medical Association, 279*, 875-877.

O'Brien, K. L., Dowell, S. F., Schwartz, B., Marcy, S. M., Phillips, W. R., & Gerber, M. A. (1998). Cough illness/bronchitis--principles of judicious use of antimicrobial agents. *Pediatrics, 101*, 178-181.

Ong, S., Nakase, J., Moran, G. J., Karras, D. J., Kuehnert, M. J., Talan, D. A., et al. (2007). Antibiotic use for emergency department patients with upper respiratory infections: Prescribing practices, patient expectations, and patient satisfaction. *Annals of Emergency Medicine, 50*, 213-220.

Palmer, D. A., & Bauchner, H. (1997). Parents' and physicians' views on antibiotics. *Pediatrics, 99*, E6.

Penders, J., Stobberingh, E. E., Thijs, C., Adams, H., Vink, C., van Ree, R., et al. (2006). Molecular fingerprinting of the intestinal microbiota of infants in whom atopic eczema was or was not developing. *Clinical and Experimental Allergy: Journal of the British Society for Allergy and Clinical Immunology, 36*, 1602-1608.

Penders, J., Thijs, C., van den Brandt, P. A., Kummeling, I., Snijders, B., Stelma, F., et al. (2007). Gut microbiota composition and development of atopic manifestations in infancy: The KOALA birth cohort study. *Gut, 56*, 661-667.

Penders, J., Thijs, C., Vink, C., Stelma, F. F., Snijders, B., Kummeling, I., et al. (2006). Factors influencing the composition of the intestinal microbiota in early infancy. *Pediatrics, 118*, 511-521.

Pennie, R. A. (1998). Prospective study of antibiotic prescribing for children. *Canadian Family Physician, 44*, 1850-1856.

Perz, J. F., Craig, A. S., Coffey, C. S., Jorgensen, D. M., Mitchel, E., Hall, S., et al. (2002). Changes in antibiotic prescribing for children after a community-wide campaign. *The Journal of the American Medical Association, 287*, 3103-3109.

Petersson, C., & Hakansson, A. (1996). High-consulting children indicate illness-prone families. A study of 38 rural and 38 urban Swedish children's health and use of medical care. *Scandinavian Journal of Primary Health Care, 14*, 71-78.

Pichichero, M. E. (1999). Understanding antibiotic overuse for respiratory tract infections in children. *Pediatrics, 104*, 1384-1388.

Reuveni, H., Sheizaf, B., Elhayany, A., Sherf, M., Limoni, Y., Scharff, S., et al. (2002). The effect of drug co-payment policy on the purchase of prescription drugs for children with infections in the community. *Health Policy, 62*, 1-13.

Roark, R., Petrofski, J., Berson, E., & Berman, S. (1995). Practice variations among pediatricians and family physicians in the management of otitis media. *Archives of Pediatrics & Adolescent Medicine, 149*, 839-844.

Ronsaville, D. S., & Hakim, R. B. (2000). Well child care in the United States: Racial differences in compliance with guidelines. *American Journal of Public Health, 90*, 1436-1443.

Rosenstein, N., Phillips, W. R., Gerber, M. A., Marcy, S. M., Schwartz, B., & Dowell, S. F. (1998). The common cold--principles of judicious use of antimicrobial agents. *Pediatrics, 126*, 313-316

Sakata, H., Fujita, K., & Yoshioka, H. (1986). The effect of antimicrobial agents on fecal flora of children. *Antimicrobial Agents and Chemotherapy, 29*, 225-229.

Scheifele, D. W., Halperin, S. A., Pelletier, L., Talbot, J., Vaudry, W., Jadavji, T., et al. (2000). Update on penicillin resistance rates among pneumococci causing invasive infection in children - Canada 1998 [Abstract]. *Paediatrics & Child Health, 5(Supplement A)*, 37A.

Schwartz, B., Bell, D. M., & Hughes, J. M. (1997). Preventing the emergence of antimicrobial resistance. A call for action by clinicians, public health officials, and patients. *The Journal of the American Medical Association, 278*, 944-945.

Seguin, L., Nikiema, B., Gauvin, L., Zunzunegui, M. V., & Xu, Q. (2007). Duration of poverty and child health in the Quebec longitudinal study of child development: Longitudinal analysis of a birth cohort. *Pediatrics, 119*, e1063-70.

Seppala, H., Klaukka, T., Vuopio-Varkila, J., Muotiala, A., Helenius, H., Lager, K., et al. (1997). The effect of changes in the consumption of macrolide antibiotics on erythromycin resistance in group A streptococci in Finland. Finnish study group for antimicrobial resistance. *The New England Journal of Medicine, 337*, 441-446.

Shaikh, N., & Harvey, K. (2009). The Cochrane library and acute otitis media in children: An overview of reviews. *Evidence Based Child Health, 4*, 390-399.

Slama, T. G., Amin, A., Brunton, S. A., File, T. M., Jr, Milkovich, G., Rodvold, K. A., et al. (2005). A clinician's guide to the appropriate and accurate use of antibiotics: The council for appropriate and rational antibiotic therapy (CARAT) criteria. *The American Journal of Medicine, 118 Suppl 7A*, 1S-6S.

Smith, S. P., Manges, A. R., & Riley, L. W. (2008). Temporal changes in the prevalence of community-acquired antimicrobial-resistant urinary tract infection affected by escherichia coli clonal group composition. *Clinical Infectious Diseases: An Official Publication of the Infectious Diseases Society of America, 46*, 689-695.

Stivers, T. (2002a). Participating in decisions about treatment: Overt parent pressure for antibiotic medication in pediatric encounters. *Social Science & Medicine (1982), 54*, 1111-1130.

Stivers, T. (2002b). Presenting the problem in pediatric encounters: "Symptoms only" versus "candidate diagnosis" presentations. *Health Communication, 14*, 299-338.

Stivers, T., Mangione-Smith, R., Elliott, M. N., McDonald, L., & Heritage, J. (2003). Why do physicians think parents expect antibiotics? What parents report vs what physicians believe. *The Journal of Family Practice, 52*, 140-148.

Thrane, N., Olesen, C., Schonheyder, H. C., & Sorensen, H. T. (2003). Socioeconomic factors and prescription of antibiotics in 0- to 2-year-old Danish children. *The Journal of Antimicrobial Chemotherapy, 51*, 683-689.

Vinson, D. C., & Lutz, L. J. (1993). The effect of parental expectations on treatment of children with a cough: A report from ASPN. *The Journal of Family Practice, 37*, 23-27.

Wang, E. E., Einarson, T. R., Kellner, J. D., & Conly, J. M. (1999). Antibiotic prescribing for Canadian preschool children: Evidence of overprescribing for viral respiratory infections. *Clinical Infectious Diseases: An Official Publication of the Infectious Diseases Society of America, 29*, 155-160.

Watson, R. L., Dowell, S. F., Jayaraman, M., Keyserling, H., Kolczak, M., & Schwartz, B. (1999). Antimicrobial use for pediatric upper respiratory infections: Reported practice, actual practice, and parent beliefs. *Pediatrics, 104*, 1251-1257.

Whitney, C. G., Farley, M. M., Hadler, J., Harrison, L. H., Lexau, C., Reingold, A., et al. (2000). Increasing prevalence of multidrug-resistant streptococcus pneumoniae in the United States. *The New England Journal of Medicine, 343*, 1917-1924.

Winters, M., Patrick, D. M., Marra, F., Buxton, J., Chong, M., Isaac-Renton, J. L., et al. (2008). Epidemiology of invasive pneumococcal disease in BC during the introduction of conjugated pneumococcal vaccine. *Canadian Journal of Public Health, 99*, 57-61.

Woolf, S. H. (1992). Practice guidelines, a new reality in medicine. II. Methods of developing guidelines. *Archives of Internal Medicine, 152*, 946-952.

Error, Misuse, and Abuse of Prescription and Over-the-Counter Medications for Young Children

Steven R. Shaw, Khing Su Lin, Tiffany W. Chiu,
Melissa Stern, Shohreh M. Rezazadeh
McGill University

Paul C. McCabe
Brooklyn College of the City University of New York

This paper presents a review of research on the use of prescription and over-the-counter medications by parents for infants and young children. The primary causes of misuse are due to medical error, administration error, independent parent medication decisions, and medication interactions. Epidemiological studies of the misuse of medications by parents for infants and young children are reviewed. In addition, methods of preventing misuse and abuse of prescription medication are described. Finally, the value of collaborative relationships among parents, medical professionals, psychologists, and educational professionals in the identification and treatment of medication misuse and abuse is explained.

In the United States, young children (i.e., less than 5 years old) and infants (i.e., less than 2 years old) require 98,000 visits to urgent care or emergency rooms each year due to medication error, misuse, or abuse (Chien, Marriott, Ashby, & Ozanne-Smith, 2003). The nature of the medical problems range from mild allergic reactions, to exacerbation of chronic medical problems, and to life-threatening seizures and anaphylactic shock (McCaig & Nawar, 2006; Moore, Weiss, Kaplan, & Blaisdell, 2002). Effective communication, management of medication administration and monitoring could prevent the majority of these adverse reactions (Osterberg & Blaschke, 2005).

To a large degree, the problem is that many medications, especially over-the-counter (OTC) medications and herbal or natural remedies, are perceived as being completely benign and without adverse effects (Eiland, Salazar, & English, 2008). For example, Ritalin (methylphenidate) for attention-deficit/hyperactivity disorder (ADHD) and Tylenol (acetaminophen) for muscle aches are often not

All correspondence should be addressed to Steven Shaw, McGill University, 3700 McTavish St., Rm 517, Montreal, QC Canada H3A 1YA. Electronic mail may be sent to steven.shaw@mcgill.ca.

perceived as having potential for serious adverse effects (Sharfstein, North, & Serwint, 2007). The result is that appropriate and reasonable levels of vigilance on the part of medical professionals and caregivers are often ignored (Ecklund & Ross, 2001). Yet, these often benign medications can have severe adverse effects such as seizures, heart arrhythmias, or liver failure that occur following medical error, misuse, or abuse (Eiland et al.; Moore et al., 2002). Vigilance on the part of physicians, teachers, psychologists, and caregivers is required to reduce error, misuse, and abuse of all medications. Without such vigilance, the adverse effects of commonly prescribed medications can negatively affect the short-term health and long-term physical and cognitive development of young children and infants.

There are differences among medications that correspond to the level, nature, and consequences of error, misuse, and abuse of medications. Although there are hundreds of medications commonly prescribed to young children and infants, there are five common types of medications that account for most emergency room and urgent care visits (Budnitz et al., 2005). These medications are: (a) stimulants, often prescribed for ADHD; (b) analgesics, prescribed for pain; (c) sedatives and sleep aides, used for chronic sleep issues; (d) OTC medications, usually used for colds and coughs; and (e) herbal remedies, self-administered and unregulated supplements used for a variety of medical and mental health issues. These five classes of medications are widely considered to be among the most benign of medications. Parents and medical professionals often do not consider the potential negative effects of these widely used medications (Jhung et al., 2005). When used as directed, these medications are among the safest in pediatric pharmacology. However, they are also the most misused medications (Cohen et al., 2008; Committee on Children and Young People, 2002).

Misuse and abuse of medications is often framed in the context of prescription drug abuse by adolescents and adults (e.g., McCabe, Cranford, Boyd, & Teter, 2007). Prescription drug use is a far more common problem in the United States than illicit drug use (Budnitz et al., 2006). For example, adolescents and adults frequently abuse sedatives and some analgesic medications (e.g., OxyContin) that have addictive properties. However, in the case of young children and infants, the intentional misuse and abuse of medications by the persons taking the medication is rarely the primary issue. For children under age 5, error, misuse, and abuse are usually generated by medical professionals and caregivers (McCabe, Teter, & Boyd, 2006). As such, assessment and intervention takes place at the health care provider and caregiver level.

There are five sources of error, misuse, and abuse described in this paper: (a) medical error involving misdiagnosis or inappropriate prescription practices of the medical professional, and pharmacist errors due to clerical errors or difficulty reading prescriptions; (b) administration errors that involve caregivers not understanding the directions for the medication regimen and caregivers changing the medication regimen without consulting the medical professional; (c) parent decisions regarding medication use that deviate from label instructions, such as diversion of medications for personal use or for use by another person, taking medications for non-approved use such as taking opioid analgesics for depression, and parent pathology such as Munchausen's Syndrome by Proxy (MSBP); (d) errors due to failure to understand the medication interactions with prescription medications, OTC medications, herbal remedies, and foods; and (e) children discovering and ingesting medications either not prescribed for them or at an incorrect dosage. Correctly identifying the cause of the error, misuse and abuse of medications for young children and infants is a critical component of identifying and treating this important issue for young children and infants.

Common Medication-Specific Issues

Stimulant Medications

Stimulant medications are used to address symptoms associated with ADHD. Within the past 20 years, there has been a substantial rise in the prescription rates of Ritalin and other stimulant medications for children 3 to 5 years old (Ghuman, Arnold, & Anthony, 2008; Riddle, 2007). Despite significant controversy concerning administration of these medications to young children, there is evidence of improvement of impulse control and overactivity (Greenhill et al., 2006).

Side effects of stimulant medications include tremors, heart arrhythmias, hypertension, and agitation (Firestone, Musten, Pisterman, Mercer, & Bennett, 1998). Psychostimulants are a Schedule II Controlled Substance (US Drug Enforcement Administration [DEA], 2004). This means that this medication has potential for abuse and addiction and the DEA strictly monitors use and prescriptions. Non-prescribed stimulant use ranges from 5 to 9% of all grade school and high school students (Wilens et al., 2008). Reasons reported for student misuse include "to get high," to stay awake longer, to improve concentration, and to control impulses (Poulin, 2007). These concerns do not usually apply to prescriptions for young children. However, parent or sibling diversion of medications away from the intended patient is common. The evidence is not clear, but Wilens and colleagues (2008) estimate that about 5% of prescriptions targeted to young children are diverted to siblings or parents. In addition to being a violation of federal law, diversion of medication directly affects the medical and mental health status of two parties: the person illegally obtaining the stimulant medication and the young child who is no longer receiving medically prescribed treatment. See Posey, Bassin, and Lewis (this issue) for a detailed review of stimulant use in young children.

Analgesics

Analgesic medications are used in the relief and management of pain. Analgesics in pediatric practice include opioid or non-opioid analgesic medications. Almost all non-opioid analgesics are non-steroidal anti-inflammatory drugs (NSAIDs), the archetypal NSAIDs being acetylsalicylic acid (Aspirin) and ibuprofen (Advil). Acetaminophen (Tylenol) is another non-opioid analgesic; however, unlike NSAIDs, acetaminophen lacks anti-inflammatory effects (Abbott & Fraser, 1998). NSAIDs act by inhibiting cyclooxygenase 1 and 2, enzymes required for the conversion of central and peripheral arachidonic acid to prostaglandins. Prostaglandins are vasodilators and pro-inflammatory compounds that account for the hyperemia, erythema, and pain associated with tissue damage. The mechanism of action of acetaminophen is the same as for NSAIDs; however, unlike NSAIDs, acetaminophen provides primarily central analgesia with a limited peripheral effect (Tobias, 2000). Frequency data of non-opioid analgesic use is limited. However, available data indicates use is common with a reported 84% of children having received acetaminophen by the age of 6 months (Li, Lacher, & Crain, 2000).

Opioid analgesics and any opioid-containing products are monitored under the Controlled Substances Act. Schedule II opioids such as morphine, codeine, and oxycodone and schedule III opioid products such as hydrocodone products and Tylenol III are frequently used in pediatric populations (DEA, 2004). The addictive and abuse potential of opioid analgesics range, depending on the drug's specific schedule, from schedule II agents as analgesics with a high potential for abuse and physical and psychological dependence, to schedule III analgesics with less potential for abuse (DEA). However, the risk of addiction is low among children receiving opioids for pain (Berde & Sethna, 2002). All opioid analgesic agents provide analgesia through interaction with one or more classes of opioid receptors, designated as *mu*, *delta*, and *kappa* opioid receptors. High densities of all three classes of receptors are found in the central nervous system with additional receptors localized in many peripheral organs. Opioid receptors are involved in opioid actions other than analgesia, and these actions include reward and the development of tolerance and dependence (Bie & Pan, 2007).

The harm of misuse of non-opioids in children tends to center on the underdosage and overdosage of medications by parents. Li and colleagues (2000) found that 51% of caregivers gave an incorrect dose of acetaminophen and/or ibuprofen, with infants more likely to receive an incorrect dose compared to older children. A greater percentage of patients received too low of a dose (37%) compared to too high (14%). Underdosing may lead to inadequate management of pain and unnecessary emergency department visits, as well as causing added stress to the parent and child (Li et al.). Ensuring appropriate analgesic dosing in children is especially important for opioid analgesics. Due to age-related physiological changes during infancy and childhood including increased metabolic rates, young children may be more sensitive to the effects of opioid analgesics. Too much of an opioid analgesic agent may cause mental or physical dependence in addition to physiological problems associated with overdosing.

Sedatives and Sleep Aids

In a survey of pediatric practitioners in the United States, over 20% of the sample reported recommending diphenhydramine (Benadryl), while other studies have found as high as 49% of pediatricians recommending antihistamines to children between birth and 2 years of age (Merenstein, Diener-West, Halbower, Krist, & Ruben, 2006; Owens, 2000). In one study, 71% of families medicated children with diphenhydramine for sleep problems. Sedatives and sleep aid medications for young children and infants are highly controversial, but continue to be administered for problems such as night terrors, delayed sleep onset, sleep schedule problems, nighttime and early morning awakenings, and parasomnias (Schnoes, Kuhn, Workman, & Ellis, 2006).

Pediatricians have reported to using antihistamines, α2-adrenergic agonists, melatonin, tricyclic antidepressants, other antidepressants, benzodiazepines, herbal remedies, sedative-hypnotics, atypical and traditional neuroleptics, and barbiturates for children's sleep difficulties (Schnoes et al., 2006). Diphenhydramine HCl, an antihistamine, is widely accepted and used as a sleep aid in the pediatric population. However, in a trial of infant response to diphenhydramine the drug was not found to be superior to placebos at commonly used dosages (Merenstein et al., 2006). Another widely used medication for sleep purposes, and second to antihistamines in popularity, is clonidine, an α2-adrenergic agonist classified as an antihypertensive.

Diphenhydramine HCl, a lipophilic competitive H1-histamine receptor blocker, crosses the blood-brain barrier to occupy sites located in the frontal lobe and deep cortical structures. Clonidine acts by stimulating noradrenergic neurons, resulting in decreased norepinephrine levels. However, the exact mechanism of this action is unknown (Pelayo & Dubik, 2008).

In addition to correct medication and dosage, timing of administration is also crucial; medicating too early may cause heightened alertness and hypnagogic hallucinations. A common side effect of diphenhydramine is impaired consciousness. Overdose can lead to fever, mydriasis (i.e., excessive dilation of pupil), blurred vision, dry mouth, constipation, urinary retention, tachycardia, dystonia, and confusion. Catatonic stupor, anxiety, visual hallucinations, seizures, and respiratory insufficiency may also occur. In very rare cases, death may result from overdose. Adverse effects of clonidine include hypotension, bradycardia, irritability, anticholinergic effects, and REM suppression (Pelayo & Dubik).

Other Over-the-Counter Medications

OTC medications are purchased without a prescription and do not generally require medical advice for purchase and use. Approximately 53% of all 3-year-olds use OTC medications over a 1-year period, and often, more than one OTC is being used at a time (Ecklund & Ross, 2001; Sharfstein et al., 2007). Toxicity by OTC medications is a significant problem for young children and infants. The Toxic Exposure Surveillance System reports that there has been approximately 90,000 calls and 3 deaths associated with OTC medications over a 3-year period from 2003-2006 (Cohen et al., 2008). Factors that influence the administration of OTC drugs to young children and infants are education level and socioeconomic status (SES) of the mother, where higher SES predicts higher use of OTC medication (Ecklund & Ross). Parent health-related anxiety, attitudes and health beliefs, perceived severity of their child's health problem, and having a child with a chronic health condition are factors that increase the likelihood of use of OTC medications (Ecklund & Ross). Despite increase of television commercials promoting OTC medication and the use of the Internet for medical information, medical providers are still the main source of OTC medication information (Ecklund & Ross; Eiland et al., 2008). Parent choice and parent decisions influenced by pediatricians are the primary contributors to the wide use of OTC medications.

One in ten US children use a cough and cold medication (CCM) in any given week (Vernacchio, Kelly, Kaufman, & Mitchell, 2008b). Reasons of CCM use are related to cough, cold, allergies, pain, and sleep problems (Vernacchio et al., 2008b). First-generation antihistamines, decongestants, and antitussives are widely used in children 2 to 5 years old (Paul et al., 2004). These drugs continue to be popular in young children, despite the paucity of data supporting their efficacy (Vernacchio et al., 2008b). Antipyretics such as ibuprofen and acetaminophen, as well as CCMs, make up the majority of OTC medications (Ecklund & Ross, 2001). The primary constituents of most CCMs are antitussives (dextromethorphan), expectorants (guaifenesin), first-generation antihistamine active ingredients (chlorpheniramine, diphenhydramine, brompheniramine), and/or decongestants (pseudoephedrine [PSE], phenylephrine; Davenport, 2009). Antitussives such as codeine involve addictive potential and may cause severe side effects (Schaefer, Shehab, Cohen, & Budnitz, 2008). One alternative to products like codeine is dextromethorphan (DXM), which does not contain any opiate activity, but is still abused for its euphoric effects (Carr, 2006).

Misuse of OTC medications is not only due to misinformation concerning the efficacy and associated risks, but also because of inaccurate dosing. Only 30% of caregivers were aware of the correct dosage for their child (Kelly, Matson, & Cowles, 2006), which is aggravated by the lack of correct dosing recommendations for children under the age of 2. Misuse of PSE may lead to adverse effects such as tremors, agitation, emesis, and tachycardia, and even death (Vernacchio, Kelly,

Kaufman, & Mitchell, 2008a). CCM overdoses have also been associated with neurologic impairment (Vernacchio et al, 2008b). Side effects of DXM range from mild (e.g., clumsiness, ataxia, hallucinations, restlessness) to severe intoxication (e.g., coma, respiratory depression, seizures) and serotonin syndrome effects (e.g., increased heart rate, shivering, sweating, dialated pupils, myoclonus, [i.e., intermittent tremor or twitching], as well as over-reponsive reflexes [Carr, 2006; Schaefer et al., 2008]).

Complementary and Alternative Medications

Homeopathic remedies, which require the precise mixing and diluting of different herbal, mineral, and animal substances based upon individual symptoms, are among the most popular alternative treatments for a variety of medical and mental health issues (Rojas & Chan, 2005). Herbal preparations are relatively inexpensive and widely available over the counter without the need for a consultation with a medical doctor. Furthermore, many parents believe that homeopathic and herbal therapy is non-invasive and safer than other forms of CAM, such as acupuncture (Bussing, Zima, Gary, & Garvan, 2002). The common belief that natural substances are always safe is simply untrue. Many individuals fail to realize the hazardous interactions that natural substances can have with other drugs and each other. Natural supplements also lack standardization and regulation (Rojas & Chan, 2005; Woolf, 2003). This results in high variability in concentration and quality among products, and instances of contamination from heavy metals, pesticides, and other toxic ingredients have been reported (Chan, 2002; Miller, Emanuel, Rosenstein, & Straus, 2004; Wong & Smith, 2006). Because natural substances are widely available without a prescription, accidental overdose is possible. Children absorb and metabolize substances differently than adults, rendering young children especially susceptible to these dangers (Woolf, 2003).

Herb-drug interactions occur due to nondisclosure of herbal treatment ingredients or mislabeling of herbal products where interactions may be attributed to misidentified plants or the presence of pharmaceutical drugs or heavy metals. Use of herbal and dietary supplements is extremely common. Approximately 3.9% of children use herbal products (Fugh-Berman, 2000). The most commonly reported product other than vitamin and mineral products was echinacea (Woolf, 2003). Parents commonly administer echinacea for the treatment of cold, flu, respiratory infection, and inflammation. Echinacea treatment is typically benign with an estimated risk of less than 1 in 100,000; however, treatment for more than 8 weeks may lead to hepatotoxicity when taken concomitantly with a hepatotoxic drug (e.g., anabolic steroids, amidarone, methatrexate, ketoconazole; Merck & Co., 2003).

Sources of Medication Error, Misuse and Abuse

As mentioned above, there are five major domains of medication error, misuse, and abuse. A significant percentage of medication error is due to medical professional error. Misunderstanding of complex medical regimens by caregivers frequently leads to error. There are also intentional deviations from the administration regimen labeled as misuse or abuse. In addition, medication interactions with other medications, herbal remedies, and food are factors contributing to adverse medication effects. Finally, medications must be secured so that inquisitive children do not access and ingest medications. In order to reduce error, misuse, and abuse of medication for young children and infants, accurate assessment of the cause of the problem is required.

Medical Professional Error

Prescribing physician error. In order to prevent errors by the prescribing physician, parents often benefit from an environment in which questions and input are encouraged. Parents often do not provide adequate information to medical professionals because they defer to an expert or are intimidated into saying little about the medical diagnosis and/or medication prescribed (DiMatteo, 2004). In order to prescribe medications with minimal probability of error, medical professionals may administer a checklist of critical information concerning potential contraindication. Items in the checklist include information about the child's weight, height, current medicines (including vitamins and herbal medicines) and allergies (Kaushal et al., 2001). Such information allows the physician to prescribe the correct dosage and to consider possible side effects. In addition, parents should be instructed to ask questions about the medication regimen prescribed to their child. Inquiring about the name of the medication and what it treats can serve as a confirmation that the correct medication has been prescribed (DiMatteo).

Filling prescription error. An effective measure to protect against errors in filling prescription is a prescription template. These are standardized order sheets where there are spaces for the child's weight, allergies, the doctor's name, phone number and signature (Kozer, Berkovitch, & Koren, 2006). Often, pharmacists have difficulty reading a physician's handwriting and can make mistakes in the dosage required or in the dilution of the medication. Therefore, educating parents about the availability of these templates can eliminate the potential for script errors. Subsequently, if the order forms are printed from a computer or filed electronically, then errors in interpretation of the prescription sheet will be less likely.

In addition, the same checklist of critical information solicited by the prescribing physician about the prescription should be asked of the pharmacist. In the pharmacy, it is possible for medications to have similar sounding names. Therefore, asking questions about the prescribed medication will serve as a check for the pharmacist to make sure that they are dispensing the right medicine (Sard et al., 2008).

Administration Errors

Not understanding or following administrative directions. In order to properly administer the drugs to their children, many medications require the child's weight in kilograms as opposed to pounds. This type of knowledge can be found in parent-held records. Most parents have these records in the form of baby books or parent-held medical records, but do not think of them as a useful tool. However, parents who were instructed either orally or in writing to use them were more likely to maintain and use their records (Glascoe, Oberklaid, Dworkin, & Trimm, 1998). Therefore, using written communication to parents highlighting the importance of this tool in administering medication to their children can prevent mistakes in dosages.

In addition, modeling can be used in order to instruct parents on how to use medication-dispensing tools effectively. For example, teaspoons and tablespoons are inefficient measuring devices. Parents who are shown how to measure medicine using a syringe can reduce the likelihood of under- or over-dosing. Furthermore, the administration of color-coded syringes that have colored lines at the correct dose can further reduce the probability of misuse. Parents should be given a color chart and written instructions on how to identify their child's color depending on their weight. Results have indicated that using this method has led to an increase in accurate measuring and a decrease of over- and under-dosing (Frush, Luo, Hutchinson, & Higgins, 2004).

Independent changes in dosing. Parents may be unaware of the consequences of mistakes in the dosage of their children's medication. Often, one parent administers the medication without the other parent knowing. This can lead to parents administering double the required dose. In order to prevent such misuse, parents can be instructed on how to use a medication log. There, parents can mark the time and date of administration to keep track of doses (Shrank, 2007).

Moreover, parents should be educated on the potential side effects of administering too much or too little of the prescribed dose, or not following the appropriate time sequences of dosages. For example, some parents wrongly believe that if a dose is skipped or missed, they can give twice the dosage at the next scheduled time of administration. Giving parents videotapes and written pamphlets/handouts have been effective in increasing a parent's knowledge about health issues (Glascoe et al., 1998). Such methods can inform parents about the harmful toxic effects that will in turn increase vigilance when administering medications to their children.

Misuse and Abuse in Administration

Diversion of medications. Parents sometimes do not know what medication to give children to soothe an ache or a pain. At times, they give children medication that is not prescribed or suitable for them without first seeking medical advice. For example, parents wrongfully give their children adult medication such as aspirin as a pain reliever when its use in young children has been linked to Reye's syndrome (Glasgow, 2006). Other common misuses of medication by parents include inappropriate use of antibiotics, such as treating children with the flu (a viral infection) with an antibiotic. Similarly, inappropriate use of anti-nausea medication is also of concern. Parents often give children anti-nausea medication to get rid of vomiting (such as when the child has stomach flu). Research findings warn against the use of anti-nausea medication in children as it can cause serious side effects (Levine, Gopal, Yanchis, & Koch, 2006).

Taking medications for non-approved use. Another issue of concern is the treatment of ailments in children with medications not intended for that use (e.g., antihistamines to help sleep; Simon & Weinkle, 1997). For example, more than half of parents interviewed admitted having given their children OTC antihistamines for their cough even though it was not advised or was found ineffective (Edwards & Fraser, 2007). A common reason reported for giving antihistamines is to help the child sleep despite research concluding that antihistamines have no effect on the child's sleep (Merenstein et al., 2006; Owens, 2000). In a recent study, surveyed parents reported attempting to reduce their child's mild fever with non-approved OTC medication, and 73% did so despite knowing it may harm their children, while 16% reported not knowing whether the medications were harmful (Walsh, Edwards, & Fraser, 2007). One study found paracetamol (also known as acetaminophen; an analgesic and antipyretic OTC medication to relieve pain and fever) to be a common unintentional overdose in children under 5 years of age (Chien et al., 2003). Studies report overdose of paracetamol is linked to acute-liver failure (Khashab, Tector, & Kwo, 2007; Larson et al., 2005). A widespread reason for parents' misuse and abuse of OTC medication is to control their child's exasperating symptoms and to lessen the burden of having to care for their sick child (Allotey, Diamond Reidpath, & Elisha, 2004).

Parent pathology. In most cases parents unintentionally give medication that is not approved or not prescribed for their children. However, some parents do this with purposeful intent and malice. Munchausen syndrome by proxy (MSBP) is a form of abuse inflicted by a parent (usually the mother) onto a child in order to seek the sympathy and attention of medical professionals and others. This condition involves a parent who concocts a medical condition for the child and brings about medical symptoms in the child (Rosenberg, 1987). The parent then attempts to prove the child's ill health to medical professionals and seeks medical support for the child (Shaw, Dayal, Hartman, & DeMaso, 2008; Sheridan, 2003). Poisoning with medications is the most prevalent practice in MSBP that gains the attention and forces immediate treatment by medical professionals (Shaw et al.; Sheridan, 2003).

Interactions

Medication interactions refer to the interference of a medication in the effectiveness or toxicity of another medication. Clinically significant interactions, most of which lead to undesirable and adverse effects and events, may result from changes in pharmaceutical, pharmacokinetic, or pharmacodynamic properties. For example, drug absorption may be altered by modifying the gastrointestinal pH. Proton pump inhibitors (PPIs) such as omeprazole change the gastrointestinal pH by reducing the acid present. Thus, co-administration of a PPI drug may potentiate or weaken medication absorption (Tom-Revzon & Adams, 2006). Pharmacodynamic interactions occur at drug action sites. Acetaminophen, and to a lesser extent, NSAIDs alter the pharmacodynamics of other medications including warfarin (Tobias, 2000). Although prescription medications are usually implicated in interactions, OTC medications, herbal preparations, and foods also create interactions that lead to adverse side effects.

Certain medication and patient factors are associated with an increased risk for drug interaction. Health professionals should pay special attention to possible drug interactions in pediatric patients as early infancy and childhood are characterized by rapid and significant age related physiological changes. The excretion and elimination processes are not fully developed until 1 year of age, resulting in extended half-life of metabolized drugs and reduced clearance as compared to adults (Martinbiancho, Zuckermann, Dos Santos, & Silva, 2007). In contrast, children 2 to 6 years of age have greater weight-normalized excretion than adults for many medications. Age-related differences in body composition exist. Infants have lower plasma concentrations of albumin and other proteins that bind medications; for medications with a high degree of protein binding, the lower plasma protein concentrations may lead to an increase in unbound drug and thus an increase in drug effect or toxicity. Age-related brain lipid content changes the permeability of the blood-brain barrier thereby altering the extent and onset of drug effect (Berde & Sethna, 2002). Given these differences, pediatric patients should be considered at risk for medication interactions.

With prescription medications. Mixing various prescriptions can have harmful side effects that might be unknown to parents. Information handouts about popular children's prescriptions can be distributed to parents. These handouts should explain the various side effects of combining two potentially harmful prescription medications together and what combinations should be avoided. Parents who were given such written advice were found to have improved knowledge of their children's medication (Glascoe et al., 1998). In addition, parents should also be advised to notify their child's physician about other medications their child is taking to avoid harmful interactions.

With OTC medications. When combining prescription with OTC drugs, parents should be educated on what to look for to ensure that the combination is not toxic. Parents can be questioned by physicians, nurses, and pharmacists in order to ensure that they can properly read and understand the labels found on the medication bottles. By modeling to look for the active ingredients found on the label, health professionals can teach parents to see if the medications contain the same active ingredients (Sharfstein et al., 2007). If so, parents should be informed that the combination of these products should not be taken together.

Moreover, parents should be encouraged to seek information from nurses, pharmacists, and physicians when they are not sure of a combination of prescription and OTC medicines. Parents can turn to the Internet as a useful resource when they need to speak with a medical professional. E-mail use between parents and physicians has been shown to provide support for medication use (Johnson & Davison, 2004). This type of communication can positively affect a child's safety. In addition, giving parents a list of trustworthy websites where they can find such information provides a solution for times when a physician is not available and a parent must find out whether an OTC medication can be mixed with their child's prescription.

With herbal treatments. Herbal medications are often unregulated and therefore it is essential that parents take precautions when mixing prescriptions and herbal medications. Parents should be instructed to access useful Internet websites such as The Physician's Desk Reference (PDR) for Herbal Medicines (http://www.pdr.net) to seek additional information about interaction effects. The site contains information about mixing herbal supplements with prescription medications.

With food. Harmful combinations of certain types of foods with medication are unknown to many parents. School professionals could provide handouts to parents making them aware of such incidences. Moreover, to ensure that the child is not eating certain foods that can have harmful side effects with their prescribed medication, it is suggested that parents be informed about the services of a dietician. A dietician can offer the child services such as an evaluation of the foods they are eating and education of what is and is not compatible with the medications they are taking (DiMatteo, 2004; Kelly et al., 2006). Records are then sent to parents, physicians, and the child's school to ensure that the child's dietary intake causes no harm to the child's health.

Accidental Ingestion

One of the most common sources of medication error, misuse, and abuse is accidental ingestion of medications by children. For infants, accidental ingestion is the most common source of emergency room visits due to medication misuse (Chien et al., 2003). Some examples of causes of emergency room visits are ingestion of gummy bear vitamins resulting in vitamin A toxicity; children swallowing parent's fosinopril (Monopril), a common blood pressure medication; children ingesting a bottle of cold syrup containing diphenhydramine (Benadryl); and children swallowing several tablets of zolpidem tartrate (Ambien). The results range from mild and easily treatable to permanently disabling or life threatening. Correct and secure storage of medications is a critical aspect of reducing the dangers of error and misuse of medications.

Intervention and Reduction of Error, Misuse, and Abuse

Most efforts to reduce error, misuse, and abuse take the form of preventative measures. Communication between parents and medical professionals is the critical factor in limiting error, misuse, and abuse of medications. Often, meetings with physicians are stressful and filled with much complex information for parents to integrate and apply. Direct instruction of parents by pediatricians, nurses, pharmacists, and others is an important measure to bring awareness to parents about the risks of OTC medication in children. This communication has the potential to lead to better medical decisions by parents regarding their child's ailments. The Committee on Children and Young People (2002) is a professional study group that underscores and encourages communication between parents and medical professionals, such as pediatricians. Pediatricians bear the responsibility to educate parents about the lack of efficacy and potential risks of some OTC medications (Budnitz et al., 2006; Kozer et al., 2006). Similarly, Carr (2006) argues that because pediatricians usually recommend OTC medication to parents for simple child ailments, physicians bear the responsibility to educate parents concerning their efficacy and risks. A simple way for this communication to take place is through educational brochures such as those promoted by the Consumer Healthcare Products Association (CHPA).

The misuse and abuse of OTC medication in children is of concern, especially given the health risks involved. Parents' error-prone and independent decisions that lead to administering OTC medications without consulting with their doctor require immediate intervention. However, parents' reported reasons for misuse and abuse are not well understood (DiMatteo, 2004; Osterberg & Blaschke, 2005; Rosenberg, 1987). Moreover, error, misuse, and abuse are extremely difficult to identify before the adverse effects become so problematic as to warrant medical attention. Additional research is required to improve identification and reasons for error, misuse, and abuse of medications. In that regard, valid and reliable measures for assessing parents' needs for the treatment of their child and their knowledge of the medication regimen need to be developed. For example, should the evaluation focus on assessing parents' knowledge about the efficacy and risks of administering OTC medication or their intent to administer non-approved medication despite their known risks?

An important step toward formulating a prevention strategy to reduce misuse and abuse of OTC medication is informing parents of the risks. The majority of parents are often unaware of the perilous risks of many medications for young children (Walsh et al., 2007). In light of this, as a form of intervention to safeguard children, parents can benefit from group treatment programs in which the aim is to educate parents about such risks and prevent any further misuse. A parent-training program that focuses on educating parents about how to make informed medical decisions for their children would be beneficial. There is currently little scientific evidence on the treatment parameters of group programs.

In the event that parent/caregiver psychopathology exists (i.e., MSBP), the case is referred to child protective service agencies, and for the suspected parent/ caregiver, psychiatric treatment such as individual psychotherapy is provided (Shaw et al., 2008). There are situations where this pathology is addressed by removing the child from the home. However, little scientific evidence exists to inform the treatment and management of MSBP (Rosenberg, 1987).

Conclusions

Medication error, misuse, and abuse in young children is occurring at an increasing rate that parallels the increase of prescription and OTC pharmacology used with the early childhood population. More parents consider the use of pharmacology acceptable with their young children to treat a host of ailments, disorders and conditions. With this increased use and availability of medications comes a heightened risk for error, misuse and abuse. The potential for serious long-term consequences, whether through medical professional or parental error or accidental ingestion, is significant.

Improvements in technology and medical service delivery are changing the way physicians prescribe medications and how those prescriptions are distributed to parents. Hand-scribbled prescription pads are gradually being replaced by handheld devices and computers that electronically transmit the prescription to the pharmacist, thus reducing the potential for transcription error. Pharmacies use sophisticated software that assesses the individual's age, weight, health conditions, medications, and other variables and compare this information to the prescribed medication to generate automatically any contraindications, warnings, and treatment protocols. The internet provides a vast amount of information for parents to examine the efficacy, risk, and treatment advisories when medications are prescribed for their children.

However, technological advances cannot replace the communication between medical providers and parents, and pharmacists and parents. Pharmacies provide quality handouts covering medication effects, side effects, and contraindications. These handouts become most effective when pharmacists support these handouts with conversation with parents (DiMatteo, 2004). Likewise, it is important that physicians take time to inform parents why a medication is being prescribed, the intended therapeutic effect, potential side effects, and any contraindications. Physicians and the entire medical team need to warmly elicit feedback from parents (who often feel intimidated in the medical setting) and encourage parents to ask questions, state concerns, and perhaps suggest alternative treatment strategies more amenable to their beliefs, misgivings about medications, and environmental variables that could interfere with the treatment protocol (such as an inconsistent home environment). Parents need to heed warnings to follow prescription directions carefully, monitor for side effects, and keep medications safely out of little hands.

Other members of the medical and mental health team, such as psychologists and social workers, can work closely with physicians and parents to help bridge the communication between all parties, encourage compliance with treatment, and assess for any signs of medication error, misuse or abuse. This is particularly important if there are indications that medications are being used for purposes in which they were not intended, such as for discipline, behavior management, to encourage drowsiness/sleep, or to induce illness in the child. Medications used in this manner suggest underlying psychopathology within the family, and psychotherapeutic and perhaps legal interventions would be necessary.

References

Abott, F. V., & Fraser, M. I. (1998). Use and abuse of over-the-counter analgesic agents. *Journal of Psychiatry & Neuroscience, 23*, 13-34.

Allotey, P., Reidpath, D. D., & Elisha, D. (2004). "Social medication" and the control of children: A qualitative study of over-the-counter medication among Australian children. *Pediatrics, 114*, 378-383.

Berde, C. B., & Sethna, N. F. (2002). Analgesics for the treatment of pain in children. *The New England Journal of Medicine, 347*, 1094-1103.

Bie, B., & Pan, Z. Z. (2007). Trafficking of central opioid receptors and descending pain inhibition. *Molecular Pain, 3,* 37-44.

Budnitz, D. S., Pollock, D. A., Mendelsohn, A. B., Weidenbach, K. A., McDonald, A. K., & Annest, J. L. (2005). Emergency department visits for outpatient adverse drug events: Demonstration for a national surveillance system. *Annals of Emergency Medicine, 45,* 197-206.

Budnitz, D. S., Pollock, D. A., Weidenbach, K. N., Mendelsohn, A. B., Schroeder, T. J., & Annest, J. L. (2006). National surveillance of emergency department visits for outpatient adverse drug events. *Journal of the American Medical Association, 296,* 1858-1866.

Bussing, R., Zima, B. T., Gary, F. A., & Garvan, C. W. (2002). Use of complementary and alternative medicine for symptoms of attention-deficit hyperactivity disorder. *Psychiatric Services, 53,* 1096-1102.

Carr, B. C. (2006). Efficacy, abuse, and toxicity of over-the-counter cough and cold medicines in the pediatric population. *Current Opinion in Pediatrics, 18,* 184-188.

Chan, E. (2002). The role of complementary and alternative medicine in attention-deficit hyperactivity disorder. *Developmental and Behavioral Pediatrics, 23,* S37-S45.

Chien, C., Marriott, J., Ashby, K., & Ozanne-Smith, J. (2003). Unintentional ingestion of over the counter medications in children less than 5 years old. *Journal of Paediatrics and Child Health, 39,* 264-269.

Cohen, A. L., Budnitz, D. S., Weidenbach, K. N., Jernigan, D. B., Schroeder, T. J., Shehab, N., et al. (2008). National surveillance of emergency department visits for outpatient adverse events in children and adolescents. *Journal of Pediatrics, 152,* 416-421.

Committee on Children and Young People. (2002). *Inquiry into the use of prescription drugs and over-the-counter medications in children and young people: The use by children and young people of prescription drugs and over-the-counter medications in children and young people.* (No. Issues Paper No 4). Sydney: NSW Government.

Davenport, P. W. (2009). Clinical cough I: The urge-to-cough: A respiratory sensation. *Handbook of Experimental Pharmacology, 187,* 263-276.

DiMatteo, M. R. (2004). The role of effective communication with children and their families in fostering adherence to pediatric regimens. *Patient Education and Counseling, 55,* 339-344.

Ecklund, C. R., & Ross, M. C. (2001). Over-the-counter medication use in preschool children. *Journal of Pediatric Health Care, 15,* 168-172.

Edwards, H., & Fraser, J. (2007). Over-the-counter medication use for childhood fever: A cross-sectional study of Australian parents. *Journal of Paediatrics and Child Health, 43,* 601-606.

Eiland, L. S., Salazar, M. L., & English, T. M. (2008). Caregivers' perspectives when evaluating nonprescription medication utilization in children. *Clinical Pediatrics, 47*, 578-587.

Firestone, P., Musten, L. M., Pisterman, S., Mercer, J., & Bennett, S. (1998). Short-term side effects of stimulant medication are increased in preschool children with attention-deficit/hyperactivity disorder: A double-blind, placebo-controlled study. *Journal of Child and Adolescent Psychopharmacology, 8*, 13-25.

Frush, K. S., Luo, X., Hutchinson, P., & Higgins, J. N. (2004). Evaluation of a method to reduce over-the-counter medication dosing error. *Archives of Pediatrics and Adolescent Medicine, 158*, 620-624.

Fugh-Berman, A. (2000). Herb-drug interactions. *The Lancet, 355*, 134-138.

Ghuman, J. K., Arnold, L. E., & Anthony, B. J. (2008). Psychopharmacological and other treatments in preschool children with attention-deficit/ hyperactivity disorder: Current evidence and practice. *Journal of Child and Adolescent Psychopharmacology, 18*, 413-447.

Glascoe, F. P., Oberklaid, F., Dworkin, P. H., & Trimm, F. (1998). Brief approaches to educating patients and parents in primary care. *Pediatrics, 101*, e10.

Glasgow, J. F. T. (2006). Reye's Syndrome: The case for a causal link with aspirin. *Drug Safety, 29*, 1111-1121.

Greenhill, L., Kollins, S., Abikoff, H., McCracken, J., Riddle, M., Swanson, J., et al. (2006). Efficacy and safety of immediate-release methylphenidate treatment for preschoolers with ADHD. *Journal of the American Academy of Child and Adolescent Psychiatry, 45*, 1284-1293.

Jhung, M. A., Budnitz, D. S., Mendelsohn, A. B., Weidenbach, K. A., McDonald, A. K., & Annest, J. L. (2005). Evaluation and overview of the National Electronic Injury Surveillance System—Cooperactive Adverse Drug Event Surveillance project. *Medical Care, 45*, S96-S102.

Johnson, K., & Davison, C. (2004). Information technology: Its importance to child safety. *Ambulatory Pediatrics, 4*, 64-72.

Kaushal, R., Bates, D. W., Landrigan, C., McKenna, K. J., Clapp, M. D., Federico, F., et al. (2001). Medication errors and adverse drug events in pediatric inpatients. *Journal of the American Medical Association, 16*, 2114-2120.

Kelly, K. O., Matson, K. L., & Cowles, B. J. (2006). Nonprescription medication use by infants and children: Product labeling versus evidence-based medicine. *Journal of Pharmacy Practice, 19*, 286-294.

Khashab, M., Tector, J. A., & Kwo, P. Y. (2007). Epidemiology of acute liver failure. *Current Gastroenterology Reports, 9*, 66-73.

Kozer, E., Berkovitch, M., & Koren, G. (2006). Medication errors in children. *Pediatric Clinics of North America, 53*, 1155-1168.

Larson, A. M., Polson, J., Fontana, R. J., Davern, T. J., Lalani, E., Hyman, L. S. et al. (2005). Acetaminophen-induced acute liver failure: Results of a United States multicenter, prospective study. *Hepatology, 42*, 1364-1372.

Levine, M. E., Gopal, V. D., Yanchis, S., & Koch, K. L. (2006). The effect of lipase supplementation on upper gastrointestinal symptoms and gastric myoelectrical activity induced by a high fat meal in healthy volunteers. *Neurogastroenterology and Motility, 18, 487*-488.

Li, S. F., Lacher, B., & Crain, E. F. (2000). Acetaminophen and ibuprofen dosing by parents. *Pediatric Emergency Care, 16*, 394-397.

Martinbiancho, J., Zuckermann, J., Dos Santos, L., & Silva, M. M. (2007). Profile of drug interactions in hospitalized children. *Pharmacy Practice, 5*, 157-161.

McCabe, S. E., Cranford, J. A., Boyd, C. J., & Teter, C. J. (2007). Motives, diversion and routes of administration associated with nonmedical use of prescription opioids. *Addictive Behaviors, 32*, 562-575.

McCabe, S. E., Teter, C. J., & Boyd, C. J. (2006). Medical use, illicit use, and diversion of abusable prescription drugs. *Journal of Psychoactive Drugs, 38, 43-58.*

McCaig, L. F., & Nawar, E. W. (2006). *National hospital ambulatory medical care survey: 2004 emergency department summary.* Advance Data from Vital and Health Statistics-CDC. Retrieved September 18, 2009, from http://www.cdc.gov/nchs/data/ad/ad372.pdf

Merck & Co., Inc. (2003). Medicinal herbs and nutraceuticals. In *The Merck Manuals Online Medical Library.* Retrieved September 18, 2009, from http://www.merck.com/mmhe/sec02/ch019/ch019a.html

Merenstein, D., Diener-West, M., Halbower, A. C., Krist, A., & Ruben, H. R. (2006). The trial of infant response to diphenhydramine: The TIRED study – a randomized, controlled, patient-oriented trial. *Archives of Pediatric and Adolescent Medicine, 160*, 707-712.

Miller, F. G., Emanuel, E. J., Rosenstein, D. L., & Straus, S. E. (2004). Ethical issues concerning research in complementary and alternative medicine. *Journal of the American Medical Association, 291*, 599-604.

Moore, T. J., Weiss, S. R., Kaplan, S., & Blaisdell, C. J. (2002). Reported adverse drug events in infants and children under 2 years of age. *Pediatrics, 110*, e543.

Osterberg, L., & Blaschke, T. (2005). Adherence to medication. *The New England Journal of Medicine, 353*, 487-497.

Owens, J. A. (2000). Challenges in managing sleep problems in young children. *Western Journal of Medicine, 173*, 38.

Paul, I. M., Yoder, K. E., Crowell, K. R., Shaffer, M. L., McMillan, H. S., Carlson, L. C., et al. (2004). Effect of dextromethorphan, diphenhydramine, and placebo on nocturnal cough and sleep quality for coughing children and their parents. *Pediatrics, 114*, e85-e90.

Pelayo, R., & Dubik, M. (2008). Pediatric sleep pharmacology. *Seminars in Pediatric Neurology, 15,* 79-90.

Poulin, C. (2007). From attention-deficit/hyperactivity disorder to medical stimulant use to the diversion of prescribed stimulants to non-medical stimulant use: Connecting the dots. *Addiction, 102*, 740-751.

Posey, W. M., Bassin, S. A., & Lewis, A. (2009). Preschool ADHD and medication…more study needed!? *Journal of Early Childhood and Infant Psychology, 5,* 57-77.

Riddle, M. A. (2007). New findings from the preschoolers with attention-deficit/hyperactivity disorders treatment study (PATS). *Journal of Child and Adolescent Psychopharmacology, 17*, 543-546.

Rojas, N. L., & Chan, E. (2005). Old and new controversies in the alternative treatment of attention-deficit hyperactivity disorder. *Mental Retardation and Developmental Disabilities, 11,* 116-130.

Rosenberg, D. A. (1987). Web of deceit: A literature review of Munchausen syndrome by proxy. *Child Abuse and Neglect, 11*, 547-563.

Sard, B. E., Walsh, K. E., Doros, G., Hannon, M., Moschetti, W., & Bauchner, H. (2008). Retrospective evaluation of a computerized physician order entry adaptation to prevent prescribing errors in a pediatric emergency department. *Pediatrics, 122,* 782-787.

Schaefer, M. K., Shehab, N., Cohen, A. L., & Budnitz, D. S. (2008). Adverse events from cough and cold medications in children. *Pediatrics, 121*, 783-787.

Schnoes, C. J., Kuhn, B. R., Workman, E. F., & Ellis, C. R. (2006). Pediatric prescribing practices for clonidine and other pharmacologic agents for children with sleep disturbance. *Clinical Pediatrics, 45*, 229-238.

Sharfstein, J. M., North, M., & Serwint, J. R. (2007). Over the counter but no longer under the radar—Pediatric cough and cold medications. *The New England Journal of Medicine, 357*, 2321-2324.

Shaw, R. J., Dayal, S., Hartman, J. K., & DeMaso, D. R. (2008). Factitious disorder by proxy: Pediatric condition falsification. *Harvard Review in Psychiatry, 16*, 215-224.

Sheridan, M. S. (2003). The deceit continues: An updated literature review of Munchausen syndrome by proxy. *Child Abuse & Neglect, 27*, 431-451.

Shrank, W. H. (2007). Educating patients about their medications: The potential and limitations of written drug information. *Health Affairs, 26*, 731-740.

Simon, H. K., & Weinkle, D. A. (1997). Over-the-counter medications:
    Do parents give what they intend to give? *Archives of Pediatric and
    Adolescent Medicine, 151*, 654-656.

Tobias, J. D. (2000). Weak analgesics and nonsteroidal anti-inflammatory agents
    in the management of children with acute pain. *Pediatric Clinics of North
    America, 47*, 527-543.

Tom-Revzon, C., & Adam, H. M. (2006). Drug interactions. *Pediatrics in
    Review, 27*, 315-317.

U.S. Drug Enforcement Administration. (2004). *Drugs of abuse/uses and effects.*
    Retrieved September 18, 2009, from http://www.usdoj.gov/dea/pubs/abuse/
    chart.htm

Vernacchio, L., Kelly, J. P., Kaufman, D. W., & Mitchell, A. A. (2008a). Cough
    and cold medication use by US children, 1999-2006: Results from the
    Sloan Survey. *Pediatrics, 122*, e323-e329.

Vernacchio, L., Kelly, J. P., Kaufman, D. W., & Mitchell, A. A. (2008b).
    Pseudoephedrine use among US children, 1999-2006: Results from the
    Slone survey. *Pediatrics, 122*, 1299-1304.

Walsh, A., Edwards, H., & Fraser, J. (2007). Influences on parents' fever
    management: Beliefs, experiences and information sources. *Journal of
    Clinical Nursing, 16*, 2331-2340.

Wilens, T. E., Adler, L. A., Adams, J., Sgambati, S., Rotrosen, J., Sawtelle, R.,
    et al. (2008). Misuse and diversion of stimulants prescribed for ADHD: A
    systematic review of the literature. *Journal of the American Academy of
    Child and Adolescent Psychiatry, 47*, 21-31.

Woolf, A. D. (2003). Herbal remedies and children: Do they work? Are they
    harmful? *Pediatrics, 112*, 240-246.

Wong, H. H. L., & Smith, R. G. (2006). Patterns of complementary and
    alternative medical therapy use in children diagnosed with autism spectrum
    disorders. *Journal of Autism and Developmental Disorders, 36*, 901-909.

Author Note

Steven R. Shaw is Assistant Professor in the Department of Educational
and Counselling Psychology, McGill University. Khing Su Lin, Tiffany W. Chiu,
Melissa Stern, and Shohreh M. Rezazadeh are students at McGill University.
Paul C. McCabe is Associate Professor at Brooklyn College-City University of
New York.

Medication Research for Young Children in Community Practice: Retrospect and Prospect. A Commentary.

Julie Magno Zito
University of Maryland

It is a pleasure to share reflections on the *Journal of Early Childhood and Infant Psychology's* (*JECIP*) special issue on medication use in very young children. The scope of topics covered is impressive - from reviews of major psychiatric drug classes such as stimulants, antidepressants and antipsychotics to classes widely used in very young children (e.g., antibiotics and over-the-counter cough and cold remedies).

As a pharmacoepidemiologist studying medication use patterns for psychiatric and behavioral disorders for the past 25 years, this occasion is also an opportunity. Looking back on knowledge of pediatric medication use is an opportunity to guide future research directions toward a *comprehensive* research model that includes independent post-marketing effectiveness and population-based safety analysis. Ultimately, the goal of such research is to improve clinical practice associated with medication use. This goal is particularly relevant to young children, a special population that is rarely evaluated in pre-marketing clinical trials.

Pharmacoepidemiology (PEPI) is the study of medication use in large populations (Strom, 2005) and this framework can be applied specifically to psychiatry and psychology (Zito, Safer, & Craig, 2008). To apply a pharmacoepidemiology framework to the evaluation of drug use in young children, a brief retrospective review starts with expanding the evidence base beyond short-term clinical trials, which are necessary but not sufficient to assess the benefits and risks for an individual in treatment. Reasons for this position stem from the U.S. drug development system that is entrepreneurially driven but relies on federal authorization for marketing based on evidence of short-term efficacy and safety in typically adult populations. In addition, our knowledge of medication use is influenced by the organization of medical care, for example in terms of continuity of care, work force dynamics, insurance coverage and access issues.

All correspondence should be addressed to Julie Magno Zito, Department of Pharmaceutical Health Service Research, University of Maryland, Saratoga Building (Room 216), 220 Arch St., Baltimore, MD 21201. Electronic mail may be sent to jzito@rx.umaryland.edu.

The Food and Drug Administration (FDA) requirements for marketing a new drug product include data typically from randomized double-blind placebo controlled experimental trials with durations ranging from weeks to several months. Generalizing from the findings of these trials is limited in terms of both efficacy and safety. The "5 toos" rule reminds epidemiologists and clinical scientists of the limited information that comes from pre-marketing clinical trials, namely:

1) Too few subjects to identify a rare adverse event;
2) Too short of a duration to assess long-term efficacy or safety;
3) Too simple in terms of diagnostic criteria to generalize to community of youth populations many of whom have comorbidities that would preclude trial participation;
4) Too narrow an age group; for example, the treatment trial for adolescent depression was restricted to age 9 years and above in assessing antidepressants (March et al., 2004); and
5) Too simple trial diagnostic criteria to generalize to the atypical symptom presentation frequently seen in community practice.

The "5 toos" rule reminds us of the need for a more *comprehensive* system to assure prescribing clinicians of an evidence base that meets their needs and evolves over time so that as more information is learned about a recently marketed product, the decision to use it will reflect an *evolving* knowledge base.

In terms of the specific benefits and risks of medication in young populations, it is well to recall that most authoritative biomedical opinion rests largely on evidence of effectiveness and safety from published proprietary clinical trials. For the patient who resembles the trial subjects, the findings often generalize but for special populations, particularly very young children, the limitations as detailed in this volume by McCabe (this issue), are substantial. These include immaturity of enzyme systems, differences in pharmacokinetic parameters, and substantial differences in adverse event profiles by age group. For example, relatively greater weight gain in youth than adults receiving atypical antipsychotics has been demonstrated from secondary analysis of trial data (Safer, 2004). Within youth groups treated with selective serotonin reuptake inhibitors (SSRIs), children were more likely than adolescents to have symptoms of activation and agitation (Safer & Zito, 2006). Moreover, activation and agitation are a major challenge to clinicians because these are treatment-emergent symptoms that may be psychiatric or behavioral in nature. Such symptoms are termed behavioral toxicity and challenge clinicians to recognize that a new adverse event may be related to the drug treatment rather than classifying such symptoms as new or underlying illness (Zito et al., 2008).

Behavioral toxicity challenges clinicians even further when the illness is depression. The controversy surrounding activation and suicidal events following treatment of depression with SSRIs illustrates the methodological problem termed *confounding by indication*. In this case, the causal inference analysis aims to assess the risk of a serious adverse event (i.e., suicidal behavior) that may be related to the underlying illness (i.e., depression) rather than to the newly initiated SSRI (Zito & Safer, 2007). Illustrating this difficult problem, is the recent tragic death of a 7-year-old Florida boy in foster care who completed suicide while treated off-label with Symbax®, a combination of olanzapine and fluoxetine. Shortly before, he was treated with Vyvanse®, an ADHD drug with FDA labeling for his age, and Zyprexa® and Lexapro®, off-label medications. This complex medication-related tragedy reduces the age for completed suicide down to childhood.

Such tragedies remind us of the need for close monitoring of drug therapies that have uncertain risk of suicidal behavior. The SSRI-suicide controversy began with adults taking fluoxetine, the first of a new molecular class, shortly after it was marketed in 1988 and reemerged when large cohorts of youth began to be treated in the late 1990s (Hunkeler et al., 2005). Such controversy in light of increasing prevalence of use supports a more comprehensive post-marketing surveillance (PMS) approach to drug safety. This system requires infrastructure that goes beyond the current passive PMS system to a more scientifically rigorous, *active* PMS system. This is particularly valuable for very young children where there is growing medication use, including complex combinations, even with a lack of adequate information on either benefits or risks. Hopefully, the newly launched FDA Sentinel system will progress toward this goal (U.S. Department of Health and Human Services).

As emphasized in several papers in this volume (McCabe; Posey et al.; Shaw, Bruce, Ouimet, Sharma, & Glaser), off-label prescribing is extensive among young children treated with antidepressants, antipsychotics, and to a lesser extent with stimulants. Off-label prescription refers to use of a medication for a treatment indication or in an age group that lacks FDA-approved information on the product labeling (Roberts, Rodriguez, Murphy, & Crescenzi, 2003). In this volume, McCabe provides data on the youngest age with labeled indications for antidepressants. Obsessive compulsive disorder is a labeled indication for four antidepressants for youth 6-10 years old. Depression is labeled for citalopram (age 12+), escitalopram (age 12+), and fluoxetine (age 7+) while many widely used products (e.g., paroxetine, sertraline, and bupropion) have no approved labeling for depression treatment in youth. Similarly, only three ADHD medications have labeled indications for youth less than 5 years of age. With the exception of risperidone for the treatment of irritability in autism, the increasing use of antipsychotics in young children is related to off-label indications, largely behavioral.

The clinical practice implications of off-label use in young children are fuzzy because the standard of care is expanding. As described here, Shaw, Bruce, and colleagues (this issue) state that "practice is ahead of the research." It is now fairly common to learn of psychotropic medication combinations (disparagingly called 'cocktails') prescribed in difficult cases despite the lack of robust, independently assessed efficacy data. It might be tempting for prescribing clinicians to view monotherapy findings from clinical trials as additive and applicable to the use of a combination of classes. But such a view is not grounded in science. In the absence of established benefits for very young children, the risk of psychotropic combinations in the very young developing child raises both scientific and ethical questions (Shaw, Bruce et al., this issue).

Effectiveness and safety of medication use is an evolving knowledge base, as is clear from advancing stimulant information from the Multimodal Treatment Study of ADHD ([MTA]; MTA Cooperative Group, 1999), which showed benefits to a larger pool of youth 7-9 years old than the later Preschool ADHD Treatment Study (PATS) did for preschoolers (Greenhill et al., 2007). Similarly, our knowledge of stimulant safety is evolving. The long-term safety data of the MTA on growth suppression indicates real deficits after 3 years of treatment, a finding that should reduce contrary opinions about the effects of stimulants on growth (Swanson et al., 2007). More recently, as amphetamine salt products have gained market share, data on the risk of cardiovascular events associated with their use has emerged (Winterstein et al., 2007) and, as noted in this volume by Posey et al., the debate continues about the value of baseline electrocardiograms.

To summarize thus far, this commentary has attempted to place the clinical science offered to the practicing clinician who works with very young children into the broader context of what we know and do not know about both population-based drug safety and the effectiveness of medications for psychiatric and behavioral disorders. Turning attention to the paper focused on antibiotic use, Kozyrskyj and colleagues (this issue) thoroughly review this important public health topic. In light of the prominence of multiply-resistant staphylococcus-aureus (MRSA) in today's health care environment, it is a welcome idea to reduce inappropriate parent demand for antibiotic treatment of upper respiratory viral infections by engaging them in 'watchful waiting.' Parents are instructed to fill a written prescription they are given only after observing that symptoms persist. This creative approach educates parents at the level of professionals and stresses the therapeutic alliance between family and professionals in a way that is likely to improve our understanding of both the illness and the treatment.

Another dimension of medication use is addressed by Shaw, Su Lin, and colleagues (this issue). The authors remind us that medication use sometimes leads to errors in dosing, accidental overdosing, and to intended or unintended abuse. One of the most compelling aspects in regard to very young children is the caution about prescribing drug regimens that are beyond the parental education and complicated by family stressors (e.g., low income, single parent households, and poor continuity of health service use). Had Rebecca Riley, the 4-year old treated with a combination of valproic acid, clonidine, dextromethorphan, and chlorpheniramine, been recognized as a child in such a dire environment, the overuse of this cocktail and her death might have been avoided (Shaw, Bruce et al., this issue).

JECIP is to be congratulated for undertaking the task of bringing together for clinical readers a treasure trove of documentation on the current knowledge base on benefits and risks of medications for very young children. Accepting the evolution of the data as experience grows in the post-marketing period will lead to more targeted research on special populations (e.g. cohorts of very young children treated with antipsychotics who are followed systematically for extended time periods) to establish 'real world' benefits and risks.

References

Greenhill, L., Kollins, S., Abikoff, H., McCracken, J., Riddle, M., Swanson, J., et al. (2007). Efficacy and safety of immediate-release methylphenidate treatment for preschoolers with ADHD. *Journal of the American Academy of Child and Adolescent Psychiatry, 45*, 1284-1293.

Hunkeler, E. M., Fireman, B., Lee, J., Diamond, R., Hamilton, J., He, C. X., et al. (2005). Trends in use of antidepressants, lithium and anticonvulsants in Kaiser Permanente-insured youths, 1994-2003. *Journal of Child and Adolescent Psychopharmacology,15,* 26-37.

Kozyrskyj, A. L., Gill, P. J., Klasson, T. P., & Forgie, M. D. (2009). Double jeopardy in the low-income child: The case of antibiotic use. *Journal of Early Childhood and Infant Psychology, 5,* 79-99.

March, J., Silva, S., Petrycki, S., Curry, J., Wells, K., Fairbank, J., et al. (2004). Fluoxetine, cognitive-behavioral therapy, and their combination for adolescents with depression: Treatment for Adolescents with Depression Study (TADS) randomized controlled trial. *Journal of the American Medical Association, 292*, 807-820.

McCabe, P. C. (2009). The use of antidepressant medications in early childhood: Prevalence, efficacy, and risk. *Journal of Early Childhood and Infant Psychology, 5,* 13-35.

MTA Cooperative Group. (1999). A 14-month randomized clinical trial of treatment strategies for attention-deficit/hyperactivity disorder. *Archives of General Psychiatry, 56*, 1073-1086.

Posey, W. M., Bassin, S. A., & Lewis, A. (2009). Preschool ADHD and medication...more study needed!? *Journal of Early Childhood and Infant Psychology, 5,* 57-77.

Roberts, R., Rodriguez, W., Murphy, D., & Crescenzi, T. (2003). Pediatric drug labeling. *Journal of the American Medical Association, 290*, 905-911.

Safer, D. J. (2004). A comparison of risperidone-induced weight gain across the age span. *Journal of Clinical Psychopharmacology, 24*, 429-436.

Safer, D. J., & Zito, J. M. (2006). Treatment-emergent adverse events from selective serotonin reuptake inhibitors by age group: Children versus adolescents. *Journal of Child and Adolescent Psychopharmacology, 16*, 203-213.

Shaw, S. R., Bruce, J., Ouimet, T., Sharma, A., & Glaser, S. (2009). Young children with developmental disabilities and atypical antipsychotic medications: Dual diagnosis, direction, and debate. *Journal of Early Childhood and Infant Psychology, 5*, 37-55.

Shaw, S. R., Su Lin, K., Chiu, T. W., Stern, M., Rezazadeh, S. M., & McCabe, P. C. (2009). Error, misuse, and abuse of prescription and over-the-counter medications for young children. *Journal of Early Childhood and Infant Psychology, 5*, 101-120.

Strom, B. L. (2005). *Pharmacoepidemiology*. New York: John Wiley and Sons, Ltd.

Swanson, J. M., Elliot, G. R., Greenhill, L. L., Wigal, T., Arnold, L. E., Vitiello, B., et al. (2007). Effects of stimulant medication on growth rates across 3 years in the MTA follow-up. *Journal of the American Academy of Child and Adolescent Psychiatry, 46*, 1015-1027.

U.S. Department of Health and Human Services. (n.d.). *FDA's Sentinel Initiative*. Retrieved June 20, 2009 from http://www.fda.gov/Safety/ FDAsSentinelInitiative/default.htm

Winterstein, A. G., Gerhard, T., Shuster, J., Johnson, M., Zito, J. M., & Saidi, A. (2007). Cardiac safety of central nervous system stimulants in children and adolescents with attention-deficit/hyperactivity disorder. *Pediatrics, 120*, e1494-e1501.

Zito, J. M., & Safer, D. J. (2007). The efficacy and safety of selective serotonin reuptake inhibitors for the treatment of depression in children and adolescents. In R. Mann & E. B. Andrews (Eds.), *Pharmacovigilance* (pp. 559-570). New York: John Wiley & Sons.

Zito, J. M., Safer, D. J., & Craig, T. J. (2008). Pharmacoepidemiology of psychiatric disorders. In A. G. Hartzema, H. H. Tilson, & K. A. Chan (Eds.), *Pharmacoepidemiology and Therapeutic Risk Management* (pp. 817-854). Cincinnati: Harvey Whitney Books.

Stressful Life Events Experienced by Clinically Referred Foster Care and Nonfoster Care Children

Robyn L. Glover & David S. Glenwick
Fordham University

Differences in the quantity and type of stressful life events experienced by foster children and nonfoster children, ages 2 through 6, were investigated. Forty-four foster children receiving services at a community mental health clinic were matched with 44 nonfoster children from the clinic based on age, gender, and ethnicity. The clinic files of the two groups then were examined with respect to the occurrence of various life events. The foster children experienced twice as many stressors as their nonfoster peers, including greater instability in their relationships with their siblings and primary caregiver, and, not unexpectedly, they had more risk factors involving maltreatment and parental substance use. Both groups experienced events related to medical/developmental and educational history at a high rate, suggesting that these are stressors relevant not only to foster care children but also to children of low socioeconomic status in general. Commonly used measures of stressful life events in young children do not include many of the items identified in this study as relevant to foster children and children living in poverty, indicating that the development of more appropriate measures is warranted.

Existing research on children living in foster care has shown that these children face a multitude of life stressors both before and during their time in foster care. Silver (1999) reported that the majority of children in foster care are born into families with extremely limited financial resources. This poverty puts children at risk for prenatal exposure to toxins, premature birth, and low birth weight. These conditions increase the likelihood that children will have special health care needs and developmental delays (Stahmer et al., 2005) which present serious challenges for caregivers who already are struggling with limited financial, social, and educational resources. Poverty also is associated with parental substance abuse, incarceration, domestic violence, and homelessness (Lee & Goerge, 1999; McGuinness & Schneider, 2007). Taken together, these factors put foster children at serious preplacement risk for physical and psychological maltreatment.

All correspondence should be addressed to David Glenwick, Department of Psychology, Dealy 236, Fordham University, Bronx, New York 10458. Electronic mail may be sent to: dglenwick@aol.com.

The maltreatment experienced by foster children before being removed from their biological families comes in many forms (Bruskas, 2008). Among children entering the child welfare system, the highest rates of abuse and neglect are reported in children under the age of 6 (Stahmer et al., 2005). In their study of the impact of welfare reform on young foster children's mental health, Klee, Kronstadt, and Zlotnick (1997) reported that 92% of the children in their sample were removed from their homes based on charges of neglect. Nearly three-quarters of these neglect charges were attributed to parental substance abuse. Klee et al. found that abandonment, abuse, prenatal drug exposure, multiple out-of-home placements, developmental delays, and emotional difficulties also were experiences common to their foster care sample. Frame (2002) uncovered similar preplacement risk factors in her study of placement outcomes for young children in foster care. Eighty percent of the infants and toddlers included in her study were placed in out-of-home care due to neglect, followed by 13.6% for physical abuse, 2.1% for sexual abuse, and 1% for emotional abuse. Morrison, Frank, Holland, and Kates (1999) reported that, in addition to becoming the victims of abuse, children later placed in foster care are exposed to high levels of violence directed toward others in their homes and in their communities.

Once removed from their biological families, foster children potentially are exposed to an additional set of stressors (Bruskas, 2008; Fein, 1991; James, 2004; Kerker & Dore, 2006), starting with the actual act of separation from their family of origin. This potentially traumatizing event can leave children with feelings of abandonment, guilt, and shame (Kerker & Dore). Foster children must cope with the difficulty of either losing contact with their biological family or of maintaining a potentially stressful relationship with that family (Eagle, 1994). Furthermore, many foster children experience multiple out-of-home placements. For example, Klee et al. (1997) reported that the number of placements for the foster children in their longitudinal study ranged from one to four, with 48% of children experiencing two or more out-of-home placements. Placement changes occur for a variety of reasons, including reunification with the biological family, unrealistic expectations of foster families, policy mandates to move children to less restrictive settings, attempts to keep sibling groups together, and unacceptable behavior by the foster child (James, 2004). Based on interviews with the caregivers of 415 children in the child welfare system, Newton, Litrownik, and Landsverk (2000) found a significant positive relationship between the number of placement changes and the total number of behavior problems presented by foster children. Newton et al. reported that even children scoring within normal limits on a measure of internalizing and externalizing behavior problems as they entered the child welfare system were highly sensitive to the detrimental effects of placement breakdowns.

Foster children removed from either their biological or foster families because of abuse may experience an increased likelihood of subsequent maltreatment in future foster care placements. From their review of studies of nonkinship foster families, Kerker and Dore (2006) concluded that previously abused children are more likely to be maltreated by subsequent caregivers than are their nonabused peers. This subsequent maltreatment rate, according to Kerker and Dore, appears to vary across studies and countries, with, for example, a 20% rate reported for an English sample (Hobbs, Hobbs, &Wynne, 1999) and rates between 1.5% and 3.5% for United States samples (Poertner, Bussey, & Fluke, 1999).

In addition to facing these foster care-specific risks, foster children are at continued risk for exposure to poverty-related stressors. Although screened for safety and appropriateness of care, foster families face similar difficulties related to financial stress and the demands of living in low-income neighborhoods (Fein, 1991; McGuinness & Schneider, 2007; Morrison et al., 1999).

Investigations of the life stressors experienced by foster children have involved a number of sources and methods, including archival records and relevant legal documents; interviews with the children themselves, foster parents, relatives, school personnel, and health care workers; demographic questionnaires; and cognitive and social/emotional assessments (e.g., Brand & Brinich, 1999; Kirby & Hardesty, 1998; Wilson, Sinclair, & Gibbs, 2000). A major problem with these data-gathering methods is that they are nonstandardized and vary from study to study. Questions regarding a particular life stressor may be addressed differently by different research groups, thus eliciting varying degrees of endorsement. For example, one frequently used stressful life events inventory contains the item "Jail sentence of parent for 30 days or less," while another contains the item "Parent getting into trouble with the law." Likewise, one inventory has as an item "Hospitalization of child," while another offers the item "Major illness or injury [of child]." Despite these items tapping similar constructs, rates of endorsement of them could vary. It should be noted that, although characteristic of the assessment of stressors in youngsters in foster care, this shortcoming does not appear to be limited to this population. In their review of issues in measuring stressors experienced by children and adolescents in general, Grant, Compas, Thurm, McMahon, and Gipson (2004) reported that only about 5% of the approximately 500 studies reviewed had used well-validated measures to assess life stressors.

With respect to children in foster care, one possible explanation for researchers' infrequent utilization of existing, psychometrically sound stressful life events measures is the fact that many of the items on these inventories are not relevant to such children. For example, the Life Events Record (Coddington, 1972), one of the most widely cited measures, focuses on events experienced by children living in two-parent families. Items include "Divorce of parents," "Addition of a step-parent to the family," "Mother beginning work," and "Change in father's occupation." These items do not capture many of the salient and stressful aspects of a foster child's experience. The frequently used Life Events Checklist (Johnson & McCutcheon, 1980) reflects a similar bias, with items on this measure including "Parents divorced," "Parents separated," and "Increased number of arguments between parents." Other measures, including the Children's Life Events Inventory (Chandler, 1981), are made up of similarly skewed item sets. Grant et al. (2004) pointed out that the majority of commonly employed life stressor measures were developed with middle-class, European American samples; such measures have been criticized for failing to address issues pertinent to children of color and those living in low-income environments.

As important as the inclusion of irrelevant items in these measures is, so too is the exclusion of life stressors that are significant in foster children's development. Items reflecting the life stressors of foster children described above are noticeably absent from existing measures. Experiences such as neglect, physical or emotional abuse, separation from both biological parents, separation from siblings, and transition from one home to another are extreme stressors not captured by the extant surveys and inventories.

Given the shortcomings of existing measures, the goal of the current study was to further elucidate those stressful life events relevant to foster children, thereby hopefully informing the item selection process in the subsequent development of valid life events instruments for this population. To do this, a sample of children in foster care was compared with a sample of children of similar socioeconomic status who were living with at least one biological parent. Specifically, foster children receiving psychological services at a community mental health clinic were matched based on age, gender, and ethnicity with nonfoster children receiving similar services at the clinic. The clinic files of the two groups then were examined with respect to the occurrence of various life events in order to elucidate those events unique to this group of foster children.

It was expected that despite some overlap (e.g., poverty-related stressors), differences in the experiences of foster and nonfoster children would be uncovered. Those stressful life events occurring with the greatest frequency in the foster care sample then would be candidates for inclusion in future inventories created for use within this population.

Method

Participants

The participants were 44 foster children and 44 nonfoster children referred for psychological services at an early childhood mental health clinic in a large northeastern city. The majority of referrals to this clinic are made by health clinics, community and protective service organizations, schools, and family members. The intake process involves a standardized interview, designed by the clinic, with the child's caregiver by a staff psychologist and observation of the child in the clinic setting, followed by the obtaining of appropriate records and documents.

Foster children were defined as children who had been formally placed into foster care through a social service agency, who were not living in the same home with either biological parent, and who had been in the foster care system for at least 3 months at the time of referral. *Nonfoster children* were defined as children who had no history of out-of-home placements and who were living with at least one biological parent at the time of referral. Children and their caregivers were eligible for inclusion if they were recommended for services after participating in the mental health clinic's intake evaluation.

Every foster child between the ages of 2 and 6 receiving an intake evaluation at the mental health center during a 2-year period was initially considered for the study. This age range was chosen as it is the fastest-growing segment of the foster care population and stressors affecting young children can develop into risk factors for later disorders (Silver, 1999). Eighty foster children were so identified. An attempt then was made to match each child on age (within 6 months), gender, ethnicity, and language spoken to a nonfoster child receiving an intake evaluation at this center during the same time period. There were 36 foster children for whom an appropriate match could not be found based on the aforementioned four variables and who therefore were removed from the sample, resulting in 44 pairs.

The children's ages ranged from 2 years, 4 months to 6 years, 3 months at the time of intake. The mean ages of the children in the foster care and nonfoster care groups were 51.64 months (SD = 10.84) and 51.03 months (SD = 11.90), respectively; there was no significant age difference between the groups, $t(86)$ = .25, *ns*. Sixty (68%) of the children were boys, and 28 (32%) were girls. With regard to ethnicity, 56 (64%) were African American and 32 (36%) Latino. Sixty-eight (77%) of the children spoke only English, and 20 (23%) spoke both English and Spanish. Thirty-eight (86%) of the foster children and 35 (80%) of the nonfoster children received Medicaid or reduced fees, indicative of family income below the poverty level; there was no significant difference on this variable between the groups, $\chi^2(1, N = 88)$ = .72, *ns*. Of the 44 foster children, 22 (50%) were placed with nonrelatives, 18 (41%) were in kinship foster care, and 4 (9%) had been adopted. This group spent a mean number of 37.37 months (SD = 19.93, range from 2 to 69) in care.

Measures

Demographic data. A demographic questionnaire created by the present investigators was used to record each child's foster care status, age, gender, ethnicity, and language spoken.

Life Stressors Inventory (LSI). An inventory of life stressors was designed for the current investigation. The items were derived from a review of the relevant theoretical (e.g., Eagle, 1994) and empirical (e.g., Frame, 2002) research on children in out-of-home-care. Life stressors identified as significant in foster children's psychological development (e.g., number of placements) were included, as were items that appear frequently on traditional stressful life events inventories (e.g., death of a parent, hospitalization). All age-appropriate items from the surveys developed by Coddington (1972) and Johnson and McCutcheon (1980) were included. Items pertaining to preadolescent and adolescent children (e.g., involvement in sports, romantic relationships, job stress) were excluded. The resulting 40-item measure grouped items in the following categories: Relationship with Primary Caregiver (6 items, e.g., "Number of changes in primary caregiver"), Stability of Home Environment (16 items, e.g., "Adult has entered or left the household"), History of Maltreatment (4 items, e.g., "History of neglect"), Biological/Constitutional Factors (5 items, e.g., "Prenatal exposure to drugs"), Medical/Developmental History (6 items, e.g., "Child medical condition"), and Educational History (3 items, e.g., "Child enrolled in special education") (see Table 1).[1] Response options were *yes, no, caregiver does not know*, and *information not in file*.

Procedures

Institutional Review Board approval for this study was obtained both from the hospital of which the clinic is a part and from the researchers' home university. The 88 children's clinic charts were analyzed with respect to the events contained in the LSI. Documents contained in these charts include intake evaluations, reports from prior testing, reports from prior medical and psychological treatment, biographical information collected from caregivers, school reports, and treatment progress reports. The documents were reviewed to determine whether the participants had experienced the stressful life events included on the LSI. One research assistant completed the LSI for each of the 88 children. A second assistant filled out the inventory for eight randomly selected children. Interrater reliability analysis indicated that the investigators agreed on 258 of the 272 (95%) items analyzed. There were no consistent patterns among the 14 items on which they disagreed, and no items were disagreed on significantly more often than others. The research assistant also filled out the demographic questionnaire for each child.

An analysis of missing data revealed that the foster care group was missing information for 11% of the items, while the nonfoster group was missing information for 3%. Of the six categories of items, Educational History was missing the highest percentage of data (31%), with 34% missing in the foster care group and 27% missing in the nonfoster care group. This likely was due to the fact that the clinic's intake form did not inquire directly about school history, and

---

[1] A copy of the inventory can be obtained from the authors.

Table 1

Life Stressors Inventory Items

Item	Group[a]		x^2	Existing measure items
	FC	NFC		
Relationship With Primary Caregiver				
Primary caregiver over age 50[b]	24	0	39.85*	
At least one change in primary caregiver[b]	40	0	73.33*	
Primary caregiver has left the home	5	0	5.30	X
Death of primary caregiver	4	0	4.19	X
Biological mother—deceased	3	0	3.51	X
Current primary caregiver serious health problem	6	3	1.11	X
Stability of Home Environment				
Biological mother—substance abuse	28	1	43.96*	
Child not living with all siblings	19	3	19.37*	
Biological father—substance abuse	11	2	17.96*	
Death of close relative	9	0	10.03	X
Child moved within last 12 months	12	3	6.51	X
Biological father—incarceration	6	3	4.67	X
Primary caregiver recently separated	1	6	3.88	X
Increased fighting among members of household	1	4	1.91	X
Custody dispute involving child	4	1	1.91	
Increased fighting between child and household	9	7	.31	X
Another child has entered or left the home	5	6	.10	X
Adult has entered or left the home	6	5	.10	X
History of Maltreatment				
History of neglect	25	0	36.92*	
History of physical abuse	15	3	11.27*	
History of sexual abuse	8	2	4.40	
Witness to violence in the home	7	7	.02	

Table 1 (continued)
Life Stressors Inventory Items

Item	Group[a]		x^2	Existing measure items
	FC	NFC		
Biological/Constitutional Factors				
Prenatal exposure to drugs	22	2	29.07*	
Prematurity	11	5	5.53	X
Low birth weight	9	4	4.44	
Biological mother—mental illness	8	4	2.18	
Medical/Developmental History				
Developmental delay--language	32	37	1.68	
Child hospitalized	3	2	.21	X
Child medical condition	19	21	.18	
Developmental delay--autistic spectrum	3	3	.00	
Developmental delay--cognitive	16	16	.00	
Educational History				
Placed in special education	15	10	2.64	
Changed schools within last 12 months	5	3	.87	X
Behavior difficulty in school	15	18	.13	X

Note. FC = Children in foster care; NFC = Children living with at least one biological parent.
[a]$n = 44$ in each group. [b]These items originally were worded as "Age of primary caregiver" and "Number of changes in primary caregiver." They were reworded as categorical variables here for comparability with the other items.
*$p < .0015$.

the obtaining of this information was left to the discretion of the intake interviewer. After Educational History, the Biological/Constitutional Factors category was missing the highest percentage of data (9%), with 19% missing in the foster care group and 0% missing in the nonfoster care group. Many foster parents reported that they were unable to answer questions in this category because the placement agency had not provided them with information regarding their foster child's birth history and biological parents.

Between-Group Differences

The foster care group had experienced an average of 8.82 (*SD* = 3.48, range from 3 to 19) stressful life events at the time of review, while the nonfoster group had experienced an average of 4.07 events (*SD* = 2.53, range from 1 to 12). An independent-samples *t* test demonstrated that this difference was significant, $t(86) = 7.33, p < .01$.

Chi-square analyses were conducted to evaluate between-group differences on LSI items, with response options being either *yes* or *no*. A Bonferroni correction due to the large number of comparisons calculated resulted in an adjusted value of $p < .0015$. As presented in Table 1, the foster care and nonfoster care groups differed significantly on eight items. Additionally, two items differed at the $p < .01$ level and eight at the $p < .05$ level.

When these results are examined by category, with respect to the Relationship With Primary Caregiver category, the foster care children were significantly more likely to have a current primary caregiver over age 50 and to have experienced at least one change in their primary caregiver. Independent-samples *t* tests treating current caregiver age and number of changes in primary caregiver as continuous variables revealed similar significant differences, $t(78) = 10.81, p < .01$, and $t(86) = 8.72, p < .01$, respectively. Of the 24 caregivers over the age of 50, 13 (54%) were kinship caregivers raising children to whom they were related.

The foster care and nonfoster care groups differed most in the History of Maltreatment (2 of 4 items) and Stability of Home Environment (3 of 12 items) categories. The foster care children were significantly more likely to have experienced neglect or physical abuse, to be living apart from at least one sibling, and to have had a biological mother and/or father with substance abuse problems. Relatedly, the final significant difference--prenatal exposure to drugs (in the Biological/Constitutional Factors category)--also involved substance abuse. In two categories, Medical/Developmental History and Educational History, the two groups did not differ significantly on any items but experienced several events at similar high rates.

Comparison with Existing Stressful Life Events Measures

As Table 1 demonstrates, many of the items found on the existing measures (Coddington, 1972; Johnson & McCutcheon, 1980) drawn upon for this study occurred infrequently in the foster care group (e.g., "Primary caregiver recently separated" and "Increased fighting among members of household"). Eighty percent of the items endorsed for fewer than six foster children can be found on existing measures. Conversely, and more importantly, many of the stressful events that the foster children did encounter (e.g., "History of neglect" and "At least one change in primary caregiver") are not included in these measures. For example, "Biological mother--substance abuse," which does not appear on the existing measures, was endorsed for 64% (28 out of 44) of foster children. Of the 10 items endorsed most frequently for foster children, only one was found on the existing measures sampled for this study.

Discussion

This study explored differences in the stressful life events experienced by low-income children in foster care and children of comparable socioeconomic status who were living with at least one biological parent. The findings indicated that the foster and nonfoster children differed significantly in both the quantity and the type of the stressful life events experienced. The foster children experienced, on average, more than twice as many stressful life events than did the nonfoster children. Also, the foster children encountered greater levels of neglect and physical abuse. This is not surprising as, by definition, foster children must experience some form of maltreatment in order to be removed from their biological families. Although expected, this finding nonetheless is striking, given the damaging long-term psychological (Edwards, Holden, Felitti, & Anda, 2003; Silver, 1999) and physical (Felitti et al., 1998) effects of child abuse and neglect.

Substance abuse appears to pose a particular challenge in the early lives of children subsequently placed in foster care. The current sample of foster care children was significantly more likely to have been born to mothers (especially) and/or fathers having a substance abuse problem and (following from maternal substance abuse) to have themselves experienced prenatal exposure to drugs or alcohol. The frequent occurrence of neglect and physical abuse was, in part, a likely consequence of this parental substance abuse.

In addition, the foster children experienced a greater number of stressors in their relationship with their primary caregiver. They had been separated from a primary caregiver (due to death or change in placement) significantly more often than had the nonfoster children. None of the nonfoster children in the sample had experienced a change in primary caregiver, while the foster group experienced an average of two and as many as six changes. Again, although this also was expected, it is important to note, given the harmful effect of disrupted caregiver relationships (Eagle, 1994).

Besides having a greater number of changes in primary caregiver, foster care children had significantly older caregivers (both kinship and nonkinship) than did nonfoster children. Twenty-four of the foster caregivers, as compared to none of the nonfoster caregivers, were over the age of 50. Based on a review of the kinship foster parent literature, Geen (2004) reported that parenting by older caregivers could be a risk factor for foster children. He indicated that kinship caregivers are significantly older than nonkinship caregivers and, as a likely result of their age, report higher rates of limiting medical conditions and/or disabilities.

In contrast to this, a survey (Goughler & Trunzo, 2005) of foster care agencies in the United States indicated that older foster parents were viewed as having a wealth of experience in child rearing which enables them to offer tolerance and flexibility in raising foster children. Thus, based on these somewhat conflicting perspectives, it is unclear whether child rearing by older individuals is more of a risk or a protective factor for foster children.

A major focus of this study was identifying stressors relevant to young children in foster care that should be added to existing inventories to improve their validity and utility with this population. Researchers in the areas of foster care and stressful life events currently are using measures that vary widely in content and quality. The development of more appropriate inventories would aid in the standardization of data collection, thus improving our knowledge of the challenges facing young children in out-of-home care. The present research found that many of the items included on widely used inventories occurred with very low frequency in the foster care group. More significantly, stressful life events that often were encountered by foster children, including change in primary caregiver and history of abuse or neglect, are missing from current measures.

In addition to identifying items that would improve data collection concerning foster children, this study also identified important stressors relevant to children of low socioeconomic status who are seen for mental health services. Many of the items relating to medical, developmental, and educational history did not differ significantly between the foster and nonfoster children because they were endorsed at a high rate for both groups. These items included the presence of cognitive or language delays, the presence of a medical condition, and placement in special education. Given the fact that these stressors occurred frequently in the current clinically referred, low-income sample, the inclusion of such items likely would increase the sensitivity of stressful life event inventories used with such populations of children.

The current results were dependent upon the amount and quality of the information contained in the documents in the participants' charts. Each chart included data from multiple reporters, who may have differed in their conceptualization of the items assessed. In addition, the validity of the information likely was influenced by self-report biases and demand characteristics. For instance, only 2 biological mothers reported that their children were prenatally exposed to drugs or alcohol, compared to 22 foster mothers. Although it is likely that rates of maternal substance abuse were indeed lower in the nonfoster care than in the foster care population, biological mothers would be expected to be far less likely to report their own drug and alcohol use than would foster mothers to report the substance use of their foster child's biological mother.

As noted above, a sizable percentage of desired data was classified as "missing." This occurred primarily for two reasons, either because the information could not be found in the chart or because the caregiver being interviewed did not have access to the requested information. Many of the foster parents could not provide birth, developmental, and placement histories because they had not received this information from the agencies that placed the children in their care. Additionally, most children do not receive medical, psychological, and developmental evaluations upon entering care, which limits the information available even to the placement agencies (Urquiza & Wirtz, 1994). Without comprehensive knowledge of the nature of their foster children's delays, it is more difficult for foster parents to connect them with the services and support that they need. Thus, the occurrence of missing data, while a threat to internal validity, also reflects one of the major challenges facing foster parents and placement agencies, as well as researchers.

Valid assessment of stressful life events would constitute a valuable first step in the identification of factors placing foster children at risk for adverse outcomes. As clinicians gain a better understanding of these factors, they can inquire directly about the stressors unique to foster children, thereby gaining information essential for effective assessment and treatment planning. Additionally, a related line of research could profitably focus on uncovering protective factors which, if properly infused into the lives of foster children, might prevent these risk factors from becoming predictive of negative outcomes.

Investigators in the area of foster care have underscored the need for the development and use of standardized instruments with this population (Urquiza & Wirtz, 1994). In addition, those studying the measurement of stressful life events in children in general have emphasized the importance of psychometrically sound and well-validated measures (e.g., Grant et al., 2004). Taken together, these calls highlight the need for the creation and standardization of stressful life events inventories that include items relevant to foster children (both younger and older) and to children living in low-income environments. The present results provide a beginning indication of what some of these items might be.

References

Brand, A. E., & Brinich, P. M. (1999). Behavior problems and mental health contacts in adopted, foster, and nonadopted children. *Journal of Child Psychology and Psychiatry, 40,* 1221-1229.

Bruskas, D. (2008). Children in foster care: A vulnerable population at risk. *Journal of Child and Adolescent Psychiatric Nursing, 21,* 70-77.

Chandler, L. A. (1981). The source of stress inventory. *Psychology in the Schools, 18,* 164-168.

Coddington, R. D. (1972). The significance of life events as etiological factors in the diseases of children: A study of normal population. *Journal of Psychosomatic Research, 16,* 205-213.

Eagle, R. S. (1994). The separation experience of children in long-term care: Theory, research, and implications for practice. *American Journal of Orthopsychiatry, 64,* 421-434.

Edwards, V. J., Holden, G. W., Felitti, V. J., & Anda, R. F. (2003). Relationship between multiple forms of childhood maltreatment and adult mental health in community respondents: Results from the Adverse Childhood Experiences Study. *American Journal of Psychiatry, 160,* 1453–1460.

Fein, E. (1991). Issues in foster family care: Where do we stand? *American Journal of Orthopsychiatry, 61,* 578-583.

Felitti, V. J., Anda, R. F., Nordenberg, D., Williamson, D. F., Spitz, A. M., Edwards, V., et al. (1998). Relationship of childhood abuse and household dysfunction to many of the leading causes of death in adults: The Adverse Childhood Experiences (ACE) Study. *American Journal of Preventive Medicine, 14,* 245-258.

Frame, L. (2002). Maltreatment reports and placement outcomes for infants and toddlers in out-of-home care. *Infant Mental Health Journal, 23,* 517-540.

Geen, R. (2004). The evolution of kinship care policy and practice. *The Future of Children, 14,* 131-149.

Goughler, D. H., & Trunzo, A. C. (2005). Unretired and better than ever: Older adults as foster parents for children. *Families in Society, 86,* 393-400.

Grant, K. E., Compas, B. E., Thurm, A. E., McMahon, S. D., & Gipson, P. Y. (2004). Stressors and child and adolescent psychopathology: Measurement issues and prospective effects. *Journal of Clinical Child and Adolescent Psychology, 33,* 412-425.

Hobbs, G., Hobbs, C., & Wynne, J. (1999). Abuse of children in foster and residential care. *Child Abuse and Neglect, 23,* 1239-1252.

James, S. (2004). Why do foster placements disrupt? An investigation of reasons for placement change in foster care. *Social Service Review, 78,* 601-627.

Johnson, J. H., & McCutcheon, S. M. (1980). Assessing life stress in older children and adolescents: Preliminary findings with the Life Events Checklist. In I. G. Sarason & C. D. Spielberger (Eds.), *Stress and anxiety* (pp. 111-125). Washington, DC: Hemisphere.

Kerker, B. D., & Dore, M. M. (2006). Mental health needs and treatment of foster youth: Barriers and opportunities. *American Journal of Orthopsychiatry, 76,* 138-147.

Kirby, K. M., & Hardesty, P. H. (1998). Evaluating older pre-adoptive foster children. *Professional Psychology: Research and Practice, 29,* 428-436.

Klee, L., Kronstadt, D., & Zlotnick, C. (1997). Foster care's youngest: A preliminary report. *American Journal of Orthopsychiatry, 67,* 290-299.

Lee, B. J., & Goerge, R. M. (1999). Poverty, early childbearing, and child maltreatment: A multinomial analysis. *Children and Youth Services Review, 21,* 755-780.

McGuinness, T. M., & Schneider, K. (2007). Poverty, child maltreatment, and foster care. *Journal of the American Psychiatric Nurses Association, 13,* 296-303.

Morrison, J. M., Frank, S. J., Holland, C. C., & Kates, W. R. (1999). Emotional development and disorders in young children in the child welfare system. In A. Silver, B. Amster, & T. Haeker (Eds.), *Young children in foster care* (pp. 33-64). Baltimore: Paul H. Brookes Publishing.

Newton, R. R., Litrownik, A. J., & Landsverk, J. A. (2000). Children and youth in foster care: Disentangling the relationship between problem behaviors and number of placements. *Child Abuse and Neglect, 24,* 1363-1374.

Poertner, J., Bussey, M., & Fluke, J. (1999). How safe are out-of-home placements? *Children and Youth Services Review, 21,* 549-563.

Silver, B. (1999). Starting young. In A. Silver, B. Amster, & T. Haeker (Eds.), *Young children in foster care* (pp. 3-32). Baltimore: Paul H. Brookes Publishing.

Stahmer, A. C, Leslie, L. K., Hurlburt, M., Barth, R. P., Webb, M. B., Landsverk, J., et al. (2005). Developmental and behavioral needs and service use for young children in child welfare. *Pediatrics, 116,* 891-900.

Urquiza, A. J., & Wirtz, S. J. (1994). Screening and evaluating abused and neglected children entering protective custody. *Child Welfare, 73,* 155-172.

Wilson, K., Sinclair, I., & Gibbs, I. (2000). The trouble with fostercare: The impact of stressful 'events' on foster carers. *British Journal of Social Work, 30,* 193-209.

Author Note

Robyn L. Glover and David S. Glenwick, Department of Psychology, Fordham University.

This article is based on the first author's predoctoral research project, completed under the supervision of the second author. The authors thank Susan Chinitz and Adam Fried for their facilitation of, and assistance in, the data collection process.

Evaluation of the Adults and Children Together (ACT) Against Violence Training Program with Child Care Providers

Volker Thomas
Purdue University

Nilufer Kafescioglu
Dougus University, Istanbul, Turkey

Dreama (Dee) Plybon Love
Purdue University

The present study aimed to develop an outcome measure evaluating the effectiveness of the Adults and Children Together (ACT) Against Violence training program by collecting pre-, post-program, and follow-up data. A two-part questionnaire was administered to 37 child care providers in a pre- and post-test control group design. Changes in the knowledge and skill level of participants were analyzed. Results of the first part of the questionnaire showed that time and group status made a difference in the average total scores. In the second part of the questionnaire, time had a significant effect but group did not. Thus, the first part may be more promising to detect participants' skill and knowledge gains.

The aim of the present study was to build on previous research by developing a reliable and valid outcome measure. More specifically, the purpose of this research was to evaluate the level of skill and knowledge gain of child care providers who participated in the ACT training program (Silva, 2002) by utilizing a research instrument. Developing an outcome measure would contribute to developing evidence-based violence prevention and early intervention programs. The research team in the present study generated a two-part instrument and tested it in a pre- and post-test control-group design to assess the effectiveness of the ACT training program.

All correspondence should be addressed to Volker Thomas, Department of Child Development and Family Studies, Purdue University, 225 Fowler Memorial House, 1200 West State St, West Lafayette, IN 47907-2050. Electronic mail may be sent to thomasv@purdue.edu.

Statistics on child abuse and neglect help highlight the prevalence of violence in young children's lives and establish the need for effective violence prevention programs. In 2005, approximately 3.3 million allegations of child maltreatment were reported nationwide to Child Protective Services and approximately 899,000 children were found to be victims of child maltreatment (U.S. Department of Health and Human Services, 2005). In most states, perpetrators of child abuse and neglect were the parents (84%) and other caregivers (11%) (e.g., foster parents, daycare staff, unmarried partner or parent, legal guardian, and residential facility staff; U.S. Department of Health and Human Services, 2005). Based on the significant number of children affected, there is an urgent need for effective prevention strategies (e.g., education for adults who care for and work with young children).

Numerous studies have addressed the extensive short- and long-term effects of maltreatment on children. These effects include severe developmental consequences (Egeland, 1988; Knutson, DeGamro, & Reid, 2004), medical (Sedlak & Broadhurst, 1996; Wharton, Rosenberg, Sheridan, & Ryan, 2000) and psychological issues (Goodwin, 1996), behavioral problems (Kelley, Thornberry, & Smith, 1997), and eventual delinquency (Widom & Maxfield, 2001). More specifically, findings have shown that maltreated children experience psychological consequences such as low self-esteem, increased fear, guilt, and self-blame (Corby, 2000). As a long-term psychological consequence, interspousal violence was found to be predicted by a history of physical abuse, witnessing domestic violence, and experiencing sexual abuse and neglect in childhood (Bevan & Higgins, 2002). Moreover, neglect in childhood has been found to be associated with increased rates of physical accidents, rashes, infections, malnutrition, physical defects, and problems in language development (Smith & Fong, 2004). As a long-term negative consequence, maltreated children were also found to show higher rates of smoking and other substance use as well as high-risk sexual behaviors (Kendall-Tackett, 2002). Kendall-Tackett also found that maltreated children were at an increased risk of developing hepatitis, diabetes, heart disease, cancer, stroke, are more likely to have surgery, and are at increased risk of having one or more chronic pain symptoms.

Many studies cited above conclude from their findings that more effective strategies need to be developed that address the effects of maltreatment on children. Besides intervention programs treating abused children, a number of violence prevention programs have been designed and researched to reduce the effects of violence on young children (Guttman & Mowder, 2005). One such program is the Adults and Children Together (ACT) Against Violence training program initiated by two national professional organizations: the American Psychological Association (APA) and the National Association for the Education of Young Children (NAEYC). The ACT training program is a unique violence prevention program, training adults as well as focusing on early childhood rather than later stages of development. The ACT program trains adults in young children's lives to become positive role models and teach children constructive conflict resolution strategies (Fuentes & Silva, 2004).

The initial ACT training program research focused on the dissemination, adoption, and implementation efforts (Silva & Randall, 2005). Indeed, researchers recommended focusing on ACT training effectiveness in order to identify program success as well as areas in need of improvement (Guttman & Mowder, 2005; Mowder & Orland, 2006). To be sure, there are relatively very few published outcome research studies on the ACT training program. Recently, however, two outcome studies assessed the effectiveness of the ACT training program (Guttman, Mowder, & Yasik, 2006; Miguel & Howe, 2006).

The Adults and Children Together (ACT) Against Violence Training Program

The ACT Against Violence Training Program was developed by APA and NAEYC to address early violence prevention. The violence prevention program has multiple components, including a national multimedia campaign as well as a training program. The national campaign focuses on raising adult awareness of the need to create supportive learning environments for young children. These supportive learning environments have been shown to buffer against the development of aggressive behavior of young children (Silva, 2002). For example, in a longitudinal study, Kokko and Pulkkinen (2000) found that a warm family environment emphasizing supportive parenting and being involved in children's lives protected children from repeating destructive behaviors. In another study, researchers evaluated the impact of the Early Risers violence prevention program with high-risk children and their parents (August, Realmuto, Hectner, & Bloomquist, 2001). The findings showed that, compared to the control group, the children and parents who participated in the program showed significant improvement in their academic achievement and school behaviors. Particularly, the most severely aggressive children showed significant improvements in their self-regulation compared to the control group.

One of the major ACT training program goals is to disseminate research-based knowledge (e.g., child development, the development of violent behaviors) to the influential adults in children's lives (e.g., parents, caregivers, teachers). The training program is described as a social-cognitive intervention (Silva & Randall, 2005). The major assumption of the intervention is based on Bandura's social learning theory proposing that children observe, learn from, and imitate the adults and others in their lives (Bandura, 1973). Thus, the ACT training program strives to teach adults how to model social skills and promote nonviolent problem-solving (Fuentes & Silva, 2004). Indeed, early childhood (i.e., 0-8 years of age) is a critical time for children to learn basic social skills which have a long-lasting impact on their lives (Guttman & Mowder, 2005; Mowder & Orland, 2006; Silva & Randall, 2005). By focusing on this age range, the ACT training program emphasizes early intervention and prevention strategies (e.g., nonviolent ways for children to solve problems; Silva & Randall).

Three main topics covered in the ACT training program are: (a) child development (e.g., brain development, cognitive development, emotional development), (b) development and consequences of violence in children's lives, and (c) early violence prevention skills. The training is presented in four modules: (a) anger management, (b) social problem solving, (c) positive discipline, and (d) monitoring media violence (Silva & Randall, 2005). These four modules include appropriate nonviolent strategies that caregivers can use and model for young children (Mowder & Orland, 2006). For example, the anger management module is designed to teach appropriate emotional expression and anger management skills. The social problem solving module focuses on developing constructive conflict resolution skills and pro-social behaviors, emphasizing the family's role in teaching children problem solving techniques. The discipline module provides developmentally appropriate avenues to deal with young children's challenging or problematic behaviors. The media violence module includes information on the effects of media violence on young children, evaluating media focused on young children, and developing strategies to reduce media impact (Silva & Randall). Thus far, the ACT training program has reached more than 100 community coordinators and more than 30,000 adults nationwide (Stambor, 2006).

Evaluation Research on the ACT Training Program

APA and NAEYC emphasize the role of evaluation in order to improve the usability and impact of the ACT program (Adults and Children Together Against Violence, 2005). With support from Center for Disease Control, The Battelle Centers for Public Health Research and Evaluation evaluated the dissemination and implementation of the ACT training program in 2003. Besides the archival and registration data, the researchers collected interview data from national program developers, and conducted telephone surveys and focus groups with ACT professionals. Findings show that 91.7% of the national program trainees and 85.3% of the Kansas City local program trainees implemented ACT activities in their workplaces or communities. The study reveals that early violence prevention awareness increased and the program had long-term positive effects on the attitudes and behaviors of the adults toward children (Silva & Randall, 2005).

The ACT training program itself has only been evaluated in a few studies. One such study was conducted by Guttman et al. (2006). The researchers compared the knowledge gain of 226 early childhood professionals and doctoral students in the New York area, receiving the ACT training program, with a comparison group of 51 participants who did not receive the training. ACT knowledge questionnaires consisting of True/False items and perception questionnaires with a Likert-type scale were created for each of the four ACT training modules and administered in a pre- and post-test design. The perception questionnaire asked participants how much knowledge they perceived to have gained by participating in the ACT training program. Further, at the end of the training, participants were asked about training usefulness in a Likert-type scale and answered a yes or no question on any difference the ACT program made for them. Guttman et al. found a significant difference between the treatment and comparison groups in knowledge gain, with the treatment group showing greater knowledge gain in each of the four modules. The treatment group also showed a significant increase in their perception of knowledge from pre-test to post-test. The media violence module appears the most useful ACT training module; overall, 94.7% of the trainees reported that the ACT training program made a difference for them. Limitations of the study were that the participants were not randomly assigned to groups and also that the knowledge gain was measured exclusively after program presentation. In the end, the study suggests ACT training program effectiveness with increased participant knowledge gains (Guttman et al.).

In another study, Miguel and Howe (2006) collected pre-, post-, and 3-month follow-up data from 51 participants in California. The researchers utilized the 14-item APA Self-Assessment Form to assess the ACT training participants' confidence with implementing the program. In addition, Miguel and Howe created a new measure called the ACT Evaluation Scenarios to assess participants' child development knowledge, problem-solving skills, and assimilation of the ACT program. The ACT Evaluation Scenarios consists of eight scenarios, similar to the ACT training curriculum, designed to reflect the age range targeted by the ACT program. In the study, participants were asked to provide answers to each scenario in a free response format.

For the 3-month follow-up, Miguel and Howe (2006) used the online version of the Batelle's study Evaluation Survey. The findings show that even after the training, participants perceived and displayed an increase in their child development and violence prevention skills and knowledge. Participants also showed increased knowledge at the 3-month follow-up. A limitation of this study was the lack of psychometric data on the ACT Evaluation Scenarios internal consistency. Although there was ACT training program effectiveness displayed, another limitation was no control group in the study.

The present study built on previous ACT training program research. Thus, a major contribution of the present study is the provision of outcome data regarding the ACT training program. To accomplish the evaluation, a two-part instrument called the ACT Evaluation Questionnaire was developed. The first part of the questionnaire consists of seven of the eight ACT Evaluation scenarios developed by Miguel and Howe (2006). In the present study, the seven scenarios were changed slightly from the original and responses were presented in a multiple choice format rather than a free response format. Further, additional questions were developed to measure ACT participant knowledge gain. The present study also provides some data regarding the 3-month follow-up effects of the ACT training program.

Method

Participants

Pilot study/first phase. Upon Institutional Review Board (IRB) approval, 240 former participants of the ACT training program were identified through APA to be invited to participate in the pilot study. Of these, 50 participants (86% women) took part in this first phase of the study. The ethnic backgrounds of the participants were as follows: 68% were Caucasian, 26% were African American, and 6% were Hispanic. Age ranges of the participants were: 16% between 24-30 years, 32% between 31-40 years, 28% between 41-50 years, and 24% were in the age range of 51-70 years. Education level of the participants varied: 10% had some college, 40% had bachelor's degrees, 28% had master's degrees, and 18% had doctoral degrees (4% did not respond).

Second phase and follow-up. After the pilot study, the original questionnaire was revised and child care providers were recruited from the Child Care Answers in Indianapolis, IN child care resource and referral database. Participants were sent out an electronic invitation both for the ACT training program and the research study. A total of 39 child care providers from four different settings in central Indiana participated in the second phase: family child care, center child care, registered ministry child care, and legally licensed exempt child care settings. There were 27 participants in the treatment group and 12 in the control group. Four participants in the treatment and three in the control group did not complete the post-test measurements. Participants received monetary compensation for their participation in each testing: $30 for participating in the pre-test, another $30 after the post-test, and $20 at the completion of the 3-month follow-up. At the 3-month follow-up, a total of 27 participants returned the follow-up questionnaires mailed to them. The demographic information on the participants of the second phase and follow-up are presented in Table 1.

Procedures

For the pilot study, former participants of the ACT training program were contacted via email and asked to respond to an electronic questionnaire. The participants had agreed to participate in the pilot study by electronically submitting

Table 1
Demographic Information of Participants

Variable	Treatment Group (*n* = 27)	Control Group (*n* = 12)	Follow-up (*n* = 27)
Gender (%)			
Male	3.7	8.3	7.4
Female	96.3	91.7	88.9
Ethnicity (%)			
Caucasian	25.9	66.7	40.7
African American	74.1	33.3	59.3
Age (years)			
20-30	11.1	25.0	3.7
31-40	22.2	25.0	29.6
41-50	29.6	8.3	22.2
51+	37.0	41.7	44.4
Education level (%)			
High School	22.2	8.3	18.5
Some College	55.6	58.3	51.9
Bachelor's Degree	18.5	33.3	22.2
Master's	3.7	0.0	3.8
Work Setting (%)			
Family Child Care	48.1	50.0	40.7
Child Care Center	14.8	8.3	18.5
Ministry Child Care	29.6	33.3	37.0
After School Care	7.4	8.3	3.7

the informed consent form. Participation in the pilot study was voluntary and confidential. Of 240 contacted, 50 former ACT participants agreed to be part of the pilot study (response rate of 20.8%).

In the beginning of the second phase of the study, the ACT program trainer and a research assistant met with a group of interested participants in an information session. The trainer briefly explained the ACT training program to the participants and left the room afterwards. The research assistant emphasized that participation in the study was voluntary and that the participants could receive the ACT training program regardless of their participation in the research project. The potential participants were also allowed to withdraw from the study at any time without any effect on their participation in the ACT training program. Confidentiality of participants was ensured by assignment of an identification number for each participant and the exclusion of the ACT program trainer in data collection.

Informed consent was obtained from participants before filling out the ACT Evaluation Questionnaire in the first session. All participants completed the ACT Evaluation Questionnaire for the first time before entering the ACT training program. Participants drew random numbers during the information session to get assigned to either a treatment or control group. However, due to scheduling issues the treatment group had a greater number of participants than the control group, because some participants were unable to attend the sessions scheduled for the control group and asked to be part of the treatment group training sessions. The ACT training program lasted for 5 weeks and consisted of weekly 90-minute sessions each. The sessions followed the ACT training modules such as young children and violence, anger management, social problem solving, discipline, and media violence. After the treatment group completed the training, both groups filled out the ACT Evaluation Questionnaire for the second time. The control group participants started the training program after the treatment group had completed their training. Three months after their respective completion of the training, participants of the treatment and control groups were sent the ACT Evaluation Questionnaire via regular mail with self-addressed and stamped envelopes and asked to participate in the follow-up data collection.

Measures

Item generation and pilot study questionnaire. The pilot study measure started with a demographic information form. In the questionnaire section, seven of the eight scenarios developed by Miguel and Howe (2006) were slightly changed to fit with the sample of the present study (child care providers) and used in a different format than its original. Miguel and Howe originally developed the scenarios similar to the ones used in the ACT training sessions. The scenarios were created in a way to assess participants' application, knowledge, and skills regarding child development and violence prevention, and their ability to generate positive nonviolent problem solving solutions. Each scenario is pertinent to a typical child care dilemma (e.g., cleaning up after play) that deals with management issues with young children. The same five questions directed at each scenario that were presented in an open-ended format by Miguel and Howe were used in the pilot phase of the present study. The questions were: (a) "Why is this happening," (b) "What can children understand and do at this age," (c) "How would you respond to this situation? What specifically would you say or do," (d) "What could you do to prevent this from happening in the future," and (e) "If you did not handle this situation very well, do you think it would have any lasting effects on the child in the future?"

The research team's contribution to the measure in the pilot phase of the present study was a response pool that was generated for the five questions that could be marked on a 5-point Likert scale ranging from "strongly agree" to "strongly disagree." Developing the response scale transformed the original Miguel and Howe (2006) scenarios with open-ended questions that could be analyzed using qualitative methods into a measure of continuous variables to which quantitative analysis could be applied. The response pool was generated by a Child Development and Family Studies faculty member experienced in instrument development, a university Extension Specialist who is responsible for disseminating knowledge generated through research to the general public by training County Extension Specialists across the state and who is also an ACT trainer, and a graduate research assistant. The responses were generated in line with the ACT curriculum and age-appropriate developmental characteristics of children from birth to age 8.

Overall, the pilot study questionnaire included seven scenarios. For each scenario respondents were asked five questions, for each question they could check one response on a 4-point Likert scale. Thus, the questionnaire had 4 times 5 (= 20) items for each of the seven scenarios adding up to 20 times 7 (= 140) possible items to be checked. The responses were analyzed and it was determined that the items with the highest endorsement would make up the multiple choice items of the revised questionnaire. Cronbach's *alpha* for internal consistency of this measure was .86. Mean scores for the items and item correlations were calculated and analyzed to determine the outliers and which items would be included, excluded, or modified. Almost half of the items were excluded or modified and replaced with new items which were worded more strongly for participants to differentiate among multiple choice options in the revised questionnaire. A total of 61 items from the pilot study questionnaire were included without any changes because their mean scores reflected an agreement among the participants. In addition, five questions directed at each scenario were reduced to four. The fifth question, "If you did not handle this situation very well, do you think it would have any lasting effects on the child in the future?" was eliminated because the question appeared to be more suitable for an open-ended format than a multiple choice format. In the end, each scenario had four questions, each with four possible responses, and one of each was designated to be "correct."

ACT Evaluation Questionnaire. The ACT Evaluation Questionnaire started with the demographic information form. The rest of the questionnaire consisted of two parts. The revised pilot study questionnaire with the multiple choice items formed the ACT Evaluation Questionnaire Part I. The final questionnaire included seven scenarios with the same four questions. The participants could choose from four multiple choice responses to answer each question. The questionnaire items were designed to differentiate the knowledge and skill level of the participants. For example, in a scenario with a 6-month-old pulling the caregiver's hair, when the question of what children understand and do at this age was posed, the four response choices provided were: (a) "They learn about the world by touching things around them," (b) "They understand when adults say, No," (c) "They understand that pulling hair hurts," and (d) "They see situations from another person's point of view." Choosing the most appropriate answer demonstrated the child care provider's knowledge of age appropriate expectations from children in the age range proposed in the scenario. In addition, other questions such as "How would you respond to this situation?" measured participants' level of problem-solving skills. Overall, the maximum score for the ACT Evaluation Questionnaire Part I was 28. Thus, a higher score on this section displayed a greater number of correct answers for the participant. For this first part of the questionnaire, the internal consistency reliability estimate Cronbach's *alpha* was .65 (including pre-, post- and follow-up measurements for both groups).

A second part, with a total of 30 items, including 9 reversed items, was added to the ACT Evaluation Questionnaire as Part II. In this section, the participants were presented with statements that are directly related to five areas of the ACT training sessions. The first included the general introduction to the ACT program, including general information regarding young children and violence. The next four areas included the four training modules: anger management, social problem solving, discipline, and media violence. Six items for each of the five areas were generated based on the main concepts of the areas. The participants were asked to rate each item on a 5-point Likert scale ranging from strongly disagree (1) to strongly agree (5). The total score ranged from 30 to 150. For the ACT Evaluation Questionnaire Part II, the Cronbach's *alpha* was .67 on the basis of treatment and control group pre-, post-test, and follow-up responses.

Data Analysis of ACT Evaluation Questionnaire

In order to test the differences in knowledge and skill levels of the treatment and control groups from pre- to post- and follow-up, the data from the ACT Evaluation Questionnaire were analyzed with a two-way mixed analysis of variance. The two-way mixed analysis of variance was chosen since it eliminates the disadvantages of missing data due to lost participants in any of the time points (Chan, 2004). In the second phase of our study, 4 participants in the treatment group and 3 in the control group did not have post-test measurements. However, the mixed model technique can be used with such unbalanced datasets. The two-way analysis of variance was appropriate since we had two independent variables (time and group) and the mixed model was appropriate since we had one between groups independent variable (group; with two conditions of treatment and control) and one repeated measures independent variable (time; with three conditions of pre-test, post-test, follow-up) to analyze.

Results

Knowledge and skill level changes on the ACT Evaluation Questionnaire were analyzed for treatment and control groups from pre-test to post-test and 3-month follow-up. Pre- and post-test means and standard deviations for treatment and control groups are presented in Table 2. In order to compare the treatment and control group scores, a two-way mixed analysis of variance was conducted with time (pre-test, post-test, and follow-up) as the within subjects factor and group (treatment versus control) as the between-subjects factor. Results for both parts of the questionnaire with F values and significance levels can be found in Tables 3 and 4.

Table 2

Means and Standard Deviations for the Treatment and Control Groups in the ACT Evaluation Questionnaire Part I and II

	Treatment Group			Control Group		
	Pre	Post	Follow-up	Pre	Post	Follow-up
ACT Evaluation Part I						
M	26.1	25.9	26.7	23.8	25.0	25.3
SD	0.4	0.4	0.4	0.6	0.7	0.5
ACT Evaluation Part II						
M	115.7	123.1	122.8	119.1	120.9	122.3
SD	1.4	1.8	2.0	2.1	2.8	3.0

Note. ACT Evaluation Part I: scores range from 0-28. ACT Evaluation Part II: scores range from 0-150.

Table 3

Two-Way Mixed Analysis of Variance for ACT Evaluation Questionnaire Part I

Source	*df*	*F*	*p*
Between-subjects effects			
Group	1,37	7.31	.010
Within-subjects effects			
Time	2,37	4.58	.017
Time x group	2,37	2.15	.131

Table 4
Two-Way Mixed Analysis of Variance for ACT Evaluation Questionnaire Part II

Source	df	F	p
Between-subjects effects			
Group	1,37	0.01	.939
Within-subjects effects			
Time	2,37	7.16	.002
Time x group	2,37	1.95	.157

ACT Evaluation Questionnaire Part I

Results from the ACT Evaluation Questionnaire Part I indicated that the effect of group was statistically significant, $F(1, 37) = 7.31, p = .01$, and there was also a significant effect for time, $F(2, 37) = 4.58, p < .05$. However, the interaction effect was not significant, $F(2, 37) = 2.15, p = .13$. Further post-hoc analyses with the Tukey-Kramer test were conducted to delineate where the significant differences were. Although the total scores on the ACT Evaluation Questionnaire Part I for all participants (both treatment and control) showed an increase from pre-test ($M = 24.91, SD = 0.35$) to post-test ($M = 25.43, SD = 0.40$), this difference was not statistically significant ($p = .31$). There was also a slight increase from post-test to follow-up ($M = 25.99, SD = 0.32$) for all participants (both treatment and control) but again this difference was not statistically significant ($p = .33$). The only statistically significant difference was found between the pre-test and follow-up scores ($p = .01$) in which participants (both treatment and control) scored higher in follow-up. When the treatment and control group mean scores were examined with all three times together (pre-test, post-test, follow-up), participants in the treatment group ($M = 26.23, SD = 0.32$) had a greater score than the control group ($M = 24.66, SD = 0.49$) at $p = .01$ significance level.

Pairwise comparisons also showed a statistically significant ($p < .05$) difference between pre-test scores of the treatment group ($M = 26.1, SD = 0.4$) and pre-test scores of the control group ($M = 23.8, SD = 0.6$). All other pairwise comparisons were statistically not significant [e.g., difference between the treatment group's pre-test ($M = 26.1, SD = 0.4$) and post-test scores ($M = 25.9, SD = 0.4$) were not significant, $p = 0.99$; difference between the post-test scores of the treatment group ($M = 25.9, SD = 0.4$) and post-test scores of the control group ($M = 25.0, SD = 0.7$) were not significant, $p = 0.86$)].

ACT Evaluation Questionnaire Part II

Results demonstrated that the effect of time was statistically significant, $F(2, 37) = 7.16, p < .01$. However, neither the effect of group, $F(1, 37) = 0.01, p =$

.94, nor the interaction effect were significant, $F(2, 37) = 1.95$, $p = .16$. Post-hoc analyses with the Tukey-Kramer test showed that participants had higher scores on average in the post-test ($M = 121.96$, $SD = 1.66$) than the pre-test ($M = 117.39$, $SD = 1.25$) with a statistical significance level of $p < .05$. Even though there was a slight increase in the mean scores from post-test ($M = 121.96$, $SD = 1.66$) to follow-up ($M = 122.53$, $SD = 1.82$), this difference was not statistically significant ($p = .95$). However, the increase in the means from pre-test to follow-up was statistically significant ($p < .01$).

Pairwise comparisons resulted in two significant differences for the treatment group. The treatment group's post-test scores ($M = 123.08$, $SD = 1.77$) were higher than their pre-test scores ($M = 115.70$, $SD = 1.39$) at a $p < .001$ level. The treatment group's follow-up scores ($M = 122.80$, $SD = 1.98$) were also higher than their pre-test scores at a significance level of $p < .01$. The other comparisons were not found to be statistically significant [e.g., difference between the post-test scores of the treatment group ($M = 123.1$, $SD = 2.0$) and post-test scores of the control group ($M = 120.9$, $SD = 2.8$) were not significant, $p = 0.98$; difference between the control group's post-test ($M = 120.1$, $SD = 2.8$) and follow-up scores ($M = 122.3$, $SD = 3.0$) were not significant, $p = 0.99$)]

Discussion

The purpose of this study was primarily to develop and assess a two-part outcome measure that would evaluate the effectiveness of the ACT training program, but also to provide additional information on the usefulness of the ACT program. For the first part of the ACT Evaluation Questionnaire, results showed a significant difference between the treatment and control group scores at different points of measurement. However, the treatment group's scores did not show any significant differences from pre-test to post-test. There were no significant differences between the post-test scores of the treatment and control group either.

In addition, since the participants in the control group went through the ACT training after their post-test measurements at the time of the completion of the treatment group's training, the control group's follow-up measurements were also expected to highlight a gain in knowledge and skill level when compared to their pre-test or post-test scores. However, these measurements did not reflect any significant differences. This finding may be explained by the high pre-test and post-test (i.e., pre-training) scores of the control group participants.

For the second part of the questionnaire, time made a difference in terms of participants' total scores, reflecting skill and knowledge gain. More specifically, the treatment group had higher scores both in their post-test and follow-up measurements when compared to their pre-test measurements. The second part of the questionnaire did not detect any difference between the scores of the treatment and control group participants.

In sum, the first part of the questionnaire was able to show significant improvements for the treatment group in follow-up when compared to the control group before the control group participants received any ACT training. The treatment group also had improved their scores in the second part of the ACT Evaluation Questionnaire immediately after they received the training and during 3-month follow-up when compared to their own measurements before receiving any training.

A major limitation of the study was the small sample size and the attrition of participants in post-test and follow-up stages of the project. Another limitation was that the study was located in only one area. These limitations make it impossible to generalize the study findings. The present study reflects some improvements when compared to previous studies due to the presence of a control group, follow-up measurements, and, for the most part, random assignment of the participants to two groups. However, random assignment could be carried out more strictly if all participants' schedules had allowed for the original assignment to groups. A unique contribution of the study was the development of multiple choice items for the first part of the ACT Evaluation Questionnaire to be used with the childhood scenarios originally created by Miguel and Howe (2006). Use of multiple choice items might add to the knowledge gained from the original open-ended format of the scale. In addition, analysis of the multiple-choice questionnaire adds quantitative aspects to the methods used in the ACT outcome studies. However, the use of the same scenarios at pre-, post-test, and follow-up measurements might have caused a memorization effect, or led participants to think about the scenarios over time, in the present study. In future research use of different scenarios to avoid memorization is recommended. The multiple choice questions can also be made somewhat more difficult to make the guessing of the correct answer more difficult which would further contribute to the reliability of this measure.

References

Adults and Children Together Against Violence. (2005). Retrieved May 2, 2007 from http://actagainstviolence.apa.org

August, G. J., Realmuto, G. M., Hectner, J. M., & Bloomquist, M. L. (2001). An integrated components preventive intervention for aggressive elementary school children: The Early Risers Program. *Journal of Consulting & Clinical Psychology, 69,* 614-626.

Bandura, A. (1973). *Aggression: A social learning analysis.* Englewood Cliffs, NJ: Prentice-Hall.

Bevan, E., & Higgins, D. J. (2002). Is domestic violence learned? The contribution of five forms of child maltreatment to men's violence and adjustment. *Journal of Family Violence, 17,* 223-245.

Chan, Y. H. (2004). Repeated measurement analysis (mixed models). *Singapore Medical Journal, 45,* 456-461.

Corby, B. (2000). *Child abuse: Towards a knowledge base* (2nd ed). Buckingham: Open University Press.

Egeland, B. (1988). The consequences of physical and emotional neglect on the development of young children. *Child Neglect Monograph: Proceedings from a Symposium* (pp. 7-19). Washington, DC: U.S. Department of Health & Human Services.

Fuentes, M. A., & Silva, J. (2004). Bullying in schools: How can the ACT against violence project help? *The Community Psychologist, 37.* Retrieved May 1, 2007 from http://smhp.psych.ucla.edu/scra/bullyinginschools.pdf

Goodwin, J. M. (1996). Adult survivors of child abuse and neglect. In S. J. Kaplan (Ed.), *Family violence: A clinical and legal guide* (pp. 209-240). Washington, DC: American Psychiatric Press.

Guttman, M., & Mowder, B. (2005). The ACT training program: The future of violence prevention aimed at young children and their caregivers. *Journal of Early Childhood and Infant Psychology, 1,* 25-36.

Guttman, M., Mowder, B., & Yasik, A. E. (2006). The ACT against violence training program: A preliminary investigation of knowledge gained by early childhood professionals. *Professional Psychology: Research and Practice, 37,* 717-723.

Kelley, B. T., Thornberry, T. P., & Smith, C. A. (1997). *In the wake of childhood maltreatment.* Washington, DC: National Institute of Justice. Retrieved May 1, 2007 from http://www.ncjrs.gov/pdffiles1/165257.pdf

Kendall-Tackett, K. (2002). The health effects of childhood abuse: Four pathways by which abuse can influence health. *Child Abuse & Neglect, 26,* 715-729.

Knutson, J. F., DeGamro, D. S., & Reid, J. B. (2004). Social disadvantage and neglectful parenting as precursors to the development of antisocial and aggressive child behavior: Testing a theoretical model. *Child Development, 30,* 187-205.

Kokko, K., & Pulkkinen, L. (2000). Aggression in childhood and long-term unemployment in adulthood: A cycle of maladaptation and some protective factors. *Developmental Psychology, 36,* 463-472.

Miguel, J. J., & Howe, T. R. (2006). Implementing and evaluating a national early violence preventing program at the local level: Lessons from ACT (Adults and Children Together) against violence. *Journal of Early Childhood and Infant Psychology, 2,* 17-38.

Mowder, M. S., & Orland, S. L. (2006). The ACT against violence training program: Targeting pre-service elementary school teachers. *Journal of Early Childhood and Infant Psychology, 2,* 39-50.

Sedlak, A., & Broadhurst, D. (1996). *Third national incidence study of child abuse and neglect: NIS 3*. US Department of Health and Human Services.

Silva, J. M. (2002). *ACT implementation handbook*. Washington DC: American Psychological Association.

Silva, J. M., & Randall, A. (2005). Giving psychology away: Educating adults to ACT against early childhood violence. *Journal of Early Childhood and Infant Psychology, 1,* 37-44.

Smith, M. G., & Fong, R. (2004). *The children of neglect: When no one cares.* New York: Brunner-Routledge.

Stambor, Z. (2006). Putting ACT to the test. *GradPSYCH, 4.* Retrieved May 3, 2007 from http://gradpsych.apags.org/jan06/act.html

U.S. Department of Health and Human Services, Administration on Children, Youth, and Families (2005). *Child Maltreatment 2005.* Washington, DC: U.S. Government Printing Office.

Wharton, R. H., Rosenberg, S., Sheridan, R. L., & Ryan, D. P. (2000). Long-term medical consequences of physical abuse. In R. M. Reece (Ed.), *Treatment of child abuse: Common mental health, medical, and legal practitioners* (pp. 117-137). Baltimore, MD: Johns Hopkins University Press.

Widom, C. S., & Maxfield, M. G. (2001). An update on the cycle of violence. *National Institute of Justice Research in Brief.* Retrieved May 1, 2007 from http://wwwlncjrs.gov/pdffiles1/nij/184894.pdf

Anxiety in Early Childhood: What Do We Know?

Cindy Altman, Julie L. Sommer, & Kara E. McGoey
Duquesne University

Anxiety is frequently cited as one of the most common mental health conditions affecting children and adolescents, yet little is presently known about the experience of anxiety among toddlers and preschool-aged children. Separation-related concerns seem to be the most typical manifestation of anxiety in young children; there is relatively less empirical support for further differentiation of anxiety during early childhood. The current literature base largely supports the contention that a complex interaction of both individual and environmental variables is implicated in the development of anxiety, and that anxiety can potentially have profound implications for the current and future functioning of young sufferers. The assessment of anxiety in early childhood should aid clinicians in understanding the etiology of the child's distress so that appropriate and individualized approaches to treatment can be planned.

Anxiety is frequently cited as one of the most common mental health problems experienced by children and adolescents (e.g., Morris & March, 2004), yet it becomes apparent in perusing recently published literature that a dearth of studies related to anxiety in toddlers and preschool-aged children have been conducted to date. As a consequence of the lack of research attention afforded to this population, relatively little is known about the experience of anxiety among young children as compared to their adolescent and adult counterparts. The potential knowledge to be gained from studies of anxiety in early childhood is vital for improving early identification of anxiety and informing future approaches to prevention and intervention of anxiety during this phase of development.

In an effort to clarify the present state of knowledge pertaining to anxiety among young children, this paper briefly summarizes the symptoms most commonly associated with anxiety in this age group and discusses multiple factors that have previously been implicated in the development of anxiety in young children. Numerous approaches to assessment and treatment of anxiety in early childhood are also presented before discussing implications for clinical practice, addressing several limitations in the reviewed literature, and suggesting

All correspondence should be addressed to Kara McGoey, Duquesne University, 209A Canevin Hall, Pittsburgh, PA 15282. Electronic mail may be sent to: mcgoeyk@duq.edu.

potential areas for future research. The intent of this work is to provide a succinct overview of the above issues in an attempt to stimulate further discussion and research in these topical areas.

Symptoms of Anxiety

As Lyons-Ruth, Zeanah, and Benoit (2003) note, the way a child functions during the early years of life is quite different from functioning at later developmental stages. This applies equally well to the experience of anxiety across the lifespan as it does to other aspects of development. A limited amount of study has focused on anxiety among young children to date. Nonetheless, researchers tend to agree that symptoms of separation anxiety, as described in the fourth edition, text revision of the *Diagnostic and Statistical Manual of Mental Disorders* (DSM-IV-TR) published by the American Psychiatric Association (APA, 2000), are the predominant manifestation of anxiety in the early years of childhood (e.g., Weems & Costa, 2005). Due to the prevalence of separation anxiety disorder in early childhood and available research devoted to this topic, the next section focuses wholly on it, while the remainder of text pertains to anxiety in more general terms.

Separation Anxiety Disorder

Separation anxiety is characterized by the experience of marked distress when separation from the home or an attachment figure occurs, or perhaps is merely anticipated by a child (APA, 2000). More specifically, children with separation anxiety may be clingy (APA), be tearful or cry inconsolably at times of separation (Schniering, Hudson, & Rapee, 2000), evidence nightmares or other sleep difficulties (Velting, Setzer, & Albano, 2002), and/or present with temper tantrums that become especially intense when separation is required (Choate, Pincus, Eyberg, & Barlow, 2005). Children with separation-related concerns also often present with somatic complaints, most commonly headaches, stomachaches, and nausea (Velting et al.). This may lead to frequent visits to the pediatrician and/or school nurse and in some cases, claims of feeling so poorly that the child cannot attend school altogether (Choate et al.; Christophersen & Mortweet, 2001).

Although anxiety surrounding separation is generally considered a normal facet of child development in the early years of life, there may be reason for concern when: (a) a child's anxiety related to separation from home or those to whom the child is attached is deemed excessive, (b) such anxiety is beyond what is expected given the child's age and developmental level, and/or (c) the anxiety is believed to adversely impact the child's everyday functioning. Only when a child's anxiety is non-normative in any of these ways and symptoms have been experienced for the requisite length of time outlined in the DSM-IV-TR (APA, 2000) is a diagnosis of separation anxiety disorder warranted, provided that other potential explanations for the child's symptoms have been investigated and ruled out.

Additional Subtypes of Anxiety

There has historically been some debate regarding whether additional subtypes of anxiety that are identified among older youth and adults are also evidenced by the very young (Spence, Rapee, McDonald, & Ingram, 2001), and there is limited available data attesting to how presentation of these varieties differs earlier versus later in life. Nonetheless, the following are additional DSM-IV-TR (APA, 2000) anxiety-related disorders (and the hallmark characteristic of each) from which young children may suffer: (a) generalized anxiety disorder – free-floating anxiety that is present across a variety of contexts; (b) obsessive-compulsive disorder – a pattern of recurrent, persistent, and distressing thoughts (e.g., fear of becoming dirty) that drive an individual to act in a certain way (e.g., repeated hand-washing) to relieve the anguish that is experienced; (c) panic disorder – the experience of unexpected panic attacks (characterized by physiological symptoms such as accelerated heart rate, increased sweat production, and dizziness), along with fear and uncertainty of when and where additional attacks may occur; (d) posttraumatic stress disorder – continual re-experiencing of a previously endured traumatic event (through dreams, flashbacks, or repetitive play, for instance) along with increased arousal, avoidance and numbing; (e) social phobia – intense concern of embarrassing oneself or being negatively evaluated by others in social or performance situations; or (f) specific phobia – marked anxiety related to a specific object (e.g., snakes) or situation (e.g., flying).

Alternative Classification

In response to numerous criticisms aimed at the use of the DSM-IV-TR (APA, 2000) classification scheme with young children, an alternative, the *Diagnostic Classification of Mental Health and Developmental Disorders of Infancy and Early Childhood: Revised Edition* ([DC: 0-3R]; Zero to Three, 2005), was developed specifically for use with the early childhood population. Although its name implies use only for children ranging in age from birth to 3, it can be utilized for children up to the age of 5 (Egger & Angold, 2006). The DC: 0-3R system is similar to the DSM-IV-TR (APA), in that it permits clinicians to make a multiaxial diagnosis. A child's clinical diagnosis is coded on Axis I; separation concerns and other anxiety-related disturbances are coded as "anxiety disorders of infancy and early childhood." Axis II classifies disorders in the caregiver-child relationship (e.g., under-involvement, abuse), while the remaining three axes of the DC: 0-3R system closely mirror their DSM-IV-TR (APA) counterparts.

The DC: 0-3R system (Zero to Three, 2005) classifies anxiety in young children as one of four specific disorders: (a) generalized anxiety disorder, (b) separation anxiety disorder, (c) specific phobia, and (d) social anxiety disorder. In addition, a diagnosis of anxiety disorder not otherwise specified can be given when children are younger than 2 years or the requisite number of symptoms for diagnosis of a specific anxiety disorder is not met. Unique to the DC: 0-3R approach is the five general characteristics of all anxiety disorders that must be met for diagnosis of any anxiety-related disturbance. These five criteria represent developmental characteristics and distinctions to define the anxiety or fear as a clinical disorder.

Relatively few studies have investigated the use of the original or revised DC: 0-3 system to date (Evangelista & McLellan, 2004). However, it seems to offer promise, in that it focuses on the manifestation of psychopathology exclusively among the very young. It also encourages a comprehensive view of a child's difficulty and contributory variables, which may facilitate planning of appropriate treatment to a greater extent than other available diagnostic systems (Evangelista & McLellan).

Regardless of the particular complement of symptoms that plague a youngster who presents with anxiety, symptom severity, degree of distress, and functional impact should all be considered before making a formal diagnosis. It is also important to take into account the length of time that symptoms have been experienced and their potential "expectedness" based on the child's developmental level (e.g., mild separation-related concerns are normative in the early years of life) or recent life events (e.g., a child who was recently separated from a parent in a shopping mall may experience more marked fears of separation than usual). Although understanding a young child's symptom presentation is important for classification and diagnostic purposes, effectively treating separation or other anxiety-related distress necessitates understanding how the child's anxiety developed, the subject of the next section.

Etiology of Anxiety

As is generally the case with psychopathology, a complex array of factors likely contributes to the development and maintenance of anxiety among young children. Previous empirical work suggests that in early childhood, a child's temperamental style (e.g., Rapee, 2002; Rapee & Jacobs, 2002) and numerous parent/caregiver-related variables (e.g., Shamir-Essakow, Ungerer, & Rapee, 2005; Weinberg & Tronick, 1998) are particularly salient in this regard. Due to the limited amount of empirical work pertaining to anxiety among young children and debate about the specific forms of anxiety from which individuals in this population may suffer, only general etiological variables have been identified.

Typical Development

To better understand how anxiety develops in young children, it is crucial to consider typical separation-related concerns, instead of merely what may occur when some facet of development goes awry. There are several lines of research that consider separation difficulties a normal part of development at certain ages and under particular circumstances. For instance, Bowlby viewed crying after a caregiver leaves to be a normal aspect of development, stating,

> Since the goal of attachment behaviour is to maintain the affectional bond, any situation that seems to be endangering to the bond elicits action designed to preserve it, and the greater the danger of loss appears to be, the more intense and varied are the actions elicited to prevent it (Bowlby, 1980, p. 42).

The "action" that Bowlby spoke of, on the part of a young child, can vary from crying to angry coercion, generally dissipating after a caregiver responds.

Hazan and Shaver (1987) expanded upon Bowlby's ideas, maintaining that potential disruption to an attachment bond between child and caregiver results in intense distress, attention-consuming reunion efforts, and sadness when reunion cannot be accomplished, on the part of both child and adult. It is therefore not surprising that crying is a common symptom of separation anxiety, which these theories suggest could serve as a way to elicit a caregiver's attention and reestablish attachment. Bowlby considered the first 6 weeks of life a stage during which the innate signal of crying brings the attachment figure closer to the child.

In other developmental research focused on infants, Mahler, Pine, and Bergman (1975) studied how separation between mother and child typically develops. They devised a multi-stage theory, termed "Psychological Birth of Self," asserting that there is a separation-individualization process where an individual establishes a sense of separateness from the primary love object and the world. In the differentiation stage, which occurs around 5-10 months of age, the child's perceptual-conscious system develops (e.g., eye sight improves), and he/she becomes aware of the mother's separateness. In the practicing stage, around 10-16 months of age, the child's locomotion develops. This permits the child to have control over his/her proximity to the caregiver, such that periodically checking back for "emotional refueling" while exerting increased independence is possible. In the rapprochement stage, occurring around 15-30 months of age, the child continues to need love and reassurance from the caregiver, despite a wealth of newly developed skills. It is common for children going through this stage to experience ambivalence about being separated versus united. It is not until the libidinal object-constancy stage, occurring at 30-36 months, that the child develops a stable inner representation of the mother so that the child can function independently when she is absent. A diagnosis of separation anxiety disorder does not, in light of this, seem appropriate for children who are younger than 3 years of age (Mahler et al.).

Common Etiological Influences

Temperament. The temperament of "behavioral inhibition to the unfamiliar" has consistently been linked to the development of anxiety problems (Kagan, Reznick, & Gibbons, 1989; Kagan & Snidman, 1991), including those in children (Biederman et al., 1993). Children with behaviorally inhibited temperaments generally appear timid and shy, and they exhibit emotional restraint when exposed to unfamiliar people, places, and contexts.

Hirshfeld and colleagues (1992) used longitudinal data to reveal that children who were defined as inhibited on four assessments occurring between 21 months and 7.5 years of age had a higher risk of anxiety disorder than those who were not inhibited. Findings of a separate longitudinal study of more than 800 children that occurred over a 12-year period indicated that males who were described as confident and eager to explore novel situations (i.e., who were non-inhibited) at the age of 5 years were less likely to have anxiety symptoms in childhood and adolescence than their less self-assured, explorative counterparts. Females described as passive, shy, and fearful at ages 3 and 5 years displayed anxiety symptoms later in life (Caspi, Henry, McGee, Moffitt, & Silva, 1995). In the absence of additional research in this area, it cannot be said with any certainty whether these findings were indeed gender specific, or if they are in fact gender neutral among individuals early in childhood.

Attachment relationship. Numerous researchers (e.g., Warren, 2004; Warren, Huston, Egeland, & Sroufe, 1997) have found qualities of the caregiver-child attachment relationship to be associated with anxiety. When a secure caregiver-child bond is observed, caregivers tend to be sensitive and responsive to their child's needs, and thus provide appropriate levels of aid and support when the child is feeling anxious or unsettled. The infant or young child comes to believe over time that distressing situations (e.g., separation) can be resolved successfully independent of the caregiver, an expectation that seemingly decreases the likelihood that the child will experience chronic anxiety (Warren). In contrast, in insecure attachment relationships, caregiving tends to be far less sensitive and responsive, which likely produces feelings of uncertainty regarding caregiver availability, concern over whether one's needs will be met, and fear of being left alone and vulnerable. According to Warren et al., the chronic anxiety and vigilance that may result when children are recipients of such care likely set the stage for the later development of anxiety.

Parental overprotectiveness. Rapee (2002) maintains that a high degree of parental overprotectiveness may also contribute to the development of anxiety-related difficulties in young children. This may work one of two ways: (a) a naturally withdrawn or inhibited child may elicit high levels of parental protection or (b) having a parent who tends to be protective may exacerbate inhibited behavior among children who evidence this temperamental trait.

Learning. Given the amount of time that children generally spend in the presence of parents or caregivers in the early years of life, it follows naturally that a number of parent/caregiver-related variables beyond the attachment relationship may be implicated in the development of anxiety in young children. With regard to learning, both parental modeling (i.e., social learning) of anxiety-related behavior (Warren, 2004) and parental reinforcement (i.e., operant conditioning) of children's anxious behavior, even if done unwittingly, have previously been associated with anxiety disorder development among youth.

An Integrated Approach

Undoubtedly, the development of anxiety among children can be preceded by an endless number of pathways. Elucidation of the particular pathway followed by a given child is likely to emerge only when a broad range of physiological, genetic, and environmental factors is considered (Weinberg & Tronick, 1998). While it may be that basic biological and behavioral factors predispose a child to develop an anxiety disorder, whether a disorder develops and what types of symptoms predominate are likely determined by a complex interaction of additional emotional, social, and cognitive variables within the child's environment (Weems & Costa, 2005). It is therefore crucial in assessing young children who present with anxiety-related concerns that consideration be given to a variety of child, family, and systemic variables that may contribute to the child's experience of symptoms.

Assessment of Anxiety

Given the paucity of research devoted to anxiety among young children, it is perhaps not surprising that little work pertaining to the assessment of anxiety specifically among this population exists. The majority of available instruments for assessing anxiety among children and adolescents have a minimum age of 6-8 years, making them inappropriate for use with the early childhood population. The techniques most commonly employed are briefly described below, although there remains a clear need for age-appropriate and developmentally sensitive methods of assessment for young children.

Traditional Methods

Clinical interviews. Several diagnostic interview schedules exist that are useful in the assessment of anxiety-related disturbances among older children and adolescents. For instance, both the Anxiety Disorders Interview Schedule for DSM-IV (APA, 1994), child and parent versions (Silverman & Albano, 1996; Silverman, Saavedra, & Pina, 2001), and the Diagnositc Interview for Children and Adolecents ([DICA]; Herjanic & Reich, 1982; Reich, 2000) are semi-structured interviews designed for children who are at least 6 years of age. The National Institute of Mental Health's Diagnostic Interview Schedule for Children ([DISC]; Shaffer, Fisher, Lucas, Dulcan, & Schwab-Stone, 2000) is a structured interview geared for children aged 9 to 17 years. These are appropriate for informing diagnosis of psychiatric conditions among older youth. They are not, however, designed for younger children and norms have not been developed for this population. The Preschool Age Psychiatric Assessment ([PAPA]; Egger & Angold, 2004) is a promising parent interview for children aged 2-5 years. The test-retest reliability and validity of this measure are sound (Egger et al., 2006), and it permits assessment of symptoms of varied anxiety disorders.

When assessing a child who presents with anxiety-related concerns during a less formalized interview, clinicians should inquire about the onset of symptoms and determine whether any stressors were present in the child's life around that time. Assessors should also seek information about various facets of development (e.g., socialization, feeding habits, sleep) to ascertain whether (and how) difficulties in these areas may relate to a child's presenting symptoms. Similarly, clinicians would do well to ask parents/caregivers about early medical issues or traumatic life events (e.g., loss of a primary caregiver) that may contribute to the experience of anxiety among children. Inquiry into family history of anxiety and other mental health issues is also essential (Warren, 2004).

During the assessment process, interviews may be conducted with multiple individuals to allow a balanced, well-rounded picture of the child to emerge (Shamir-Essakow et al., 2005) and to ascertain the consistency of the child's behavior across situational contexts. Spence and colleagues (2001) asserted that this practice may be somewhat suspect due to discrepancies between mother- and father-reported symptoms of anxiety in their preschool-aged children. Specifically, these researchers found that mothers tended to report more symptoms than did fathers. The use of observations may prove helpful (Glennon & Weisz, 1978) in determining which parent's report is more accurate. This practice may be especially useful when mothers are anxious or depressed themselves, as this may result in biased reporting (Najman et al., 2000).

Questionnaires and rating scales. As indicated by Egger and Angold (2006), questionnaires and rating scales are useful methods by which to obtain information from parents, teachers, and other important adults in a child's life. Parent-report methods are often perceived as particularly beneficial, as parents can most readily provide information about their child's functioning across situations, contexts, and times. The use of questionnaires and rating scales is also ideal in research and practice because these measures are generally inexpensive and simple to administer and score (Rapee, 2002). Several scales exist that may be both useful and appropriate in the assessment of young children who present with anxiety-related concerns. These include, although are not necessarily limited to: the Achenbach scales (i.e., Child Behavior Checklist [CBCL] and Teacher Report Form [TRF]; Achenbach, 1992), the Infant-Toddler Social and Emotional Assessment ([ITSEA]; Carter & Briggs-Gowan, 2000), the Preschool Anxiety Scale ([PAS]; Spence et al., 2001), the Fear Survey Schedule for Infants and Preschoolers (Warren, 2004), Children's Moods, Fears and Worries (Bayer, Sanson, & Hemphill, 2006), and The Infant-Preschool Scale for Inhibited Behaviors (Warren, 2004).

Behavioral observations. Considering the limited ability of young children to accurately self-report and potential bias in parent reporting, clinicians may find that behavioral observations offer unique information about the child being assessed. In prior studies, infant and toddler behaviors in response to caregiver separation and reunion, new situations, and strangers have been utilized in observational assessments of anxiety among young children (Glennon & Weisz, 1978; Hudson & Rapee, 2002). These situations are often contrived and may thus inaccurately reflect a child's behavior in his/her natural environmental context. To ensure that observational data is meaningful, Warren (2004) advocates that children be observed in multiple contexts, on numerous occasions, and in their everyday environments (e.g., home, daycare, preschool) for potential indices of anxiety. These may include, among others, frequent crying, clinginess, social withdrawal, tense muscles, noncompliance, and temper tantrums when required to separate from a caregiver. Such practice permits comparison of the child's behavior across settings and allows assessors to gain insight into how a child's relationships with his/her caretakers, as well as the environment, may be implicated in the development of anxious symptoms. Observations that are classroom-based permit comparison between the target child's behavior and that of a peer, which provides useful information about the normality and appropriateness of the frequency, intensity, and duration of the child's anxious symptoms.

Alternative Methods

Several alternative methods of assessing anxiety in young children have been suggested in the literature. For instance, Warren and Dadson (2001) propose that a series of dramatic stories, generally initiated by examiners, be enacted through doll play. Potential indicators of anxiety-related problems during doll play may include a child making a doll cry upon separation from a caregiver or when faced with a frightening situation. Youngsters could also be shown pictures of a child in a potentially anxiety-arousing situation or a cartoon depicting a child having a scary dream; their responses to these stimuli can then be monitored for anxiety. A child may likewise be presented with two puppets that claim to feel opposing feelings (e.g., afraid, not afraid) and then be asked to identify which he/she feels most like (Warren & Dadson). Art may be an additional technique appropriate for use in the assessment of anxiety in young children, as drawing is a mechanism that children use to express themselves. This and other play-based techniques have the added benefit of having potential therapeutic value; in the case of an anxious child, play can facilitate recognition of anxiety, experience of fears, and learning effective and age-appropriate skills for coping with these emotions (Kottman, 2001).

In determining the most appropriate way to assess a young child's experience of anxiety, it is important to bear in mind that assessment measures used with older youth often have limitations when used to assess and diagnose the preschool population (e.g., young children are unable to read or to comprehend complex verbal information). Alternative approaches may be helpful in determining the child's strengths, whereas more traditional measures may primarily expose areas of weakness. The former is far more beneficial in intervention development, as knowledge of a child's strengths can be used to inform treatment planning. A strengths-focused approach to assessment is consistent with the nature of authentic assessment of young children, for which Neisworth and Bagnato (2004) staunchly advocate.

Treatment of Anxiety

The relevant literature that is currently available does not involve empirical testing of prevention or treatment approaches for young children who experience anxiety, but rather outlines broad-based principles of what interventions should entail. The approaches to treatment that are most frequently discussed among researchers are summarized briefly below.

Prevention-Oriented Approaches

Donovan and Spence (2000) call for approaches geared toward the prevention of anxiety among young children. These authors contend that such aims can effectively be accomplished in a number of ways, including direct instruction in the use of coping skills for anxiety-arousing situations, modeling of appropriate behavior when feeling anxious, pre-exposure to feared situations (e.g., taking a child to school to meet his/her teacher prior to the start of the school year), and parent education/skills training. Schools may be an ideal setting in which to provide preventive services since large numbers of children can be targeted within this context.

Intervention-Oriented Approaches

Parent training and education. Due to the abundant parent-related variables associated with the development of childhood anxiety disorders, parental involvement in the treatment of these conditions is essential. Numerous researchers (e.g., Rapee & Jacobs, 2002) have reported the benefits of providing basic education to parents about symptoms of childhood anxiety, commonly associated risk factors in young children, and techniques that may help to manage a child's anxiety. Rapee and Jacobs found that both immediately after training and at 6-month follow-up, young children whose parents participated in such educational initiatives evidenced less behavior indicative of withdrawal than they did at the outset of the study. Rapee, Kennedy, Ingram, Edwards, and Sweeney (2005) similarly report that when parents who participated in a parent education program were compared to those who did not, the children of the former showed a significantly greater decrease in subsequent presence of disorder than the latter group did.

Psychotherapy. According to the Anxiety Disorders Association of America (ADAA, 2006b), psychotherapy is a common component in the treatment of anxiety disorders in early childhood, yet few empirical studies presently exist to provide evidence of the efficacy of this practice. In order for young children to profit from psychotherapy, it is essential that the methods employed by clinicians be age and developmentally appropriate. This likely requires that clinicians elicit information from children through means quite different from those utilized with adolescent and adult clients (e.g., storytelling, play). Engaging children in "talk therapy" or employing cognitive behavioral techniques are likely to prove less effective when working with young children, as they may exceed child clients' emerging language and cognitive capabilities (Kottman, 2001).

Regardless of the particular manner in which psychotherapy is provided to young children, Warren et al. (1997) contend that a primary role of the clinician is to act as a "secure base" for the child. This is of particular importance when separation-related concerns are prominent and disturbance in the caregiver-child attachment relationship precludes the child from experiencing the caregiver in such a way. In order to accomplish this, Warren et al. assert that clinicians should be reliable, attentive, empathic, and responsive. In the clinician's demonstration of these qualities, the child experiences the needed comfort and security that may be absent in his/her other relationships. By responding to young children in this manner consistently, clinicians ultimately aspire to alter the child client's perception of what to expect from future relationships and interactions. Failing to address such issues in treatment may have profound negative implications for a child's ability to successfully establish and maintain subsequent meaningful relationships (Warren et al.)

Choate and colleagues (2005) investigated the effectiveness of a particular therapeutic approach, Parent-Child Interaction Therapy (PCIT), with three families with 4-8 year old children with diagnoses of separation anxiety; two children had additional diagnoses. PCIT focused on allowing the children to direct parent-child interactions and thereby experience increased levels of control. Parents were taught to restate questions as descriptions, be enthusiastic toward their child, ignore negative behaviors, praise positive behaviors, and reflect the child's emotions and behaviors. The parents were further instructed in how to phrase directions, issue praise for following directions, and implement time-out for non-adherence to parental directives. None of the child study participants met diagnostic criteria for separation anxiety disorder at the conclusion of treatment, and normative levels of separation anxiety were present during a follow-up telephone interview.

Pharmacological approaches. The extant literature makes apparent that using medication in the treatment of young children with anxiety is currently the source of much disagreement; this debate is complicated by the shortage of empirical evidence to support the views of those on either side. The Anxiety Disorders Association of America (ADAA, 2006a) recommends that medication only be prescribed for the treatment of anxiety disorders in children when symptoms are severe, cause the child subjective distress, and/or contribute to functional impairment in the child's daily life. However, this criterion offers little guidance as to whether it is most appropriate to prescribe medication immediately following symptom onset or only after an intervention of lesser intensity fails to be effective. Some contend that prescription is only appropriate if psychotherapy alone is ineffective, while others argue equally as strongly that some children (particularly those with debilitating levels of anxiety) may be unsuccessful in treatment without medication to permit some initial symptom relief (ADAA, 2006a).

Implications for Clinical Practice

When working with young children with anxiety, the role of the clinician goes beyond mere assessment, diagnosis, and intervention planning. Even though each of these roles is critical, practitioners working in early childhood settings (e.g., preschools, early intervention classrooms) may also find consultation to be a vital component of their practice. Because parents, teachers, and school personnel may be ill-informed regarding the identification and treatment of anxiety in young children, educational efforts may need to be undertaken. Such initiatives may focus on common symptoms of anxiety, how to structure children's environments to minimize the likelihood that anxiety will be experienced, and techniques for addressing children's anxiety within these contexts. Clinicians may also find themselves in situations in which counseling an anxious young child seems warranted. As previously mentioned, it is imperative that all interactions and materials employed be both age and developmentally appropriate if such a service is provided within early childhood settings.

On a somewhat broader level, clinicians should utilize appropriate screening methods to identify children with mental health problems, ideally at an early age so that symptoms do not worsen and are still amenable to change. The best available tools for this purpose among young children are likely broad band assessment measures that tap a variety of domains of psychopathology (e.g., anxiety, depression, hyperactivity) and identify youth who present with symptom levels considered at-risk or clinically significant when compared to same-age peers. One such example is the Behavior Assessment System for Children, Second Edition ([BASC-2]; Reynolds & Kamphaus, 2004), which includes parent and teacher rating scales specifically geared toward children between 2 and 5 years of age. Older versions of this assessment tool have been used in clinical research with young children successfully (e.g., Harvey, Friedman-Weieneth, Goldstein, & Sherman, 2007).

The Preschool and Kindergarten Behavior Scales, Second Edition ([PKBS-2]; Merrell, 2002) may likewise be useful in the assessment of mental health concerns among young children. It is a normed and nationally standardized screening instrument that permits parents and teachers to report social and behavior problems among children aged 3 to 6. It contains three supplemental scales, one of which taps anxiety and somatic complaints. Major areas of concern can be followed up with the Childhood Behavior Checklist 2-3 (Achenbach, 1992), which is highly correlated with the PKBS-2, but has better norms and predictive and criterion validity data (Brassard & Boehm, 2007).

Clinicians who desire to have a systems-level impact may serve as liaisons between families and outside treatment agencies, advocate for legal policies that are designed to promote mental health among young children and improve access to services, and engage in research pertaining to anxiety and anxiety-related disorders in early childhood, as well as other common mental health concerns among this population (U.S. Public Health Service, 2000).

Along with the above, clinicians are advised to consider individual difference variables (e.g., culture, ethnicity, socioeconomic status) in their work with young children, just as they would with an older clientele (Rae & Fournier, 2004). It is also advisable for clinicians to inform young children, in a manner commensurate with their abilities, about the nature of services that will be provided prior to undertaking assessment and intervention activities with them. Consideration of the child's preferences and best interests is likewise paramount (Rae & Fournier).

Clinicians should also be aware that young children with anxiety problems are often non-disruptive and compliant; as a result, their difficulties may go undetected or be minimized by parents and teachers (Donovan & Spence, 2000). This seemingly underscores the need for those who work with young children to gather data through methods (e.g., behavioral observation) other than parent and/ or teacher report since the accuracy of information provided by these individuals may be questionable.

Conclusions and Future Directions

There is a general contention among researchers that anxiety is a common experience among children and adolescents (e.g., Morris & March, 2004), yet relatively little is presently known about the unique manner in which anxiety manifests early in childhood. Separation-related anxieties seem to predominate among toddlers and preschool-aged children. The challenge facing clinicians is differentiating typical from pathological levels of anxiety during this stage of development. In making this determination, consideration of factors such as symptom severity, degree of distress, and length of time that symptoms have been present is essential. Because anxiety can potentially have profound implications for the current and future functioning of young sufferers, early identification and intervention are crucial.

Assessment of anxiety in early childhood should make use of developmentally appropriate methods (e.g., play) and utilize a multi-source, multi-method approach so that a holistic picture of the child emerges. Only when such an assessment is undertaken can clinicians gain insight into the complex array of factors likely to be implicated in the etiology and maintenance of the child's distress. This understanding is paramount since it forms the basis of clinicians' individualized treatment planning; only when intervention attempts are appropriate to the child and his/her unique pathway to disorder can they be expected to be effective.

It is clear that future investigative efforts are essential to further the current understanding of how anxiety manifests in young children. This clarification is important so that diagnostic criteria, assessment tools, and treatment regimens can be developed and/or modified to be appropriate for this age group. Longitudinal work seems especially timely, so that insight into the developmental trajectories and long term implications of fearfulness and anxiety in early childhood can be gleaned (Warren, 2004). Weems and Costa (2005) recommend that future cross-sequential studies (which combine longitudinal and cross-sectional methodology) would likewise be informative because they would permit the simultaneous examination of age group differences and longitudinal developmental trends.

Because most existing research into anxiety in early childhood has been conducted using demographically homogeneous samples, little is presently known about potential differences in anxiety among young children of diverse racial, ethnic, and socioeconomic backgrounds, suggesting that research efforts to investigate differences that may be attributable to such diversity-related factors are necessary. Also of note, few available studies focus on anxiety and other psychiatric disorders among primary care or community samples of preschool-aged children (Egger & Angold, 2006), instead relying on clinic-based samples. Data derived from the former populations is necessary to more clearly delineate what constitutes a "typical" experience of anxious symptoms among children this age. Differentiating typical from pathological levels of anxiety in early childhood is undoubtedly challenging and currently an area of much debate; any data that may clarify this distinction has widespread applications for both future research and practice endeavors.

References

Achenbach, T. M. (1992). *Manual for the Child Behavior Checklist / 2-3 and 1992 profile*. Burlington, VT: University of Vermont, Department of Psychiatry.

American Psychiatric Association. (1994). *Diagnostic and statistical manual of mental disorders* (4th ed.). Washington, DC: Author.

American Psychiatric Association. (2000). *Diagnostic and statistical manual of mental disorders* (4th ed., text revision). Washington, DC: Author.

Anxiety Disorders Association of America. (2006a). *Anxiety medication and kids*. Retrieved October 25, 2006 from http://www.adaa.org/GettingHelp/FocusOn/children&Adolescents/AMK.asp

Anxiety Disorders Association of America. (2006b). *October monthly feature: Anxiety disorders in children*. Retrieved October 25, 2006 from http://www.adaa.org/GettingHelp/MonthlyFeatures.asp

Bayer, J. K., Sanson, A. V., & Hemphill, S. A. (2006). Children's moods, fears, and worries: The making of an early childhood parent questionnaire. *Journal of Emotional and Behavioral Disorders*, *14*, 41-49.

Biederman, J., Rosenbaum, J. F., Bolduc-Murphy, E. A., Faraone, S. V., Chaloff, J., Hirshfeld, D., et al. (1993). A 3-year follow-up of children with and without behavioral inhibition. *American Academy of Child and Adolescent Psychiatry*, *32*, 814-821.

Bowlby, J. (1980). *Attachment and loss: Vol. 3. Sadness and depression*. New York: Basic Books.

Brassard, M. R., & Boehm, A. E. (2007). *Preschool assessment: Principles and practices*. New York: Guilford.

Carter, A. S., & Briggs-Gowan, M. (2000). *The Infant-Toddler Social and Emotional Assessment*. Unpublished manual, University of Massachusetts at Boston and Yale University, New Haven, CT. Available by request at alice.carter@umb.edu

Caspi, A., Henry, B., McGee, R. O., Moffitt, T. E., & Silva, P. A. (1995). Temperamental origins of child and adolescent behavior problems: From age three to age fifteen. *Child Development*, *66*, 55-68.

Choate, M. L., Pincus, D. B., Eyberg, S. M., & Barlow, D. H. (2005). Parent-child interaction therapy for treatment of separation anxiety disorder in young children: A pilot study. *Cognitive and Behavioral Practice, 12*, 126-135.

Christophersen, E. R., & Mortweet, S. L. (2001). Diagnosis and management of anxiety disorders. In E. R. Christophersen & S. L. Mortweet (Eds.), *Treatments that work with children: Empirically supported strategies for managing childhood problems* (pp. 49-78). Washington, DC: American Psychological Association.

Donovan, C. L., & Spence, S. H. (2000). Prevention of childhood anxiety disorders. *Clinical Psychology Review, 20*, 509-531.

Egger, H. L., & Angold, A. (2004).The Preschool Age Psychiatric Assessment (PAPA): A structured parent interview for diagnosing psychiatric disorders in preschool children. In R. Del Carmen-Wiggins & A. Carter (Eds.), *Handbook of infant, toddler, and preschool mental assessment* (pp. 223-243). New York: Oxford University Press.

Egger, H. L., & Angold, A. (2006). Common emotional and behavioral disorders in preschool children: Presentation, nosology, and epidemiology. *Journal of Child Psychology and Psychiatry, 47*, 313-337.

Egger, H. L., Erkanli, A., Keeler, G., Potts, E., Walter, B. K., & Angold, A. (2006). Test-retest reliability of the Preschool Age Psychiatric Assessment. *Journal of the American Academy of Child and Adolescent Psychiatry, 45*, 538-549.

Evangelista, N., & McLellan, M. J. (2004). The Zero to Three Diagnostic System: A framework for emotional and behavioral problems in young children. *School Psychology Review, 33*, 159-173.

Glennon, B., & Weisz, J. R. (1978). An observational approach to the assessment of anxiety in young children. *Journal of Consulting and Clinical Psychology, 46*, 1246-1257.

Harvey, E. A., Friedman-Weieneth, J. L., Goldstein, L. H., & Sherman, A. H. (2007). Examining subtypes of behavior problems among 3-year-old children, Part 1: Investigating validity of subtypes and biological risk-factors. *Journal of Abnormal Child Psychology, 35,* 97-110.

Hazan, C., & Shaver, P. (1987). Romantic love conceptualized as an attachment process. *Journal of Personality and Social Psychology, 52*, 511-524.

Herjanic, B., & Reich, W. (1982). Development of a structured psychiatric interview for children: Agreement between child and parent on individual symptoms. *Journal of Abnormal Child Psychology, 10*, 307-324.

Hirshfeld, D. R., Rosenbaum, J. F., Biederman, J., Bolduc, E. A., Faraone, S. V., Snidman, N., et al. (1992). Stable behavioral inhibition and its association with anxiety disorder. *Journal of the American Academy of Child and Adolescent Psychiatry, 31*, 103-111.

Hudson, J. L., & Rapee, R. M. (2002). Parent-child interactions in clinically anxious children and their siblings. *Journal of Clinical Child and Adolescent Psychology, 31*, 548-555.

Kagan, J., Reznick, J. S., & Gibbons, J. (1989). Inhibited and uninhibited types of children. *Child Development, 60*, 838-845.

Kagan, J., & Snidman, N. (1991). Temperamental factors in human development. *Amercian Psychologist, 46*, 856-862.

Kottman, T. (2001). Introduction to play therapy. In T. Kottman (Ed.), *Play therapy: Basics and beyond* (pp. 3-21). Alexandria, VA: American Counseling Association.

Lyons-Ruth, K., Zeanah, C. H., & Benoit, D. (2003). Disorder and risk for disorder during infancy and toddlerhood. In E. Mash & R. Barkley (Eds.), *Child psychopathology* (2nd ed., pp. 589-631). New York: Guilford.

Mahler, M. S., Pine, F., & Bergman, A. (1975). *The psychological birth of the human infant: Symbiosis and individuation.* New York: Basic Books.

Merrell, K. W. (2002). *Preschool and kindergarten behavior scales* (2nd ed.). Austin, TX: Pro-Ed.

Morris, T. L., & March, J. S. (Eds.). (2004). *Anxiety disorders in children and adolescents* (2nd ed.). New York: Guilford.

Najman, J. M., Williams, G. M., Nikles, J., Spence, S., Bor, W., O'Callaghan, M., et al. (2000). Mothers' mental illness and child behavior problems: Cause-effect association or observation bias? *Journal of the American Academy of Child and Adolescent Psychiatry, 39*, 592-602.

Neisworth, J. T., & Bagnato, S. J. (2004). The mismeasure of young children: The authentic assessment alternative. *Infants and Young Children, 17*, 198-212.

Rae, W. A., & Fournier, C. J. (2004). Ethical and legal issues for pediatric psychology and school psychology. In R. DelCarmen-Wiggins & A. Carter (Eds.), *Handbook of infant, toddler, and preschool mental health assessment* (pp. 721-738). New York: Oxford.

Rapee, R. M. (2002). The development and modification of temperamental risk for anxiety disorders: Prevention of a lifetime of anxiety? *Biological Psychiatry, 52*, 947-957.

Rapee, R. M., & Jacobs, D. (2002). The reduction of temperamental risk for anxiety in withdrawn preschoolers: A pilot study. *Behavioural and Cognitive Psychotherapy, 30*, 211-215.

Rapee, R. M., Kennedy, S., Ingram, M., Edwards, S., & Sweeney, L. (2005). Prevention and early intervention of anxiety disorders in inhibited preschool children. *Journal of Consulting and Clinical Psychology, 73*, 488-497.

Reich, W. (2000). Diagnostic Interview for Children and Adolescents (DICA). *Journal of the American Academy of Child and Adolescent Psychiatry, 39*, 59-66.

Reynolds, C. R., & Kamphaus, R. W. (2004). *BASC-2: Behavior Assessment System for Children* (2nd ed.). Circle Pines, MN: American Guidance Service.

Schniering, C. A., Hudson, J. L., & Rapee, R. M. (2000). Issues in the diagnosis and assessment of anxiety disorders in children and adolescents. *Clinical Psychology Review, 20,* 453-478.

Shaffer, D., Fisher, P., Lucas, C. P., Dulcan, M. K., & Schwab-Stone, M. E. (2000). NIMH Diagnostic Interview Schedule for Children Version IV (NIMH DISC-IV): Description, differences from previous versions, and reliablity of some common diagnoses. *Journal of the American Academy of Child and Adolescent Psychiatry, 39,* 28-38.

Shamir-Essakow, G., Ungerer, J. A., & Rapee, R. M. (2005). Attachment, behavioral inhibition, and anxiety in preschool children. *Journal of Abnormal Child Psychology, 33,* 131-143.

Silverman, W. K., & Albano, A. M. (1996). *Anxiety Disorders Interview Schedule for Children for DSM-IV* (child and parent versions). San Antonio, TX: Psychological Corporation/Graywind.

Silverman, W. K., Saavedra, L. M., & Pina, A. A. (2001). Test-retest reliability of anxiety symptoms and diagnoses with Anxiety Disorders Interview Schedule for DSM-IV: Child and parent versions. *Journal of the American Academy of Child and Adolescent Psychiatry, 40,* 937-944.

Spence, S. H., Rapee, R., McDonald, C., & Ingram, M. (2001). The structure of anxiety symptoms among preschoolers. *Behaviour Research and Therapy, 39,* 1293-1316.

U. S. Public Health Service. (2000). Report of the surgeon general's conference on children's mental health: A national action agenda. Washington, DC: Department of Health and Human Services. Retrieved October 30, 2006 from http://www.hhs.gov/surgeongeneral/ topics/cmh/cmhreport.pdf

Velting, O. N., Setzer, N. J., & Albano, A. M. (2002). Anxiety disorders. In D. T. Marsh & M. A. Fristad (Eds.), *Handbook of serious emotional disturbance in children and adolescents* (pp. 204-227). New York: John Wiley and Sons.

Warren, S. L. (2004). Anxiety disorders. In R. DelCarmen-Wiggins & A. Carter (Eds.), *Handbook of infant, toddler, and preschool mental health assessment* (pp. 355-375). New York: Oxford.

Warren, S. L., & Dadson, N. (2001). Assessment of anxiety in young children. *Current Opinion in Pediatrics, 13,* 580-585.

Warren, S. L., Huston, L., Egeland, B., & Sroufe, A. (1997). Child and adolescent anxiety disorders and early attachment. *Journal of the American Academy of Child and Adolescent Psychiatry, 36,* 637-644.

Weems, C. F., & Costa, N. M. (2005). Developmental differences in the expression of childhood anxiety symptoms and fears. *Journal of the American Academy of Child and Adolescent Psychiatry, 44,* 656-663.

Weinberg, M. K., & Tronick, E. Z. (1998). The impact of maternal psychiatric illness on infant development. *Journal of Clinical Psychiatry, 59,* 53-61.

Zero to Three. (2005). *Diagnostic classification: 0-3R: Diagnostic classification of mental health and developmental disorders of infancy and early childhood* (Rev. ed.). Washington, DC: Author.

Preschool Assessment:
The Diagnostic Classroom Model

Beth T. Clingenpeel, Kelli R. Good,
& Karen J. McCleu-Jackson
Virginia Beach City Public Schools

Early childhood assessment has evolved to an environmental model encompassing not only child attributes, but ecological factors relating to child functioning within systems as well. The purpose of this article is to describe the successful use of a diagnostic classroom model for preschool assessment in a public school district in southeastern Virginia. The diagnostic classroom model is a structured learning environment where dynamic assessments of children aged 3 through 5 can occur by allowing children to be observed in a more natural setting over time. As a mode for assessment, the diagnostic classroom addresses two key features of best practices of early childhood assessment: families play a vital role in the process and methods accommodate children's developmental status. Descriptions of the classroom and stakeholder satisfaction data are discussed.

As a nation, there has been a growing public commitment to early childhood education programs, not only with the passage of federal laws and amendments, but also with increased awareness of the importance of early identification of developmental and learning problems in infants and young children. It is well documented how important environmental stimulation is for a child's development, from improved intellectual performance and peer orientation to more long-lasting positive effects of fewer grade retentions, lower delinquency, and less welfare (Barnett, Lamey, & Jung, 2005; Berrueta-Clement, Schweinhart, Epstein, & Weikert, 1984; Lazar & Darlington, 1982; Zigler & Muenchow, 1992). Intervention services for young children's psychological and developmental difficulties have been shown to be beneficial and cost-effective (Schwinhart, Barnes, Weikart, Barnett, & Epstein, 1993), as they help prevent the need for more costly and long-lasting intervention services in the future. One of the first tiers of support for young children is assessing their needs and determining what interventions are appropriate. Much has been written about the importance of fair

All correspondence should be addressed to Beth T. Clingenpeel, Psychological Services, Virginia Beach City Public Schools, Laskin Road Annex, 1413 Laskin Road, Virginia Beach, Virginia 23451. Electronic mail may be sent to: btcwsu@cox.net and accurate identification of the developmental needs of young children (Bagnato & Neisworth, 1991). Most early childhood education organizations, such as the National Association for the Education of Young Children and the High/Scope Educational Research Foundation have concluded that assessment is a necessary component of high quality early childhood programs (Brickman & Taylor, 1991; Sandall, McLean, & Smith, 2000).

The purpose of this article is to describe one approach to early childhood assessment utilized by a particular school district in southeastern Virginia. The model described evolved from a single assessor model to a more holistic and naturalistic approach in support of the trend in preschool assessment in the mid-1990s to adopt an environmental model (Bowers, 2002). The current model encompasses many of the recommended practices of early childhood assessment in addition to detailing the complexity and difficulty of striving for best practice within the realities of operating in a public school system with limited resources, personnel, and monetary funds.

One of the goals when developing the model was to address the limitations of a compartmentalization approach to child assessment and to embrace best practices by incorporating a more holistic view of children within natural settings. There is widespread agreement on the part of educators and other early childhood specialists that the goal of assessment is to improve learning experiences for all young children (Brassard & Boehm, 2007). The assessment of young children involves a range of procedures used to gather information about their functioning, including standardized testing, observation, parent and teacher interviews and ratings, evaluation of work samples, review of records, and a focus on learning environments (Brassard & Boehm, 2007). The purposes of early childhood assessment are just as varied as the procedures used. Brassard and Boehmn (2007) outlined eight functions of the assessment of preschoolers that can be summarized into four key areas: (a) describe children's strengths and needs across developmental areas, in order to predict possible developmental delay and determine eligibility for special education; (b) provide information to plan instructional activities and curriculum; (c) plan and monitor intervention activities; and (d) evaluate program effectiveness. No one assessment procedure can address these various functions, and different methods need to be used depending on the purpose for which the assessment is conducted.

Designing an assessment to meet a specified purpose using varied and multiple procedures is difficult enough, but working with young children ages 2 through 5 also presents its own set of challenges. These challenges can include: the difficulty most young children have in complying with a predetermined structured protocol; the need to gather representative samples of children's behavior despite the short amount of time children typically stay engaged in tasks; the need to elicit information about what skills children can perform in light of the difficulty most young children have with unfamiliar adults in novel situations; and the need to include the perspective of parents regarding their children's skills, needs, and progress in the face of a limited amount of time with families to provide this type of information (Greenwood, Luze, & Carta, 2002). In addition, issues of technical adequacy of test results, such as reliability and validity often come into question when working with young children whose development tends to be uneven and rapid. To improve the reliability and validity of assessment results, Bagnato and Neisworth (1991) recommended that assessments include multiple sources of information and multiple approaches, as well as be conducted in multiple settings across time in order to yield a comprehensive understanding of young children's skills and needs.

Given an adequate understanding of the purposes for assessment and the difficulties inherent when evaluating young children, the method of assessing preschool-aged children within Virginia Beach City Public Schools slowly transformed over the last 25 years to incorporate best practices. The Virginia Beach City Public School System is the third largest school system in Virginia and among the 50 largest school divisions in the United States based on student enrollment. Virginia Beach City Public Schools serve approximately 70,000 students and currently include 56 elementary schools, 15 middle schools, 11 high schools, and a number of secondary and post-secondary specialty centers. As of the 2005-2006 school year, the population of the school system was comprised of 58% Caucasian, 28% African American, 6% Asian, 5% Hispanic, and 3% other or unspecified students. Also, the city of Virginia Beach houses four military installations, resulting in many families being relocated to and from the city.

The early childhood assessment model of focus is within the Virginia Beach City Public Schools and a part of the smaller operating unit called the Preschool Assessment Center (PAC). The PAC operates year round and evaluates children 2 to 5 years of age. The primary focus of the PAC is to assess children's strengths and needs across developmental areas to determine the need for early intervention services. Approximately 1200 initial screening appointments are made during a 12-month period, and of these 1200 initial calls from families expressing concerns about their children's functioning, approximately one-third are referred for a more comprehensive evaluation to determine if the children qualify for early childhood special education services due to significant developmental delays. The PAC completes between 375 and 400 comprehensive evaluations each year.

Prior to the 1990s, the PAC operated by asking parents to bring their children to several appointments, in which evaluators conducted separate formalized assessments of specific areas. This resulted in a compartmentalized view of a child, in which a child's functioning was dissected into small parts by separate individuals without any attempt to examine the child as a whole and without any attention to environmental contributions. A team approach was adopted in the early 1990s, whereby a speech therapist, developmental specialist, and school psychologist conducted their evaluations at the same time in what was coined an arena format. This meant the parents brought their children to one appointment and the three specialists worked together with the child and parent to complete an assessment. Formalized measures were used in addition to informal, play-based tools, such as following the child's lead and using his or her natural play interests to gauge performance and developmental standing. The arena format resulted in less overlap between assessors and less inconvenience to families having to previously negotiate multiple appointment times. In addition to a speech therapist, developmental specialist, school psychologist, and parent forming the multidisciplinary team, a school social worker was also a part of the team. The school social worker interviewed the parent preferably within the home environment and obtained a developmental history of the child, the parent's perspective of his or her child's functioning, and ratings from family members of the child's social functioning. The interview was conducted at a place and time convenient for the parent. The school social worker was encouraged to meet with the parent in the home with the child present in order to observe the child in his or her natural environment. The arena format is currently being used in the PAC to assess children ages 2 through 5 suspected of developmental delays in addition to a diagnostic classroom model of early childhood assessment, which was proposed as an alternative method to the arena assessment in the spring of 2002, and adopted in the school year 2003-2004.

The arena assessment is believed to be an improvement over the single assessor model used in Virginia Beach City Public Schools prior to the early 1990s. However, the arena assessment is not without its share of shortcomings. Children are asked to perform their best in an unfamiliar situation with unfamiliar adults in a short amount of time. A typical arena assessment lasts from 80 to 120 minutes. Young children tend to fatigue and have lapses in their attention during the arena assessment. Certain children who have severe language impairments or physical disabilities do not perform well on the formal instruments and standardized conditions of the arena assessment. Also, an increasing number of referrals for evaluations to the PAC were the result of behavior concerns. Assessing for potential behavior problems in an arena format is wrought with challenges and limited opportunities to observe social and emotional functioning. To address these concerns with the arena assessment, a diagnostic classroom assessment model was proposed. The diagnostic classroom model most directly evolved from the preschool team members striving to overcome the limitations of the arena assessment format.

The diagnostic classroom model of early childhood assessment is defined by the PAC as a structured learning environment created to provide an atmosphere conducive to evaluating a child's (3-5 years) developmental skills and needs. Although the PAC serves children at age 2, these youngsters typically are evaluated through the arena format given the social nature of the diagnostic classroom and the need to separate from parents for substantial periods of time to attend the classroom. The purpose of the diagnostic classroom is to create a setting in which more dynamic and naturalistic assessments can occur, as such a classroom affords children time to acclimate to their surroundings, to establish rapport with evaluators, and to demonstrate their skills on their own terms in a developmentally appropriate and stimulating setting. As opposed to a pre-determined, one-time protocol for assessment, the diagnostic classroom model offers evaluators the chance to respond to changing variables both within and outside the child. The diagnostic classroom allows children to be observed in a more natural setting over time and addresses a chief complaint from families that a 90-minute arena evaluation was not enough opportunity to learn about their children. The use of a classroom format for assessment also gives evaluators more flexibility to tailor assessment instruments to the strengths and needs of the children. Furthermore, children's interactions with others and play could be observed in the classroom. Another advantage of the diagnostic classroom is the ability to watch a child's rate of learning firsthand. In short, the diagnostic classroom as a mode for assessment addresses two key features of best practices of early childhood assessment: families must play a vital role in the assessment process and assessment methods and materials must accommodate children's developmental status (Sandall et al., 2000).

The diagnostic classroom embodies many of the features of a current preschool assessment approach described by Brassard and Boehm (2007). The multifactor ecological model views preschool assessment as an ongoing problem-solving task with the goals of understanding the child within his or her daily environments and planning appropriate instruction and other forms of intervention. A basic tenet of the multifactor ecological model is the interplay of adult, child, environmental, and situational factors influencing children's skill development and behavior, resulting in the need for assessors to collect information from and about all of the persons and settings relevant to a particular child (Brassard & Boehm, 2007). A multifaceted approach is recommended, in which assessors use a variety of methods to collect information from many sources. Thus, a comprehensive assessment results in understanding a child across developmental areas of functioning (e.g., cognitive, motor, language, social and emotional) within the context of his or her past and present environmental settings and situational influences.

Although developed from the goal of improving the arena assessment format, the diagnostic classroom model has evolved into using many components of an ecological theoretical framework for assessment (Bracken & Nagle, 2007). The diagnostic classroom model recognizes and addresses the multiple and interactive contexts and relationships that affect a child's development, including family and educational systems, home environments, and maturation of the child. However, in keeping with best practice guidelines for assessment in general, the diagnostic classroom model does not rely solely on one theoretical framework, but uses multiple methodologies (National Association of School Psychologists, 2003).

Description of the Diagnostic Classroom

The diagnostic classroom operates year round and is housed within an elementary school in Virginia Beach City Public Schools. It literally is one classroom set up with a developmentally appropriate early childhood curriculum (Bredekamp, 1987). Children attend the diagnostic classroom for 4 weeks with no more than 12 children enrolled at one time. After tweaking with the days of attendance when the classroom was first established, 4 weeks was determined to be the ideal timeframe for securing a thorough and comprehensive evaluation of the children within the confines of an academic calendar, allowing for eight sessions in one year. There is a morning and afternoon session, so children attend either in the morning or afternoon for a total of 3.5 instructional hours, 5 days a week. Two teachers trained in early childhood special education and an aide work with the children and operate a typical preschool day. In addition, early childhood specialists (speech and language pathologists, school psychologists, school social workers) are frequently observing, facilitating, and interacting in the classroom.

Consistent with best practices in early childhood education, the children in the diagnostic classroom are exposed to structured and unstructured instructional situations; developmentally appropriate materials and equipment are available both indoors and outdoors; and routine tasks are incorporated as a part of the daily schedule, such as eating snack and washing hands (Sandall et al., 2000). The environment is designed to promote children's exploration, engagement, play, and participation. Routines and transitions between activities occur with a focus on child-initiated learning. There are distinct centers children chose to play in and environmental supports to aid children's learning about personal space, self-regulatory behaviors, and social skills. The curricula include all areas of development (physical, emotional, social, language, pre-academic, and cognitive) in an integrated approach. A variety of activities is provided which are relevant to children's lives and accommodate the developmental needs of the children enrolled.

The diagnostic classroom operates from the premise that children thrive in a structured environment that is also flexible to allow them freedom to pursue their interests. A class schedule is used with visual reminders of the daily activities and a bell is rung to indicate transition between the activities. The preschool morning or afternoon session in the diagnostic classroom includes: arrival/greeting, table toys, circle including music and movement, free choice in centers, clean up, snack, outdoor play, story time, and departure. Children transition from one activity to the next by singing songs and they rotate different roles in the classroom, such as ringing the bell to indicate a transition, calendar helper at circle, and line leader. Each child is assigned a special shape or animal with his or her name on it to help them locate their cubby and their seat at circle, thus fostering the idea of environmental support to aid independence.

The available centers that children can choose during center time include: blocks, house/dramatic play, table toys, library or quiet area, art, and sand table (Voorhees, Aveno, Landon, & Massie, 1993). Since the focus of the diagnostic classroom is to assess children suspected of developmental delays within a more natural early childhood setting, the teachers deliberately plan activities and allow exploration of certain materials to observe the children's reaction to certain textures and novel experiences. As a part of center time, the school social workers offer weekly mini social skill lessons for the children. Prior to the start of each 4-week session, an open house is scheduled, in which families are invited to meet the specialists, see the classroom, and learn how the diagnostic classroom operates through a slide show and question-and-answer session. The families are encouraged to bring their children to the open house, since childcare is provided, and it is a chance for those children enrolled to become acquainted with the diagnostic classroom and their teachers prior to starting.

Role of Families

Families are an integral part of the assessment process from initial screening to eligibility placement decisions. They have the freedom to determine their role in the process, since many options are offered for participation, and their choice is respected on the continuum of limited to involved. Families are welcome in the diagnostic classroom at all times and they are encouraged to observe and participate in the classroom activities. The diagnostic classroom teachers communicate with the families almost daily and send home weekly progress notes. Families are asked to complete many different forms and rating scales, providing vital input about their concerns and perceptions. Families are interviewed at home by social workers, providing input on social and adaptive behavior skills and general functioning within home routines. They are invited to attend an informational session about parenting strategies, behavior management, and the special education process offered at night by the school social workers. Given the frequent communication between families and the specialists during the course of the 4-week period, consultation often occurs with the families pertaining to an array of issues surrounding their children from medical concerns to behavior strategies. Transportation is provided to the diagnostic classroom for those families who do not have the means.

Role of Early Childhood Specialists

The diagnostic classroom operates in 4-week periods during which the teachers, school psychologists, speech and language pathologists, and school social workers assess each child enrolled. Physical and occupational therapists operate a group for the children to attend weekly, in which activities allowing for closer examination of fine and gross motor skills are presented. For the first week of enrollment, the children become acquainted with the routines of the diagnostic classroom, and the early childhood specialists observe and facilitate. During the 3 remaining weeks is when individual assessments typically occur, in which the children may be removed from the classroom for brief time periods to undergo standardized assessment procedures. Since current Virginia state guidelines require evidence that a child's delays deviate substantially from that of his or her peers, norm-referenced tests are used as one part of the overall evaluation.

One of the advantages of the diagnostic classroom is the opportunity to tailor the choice of standardized, norm-referenced instruments to address the needs of a particular child based on observing him or her functioning over time within an early childhood educational setting. However, results from formal procedures are small in comparison to the wealth of information gleaned from observing the children. In fact, the majority of the information gathered from each early childhood specialist on the children in the diagnostic classroom overwhelmingly is derived from observing them during the 4 weeks. This is in line with the recommended practice of focusing on children's behaviors during naturally occurring events (Brassard & Boehm, 2007). A wide range of behaviors can be assessed through observation, including peer interactions, attention and persistence, play, language use, self-help skills, fine and gross motor skills, emotional regulation, and coping strategies. Also, observation can help validate the information gathered from formal testing procedures.

At the conclusion of the 4-week period, each specialist in collaboration with one another provides a detailed report of each child's current level of functioning for determining eligibility for special education services. Each specialist produces his or her own report, which includes assessment results from a variety of measures (standardized instruments, observation, teacher and parent rating scales, checklists, evaluation of work samples, and review of records). All domains of development are discussed in a multidisciplinary format (National Association of School Psychologists, 2002). Typically, with some overlap between evaluators consistent with developmental theory of the integratedness of children's skills, the teachers address physical areas of development and pre-academic skills, the speech and language pathologists discuss language development, the school psychologists focus on social and emotional and cognitive development, and the school social workers speak to family perceptions and the home environment. In addition to results gathered from enrollment in the diagnostic classroom, one member of the multidisciplinary team will observe the children at preschool or daycare if they typically attend such settings when not enrolled in the diagnostic classroom and incorporate these observations into their results. An integrated assessment of developmental domains is the outcome, in which children were allowed to demonstrate their competencies in a comfortable setting of interest to them (Temple University Forum on Preschool Assessment, 2003).

Utility of the Diagnostic Classroom

The diagnostic classroom model has been operating for 4 years with much success. The model addresses the limitations of an arena format and has produced unintended positive outcomes as well. As were the goals when designing the diagnostic classroom model, it has resulted in more tailored assessments and better descriptions of child functioning. This has lead to more meaningful Individualized Education Plans (IEP) based on surveys administered to early childhood special educators who teach children enrolled in classrooms for developmental delays, in which 85% said that they developed more functional intervention plans as a result of reading information gathered on children from the diagnostic classroom versus the arena format. If one of the goals of assessment is to improve learning experiences for children, the diagnostic classroom has achieved this end. One measure of the success of any assessment model is to determine how well the goals of assessment were met. If the diagnostic classroom model were judged by how well it identified those children with needs requiring special education services, the diagnostic classroom model has fared extremely well. Over the past four years, 528 evaluations were conducted in the diagnostic classroom and only one case was referred for a re-evaluation (a request for another evaluation of a preschool-aged child who was previously evaluated within the 2 to 5 age range through the PAC). By comparison, there have been 33 requests for re-evaluations just since last year from those cases initially evaluated through the arena format. These data indicate that the diagnostic classroom model identifies children's needs and lines up appropriate resources to address those needs overwhelmingly correct the first time.

The cost of operating the diagnostic classroom is slightly more expensive than arena assessments, since one additional staff member was needed (classroom aide) and transportation to and from the diagnostic classroom is provided by the school system. A cost-effectiveness study has not been completed to date; however, anecdotal records suggest that the diagnostic classroom model does well at identifying children's needs and does not result in repeat evaluations of the same children as does the arena format. Thus, any extra costs incurred upfront are largely recouped through effective outcomes for children and their families in the long run.

Currently, the Virginia Beach City Public School System operates a self-contained model for serving preschool-aged children with significant developmental delays in addition to a resource model for those children with less severe delays. The overwhelming majority (85%) of teachers who work in the classrooms and receive the children who attended the diagnostic classroom and were found to exhibit significant delays across a number of developmental domains indicated that the diagnostic classroom provides an overall better picture of child functioning, thus rendering the writing of an IEP more practical and suitable to the expectations of the intervention classrooms. The curricula in the diagnostic classroom mirror that in the intervention classrooms, so the diagnostic classroom model assesses those child skills linked directly to intervention. A more ecologically valid assessment results because aspects of the classroom setting were incorporated, and teachers were provided with useful information for curriculum planning (Temple University Forum on Preschool Assessment, 2003). This type of assessment linked to intervention also results in recommending that certain children, depending on their performance in the diagnostic classroom, be served in a less restrictive setting than the intervention classrooms, such as receiving services at home or in a community-based preschool. In line with the move for more inclusive early childhood education, the public school intervention classrooms are reserved for those children with the most significant developmental delays, while the others are served amongst their typically developing peers (Guralnick, 2001).

Further evidence for the diagnostic classroom model resulting in more rich and meaningful description of child functioning is from family survey results. At the conclusion of the 4 weeks and after the eligibility meeting, a short survey is sent home for the families to complete. The survey asks for parent's satisfaction with the diagnostic classroom using a 4-point Likert scale with seven questions. For example, one of the questions reads, "The assessment process has helped me to have a better understanding of my child's strengths and weaknesses." With approximately 33% of the parents completing the survey over the course of the 4 years, the vast majority of them (93%) responded favorably, indicating that they were satisfied with the model, they felt their children were accurately described, and they would recommend the diagnostic classroom to other parents. Most of the families also provided feedback in their own words in the space provided on the survey. The majority of those comments spoke to seeing growth in their children over the 4-week period enrolled in the classroom and how they appreciated the length of time used to understand their children. For example, one parent wrote:

> I don't believe there is any other way to get a true picture of a child other than through interaction and observation over time. Knowing that our son was with true professionals in their fields provided us with a sense of relief and hope that any educational and social issues would be identified. Our son has grown and matured since he attended the diagnostic classroom.

One of the unintended results of the diagnostic classroom shared by the families was that they saw the value of and the positive impact early childhood education can have on children. They reported feeling more equipped to find high quality preschool programs in the community for their children to attend and they learned teaching strategies and managing skills to work with their children at home.

In addition to high satisfaction from teachers and families, the diagnostic classroom model has evolved to be a fitting format for assessing behavior problems in preschool children. Those children who are referred to the PAC due to behavior concerns are enrolled in the diagnostic classroom. The PAC currently evaluates preschool-aged children suspected of developmental delays in either an arena format or the diagnostic classroom model. Given the opportunities to observe children in the diagnostic classroom, it is the natural choice for those children with behavioral issues. One of the benefits of the diagnostic classroom is the prospect of trying to tease out environmental contribution to social and emotional issues. For 4 weeks, children are exposed daily to a stimulating and developmentally appropriate environment with sensitive and supportive adults. It is contextually meaningful to compare the functioning of children in the diagnostic classroom versus their functioning in other settings, such as daycares or preschools they typically attend. In some cases, the children have problems in both settings and at home, giving credence to the conclusion that these children have behavior problems which need to be addressed through a variety of interventions, including special education. In other cases, the children do not demonstrate behavior problems at the diagnostic classroom, although they continue to do so in other settings. The needs of these children are often addressed through specially designed interventions for those particular environments and not through special education services. Often times the teachers in the diagnostic classroom in collaboration with the school psychologists modify the environment in such a way to allow the children to be successful, and these ideas are shared with others. The diagnostic classroom model in combination with observation of children in their natural settings has been a very beneficial way for assessing social and emotional issues and understanding their inherent complexity.

Limitations of the Diagnostic Classroom

The diagnostic classroom has overall been a welcomed and positive addition to the operation of the PAC. The lengthy time invested in each child enrolled in the classroom and the limited resources available to operate only one classroom consequently results in the need to continue to use an arena format for assessment as well. The practice amongst the preschool team members has been to refer those children with more complex behavior or developmental issues to the diagnostic classroom and to assess those children with suspected language impairments or less multifaceted problems and who are 2 years old in an arena format. Although other forms of assessment are utilized in the diagnostic classroom, such as providing information to plan instructional activities and curriculum, the overarching purpose for assessment is to determine eligibility for special education services. This can be viewed as a limitation, since the diagnostic classroom affords opportunities to assess learning potential and to monitor progress; however, these types of assessments are not implemented to their capability at this time. Although the diagnostic classroom model is more authentic than the arena format, it does not completely address the current push for authentic assessment in early intervention (Bagnato, 2007).

Authentic assessment advocates for the assessment process to be a collection of accurate and ongoing observational information about a child's status and progress within natural early learning experiences in everyday situations and routines by those most familiar to the child (e.g., parents, teachers, and providers). The assessment of young children should resemble authentic, curriculum-based samples of everyday problem-solving and living skills in play or other natural learning situations, and include direct observation, interviews, and rating scales (Bagnato, 2007). This approach to assessment allows early childhood specialists to assume a more consultative and intervention role (Hojnoski & Missall, 2006). The diagnostic classroom combines traditional norm-referenced testing, including the use of rating scales and interviews with informal observations of children's behavior within an early childhood educational setting to determine children's needs. It is a step in the right direction but not at the point of evaluating and intervening in children's natural contexts.

The emphasis on an educational setting is an important distinction of the diagnostic classroom. It was designed to reflect the routines, curriculum, and structure of a typical early childhood special education classroom of Virginia Beach City Public Schools. As such, its operation resembles that of a developmentally appropriate preschool curriculum, and serves as an important context for assessing children's functioning within an educational environment and their subsequent assimilation if found eligible for classroom-based services. The current practice of specialists within the diagnostic classroom tailoring time to traditional testing could be improved upon by allotting more focus on meaningful assessment procedures, such as aligning curriculum-based competencies to daily routines (Bagnato, 2007) and using play more frequently to determine young children's skills (Ross, 2002). There is a movement toward the use of criterion-referenced assessment procedures linked directly to curriculum for all purposes including eligibility determination (Slentz & Hyatt, 2008). The diagnostic classroom model provides a format for such procedures to be implemented, although it has not fully incorporated a criterion-referenced procedure due in part because the school district as a whole has not adopted a universal curriculum used in the classrooms serving those children with developmental delays.

Another limitation of the diagnostic classroom is how parents are incorporated into determining children's needs and planning for interventions. Parents are included in all aspects of the assessment process from screening to eligibility determination, although their inclusion is not at the level of "parents as partners" as advocated by The Division for Early Childhood (Sandall et al., 2000). More could be done to ensure that parents' thoughts and wants are given the same attention as those of other preschool team members, especially in regards to realizing that parents are the constant in their children's lives and interventions incorporating them are more far reaching than other interventions. One promising area for including parents more as partners at the preschool level is the family-centered intervention planning using a routines-based approach (McWilliam, 1992).

With the emphasis more on families, the diagnostic classroom could offset another limitation of offering meaningful, long-lasting services to only those children who qualify for special education. Not unique to the diagnostic classroom is its limited reach to only those children with the most severe developmental delays. By incorporating families into the assessment process more through the routines-based interview, potential concerns identified in the children's natural contexts could be addressed within the time frame that the children are being evaluated with lasting positive effects.

Implications of the Diagnostic Classroom

The diagnostic classroom as described in this article offers early childhood practitioners an attractive alternative to preschool assessment. The model has been in operation successfully for 4 years with data to support its use. When interpreting the data presented in this article, it is important to note the response rate from the family survey (the majority of parents did not respond), and that the comparison with arena assessment was not conducted by an empirically driven, experimental design. Despite the caveats associated with the data, the diagnostic classroom is one of the best models available for balancing the need to compare a child's functioning to a peer group while at the same time implementing natural, whole-child assessment procedures when determining traditional eligibility for special education services. Although it does not address all the limitations of conventional testing practices, it is a step in the right direction for meeting eight critical qualities of best-practice early childhood assessment: utility, acceptability, authenticity, collaboration, convergence, equity, sensitivity, and congruence (Bagnato & Neisworth, 1999). Those who work with young children know that small steps on the path of success can have widespread influence and lead to even greater accomplishments. The diagnostic classroom model, as an approach to preschool assessment for determining the need for special education services, is in need of continued research, especially regarding its cost-effectiveness. A systematic evaluation of its methods would be an appropriate next step to delineate its utility in comparison to specific other approaches to preschool assessment.

References

Bagnato, S. J. (2007). *Authentic assessment for early childhood intervention: Best practices.* New York, NY: Guilford Press.

Bagnato, S. J., & Neisworth, J. T. (1991). *Assessment for early intervention: Best practices for professionals.* New York: Guilford Press.

Bagnato, S. J., & Neisworth, J. T. (1999). Collaboration and teamwork in assessment for early intervention. *Child and Adolescent Psychiatric Clinics of North America, 8(2),* 347-363.

Barnett, W. S., Lamey, C., & Jung, K. (2005). *The effects of state prekindergarten on young children's school readiness in five states.* U.S. Department of Health and Human Services, Administration for Children and Families, National Child Care Information Center. Retrieved from: http://nieer. org?resources/research/multistate/fullreport.pdf.

Berrueta-Clement, J., Schweinhart, L., Barnett, W., Epstein, A., & Weikart, D. (1984). *Changed lives: The effects of the Perry Preschool Program on youths through age 19.* Ypsilanti, MI: High/Scope Press.

Bowers, S. (2002). *Assessing young children: What's old, what's new, and where are we headed?* Retrieved from: www.earlychildhood.com

Bracken, B. A., & Nagle, R. J. (2007). *Psychoeducational assessment of preschool children* (4th ed.). Mahwah, NJ: Lawrence Erlbaum Associates Publishers.

Brassard, M. R., & Boehm, A. E. (2007). *Preschool assessment: Principles and practices.* New York: Guilford Press.

Bredekamp, S. (1987). *Developmentally appropriate practice in early childhood programs serving children from birth through age 8.* Washington, DC: National Association for the Education of Young Children.

Brickman, N. B., & Taylor, L. S. (1991). *Supporting young learners: Ideas for preschool and day care providers.* Ypsilanti, MI: High/Scope Press.

Greenwood, C. R., Luze, G. L., & Carta, J. J. (2002). Best practices in assessment of intervention results with infants and toddlers. In A. Thomas & J. Grimes (Eds.), *Best practices in school psychology* (4th ed., pp. 1219-1230). Washington, D.C: National Association of School Psychologists.

Guralnick, M. J. (2001). *Early childhood inclusion: Focus on change.* Baltimore, MD: Paul H. Brookes.

Hojnoski, R. L., & Missall, K. N. (2006). Addressing school readiness: Expanding school psychology in early education. *School Psychology Review, 35,* 602-614.

Lazar, I., & Darlington, R. (1982). Lasting effects of early education: A report from the Consortium for Longitudinal Studies. *Monographs of the Society for Research in Child Development, 47*(2-3, Serial No. 195), pp. 1-151.

McWilliam, R. A. (1992). *Family-centered intervention planning: A routines-based approach*. Tucson, AZ: Communication Skill Builders.

National Association of School Psychologists. (2002). *Position statement on early childhood assessment*. Bethesda, MD: Author.

National Association of School Psychologists. (2003). *Position statement on school psychologists' involvement in the role of assessment*. Bethesda, MD: Author.

Ross, R. P. (2002). Best practices in the use of play for assessment and intervention with young children. In A. Thomas & J. Grimes (Eds.), *Best practices in school psychology* (4th ed., pp. 1263-1280). Washington, D.C: National Association of School Psychologists.

Sandall, S., McLean, M. E., & Smith, B. J. (2000). *DEC recommended practices in early intervention/early childhood special education*. Longmont, CO: Sopris West.

Schwinhart, L. J., Barnes, H. V., Weikart, D. P., Barnett, W. S., & Epstein, A. S. (1993). *Significant benefits: The High/Scope Perry Preschool study through age 27*. Ypsilanti, MI: High/Scope Press.

Slentz, K. L., & Hyatt, K. J. (2008). Best practices in applying curriculum-based assessment in early childhood. In A. Thomas & J. Grimes (Eds.), *Best practices in school psychology* (5th ed., pp. 519-534). Washington, D.C: National Association of School Psychologists.

Temple University Forum on Preschool Assessment. (2003). *Using science to inform preschool assessment*. Philadelphia, PA: Center for Improving Resources in Children's Lives.

Voorhees, M. D., Aveno, A., Landon, T., & Massie, C. (1993). Preparing the classroom environment. In A. Aveno (Ed.), *Inclusive preschool programs: A guide for making them work*. Charlottesville, VA: University of Virginia, Department of Curriculum, Instruction, and Special Education.

Zigler, E., & Muenchow, S. (1992). *Head Start: The inside story of America's most successful educational experiment*. New York: Basic Books.

Author Note

Beth T. Clingenpeel, Kelli R. Good, and Karen J. McCleu-Jackson are school psychologists for Virginia Beach City Public Schools.

www.ingramcontent.com/pod-product-compliance
Lightning Source LLC
Chambersburg PA
CBHW071122280326
41935CB00010B/1093